The Web of
Violence

The Web of Violence

From Interpersonal to Global

Edited by

Jennifer Turpin and
Lester R. Kurtz

University of Illinois Press
Urbana and Chicago

Manufactured in the United States of America
1 2 3 4 5 C P 5 4 3 2 1

This book is printed on acid-free paper.

Library of Congress Cataloging-in-Publication Data
The web of violence : from interpersonal to global / edited by Jennifer Turpin and Lester R. Kurtz.
p. cm.
Includes bibliographical references and index.
ISBN 0-252-02261-0 (cloth : acid-free paper).
ISBN 0-252-06561-1 (pbk. : acid-free paper)
1. Violence. 2. Violence—Psychological aspects. 3. Violence—Prevention. I. Turpin, Jennifer E. II. Kurtz, Lester R.
HM281.W4 1997
303.6—dc20 96-4450
CIP

Dedicated to

Solveig A. Turpin and William F. Turpin and to

Poeta and Patience Asher-Kurtz

Contents

Acknowledgments

Many people helped us to complete this book. We thank our spouses, Robert Elias and Sarah Beth Asher, for their support. We are grateful to those who read versions of our work and provided feedback, including Robert Elias, Paul Joseph, Sam Marullo, Mike Webber, and Tami Spector. Stanley Nel, Dean of the College of Arts and Sciences at the University of San Francisco, provided support for this research, as did Associate Dean Gerardo Marín and the members of the Faculty Development Committee at USF. The assistance of Theresa Sears, managing editor at the University of Illinois Press, in the later stages of this project has been invaluable. We thank them all.

Introduction: Violence—The Micro/Macro Link

Jennifer Turpin and Lester R. Kurtz

Warfare, terrorism, urban violence, woman abuse: violence today is pervasive and inescapable. Over fifty large-scale wars now rage around the globe (Gurr 1993; SIPRI 1993). About three million violent crimes occur in the United States each year (U.S. Dept. of Justice 1992). Indeed, the U.S. Centers for Disease Control and Prevention (CDC) and the American Medical Association (AMA) have concluded that violence is an epidemic in the United States. This is particularly the case with violence against women: one in four women is sexually assaulted, and every eighteen seconds a woman is battered (Faludi 1991). There is a paradox about violence. Since most people believe they can be secure only by repelling violence with violence, they simultaneously deplore and condone it. The use of violence is considered taboo almost universally in modern society except under certain conditions. It is widely abhorred yet widely used to promote social control in settings ranging from the household to the global socioeconomic order. Because of that ambivalence, elaborate social mechanisms have been institutionalized to distinguish between legitimate and illegitimate violence.

Not only are individuals threatened by violence, but so are whole societies, and now—in the nuclear age—the species itself. Ironically, the very structures supposedly created to provide security against violence instead threaten everyone. Violence is not only pervasive in modern society, it is highly organized and efficient. As Randall Collins (1974a) observes, the highly personal violence of preindustrial societies has yielded to the kind of bureaucratized violence found in Nazi concentration camps and high-altitude bombing. The saturation of public spheres with violence, from war to street crime, and its celebration in popular culture may desensitize people to its use in private spheres.

Understanding human violence is one of the central tasks of our time, yet we still know very little about it. Hundreds of studies examine specific kinds of violence (e.g., Brownmiller 1975; Burt 1980; Durkheim and Denis 1915; Erikson 1966; Fromm 1973; Gerson 1986; Givens and Nettleship 1976; Hoefnagels 1977; Kwitny 1984; Lifton and Falk 1982; Pearce 1982; Rieder 1984; Sanders 1983; Schwendinger and Schwendinger 1983; Sorel [1950] 1961; Stockwell 1978; Wright 1942),[1] yet there have been few systematic efforts to explore patterns and underlying themes across micro- and macrolevels (Blumenthal, Chadiha, Cole, and Jayaratne 1975; Singer and Small 1972). Indeed, the study of violence has become so bureaucratized that we have neglected the search for fundamental causes despite efforts by earlier social thinkers to develop broad theories about violence and appropriate responses to it (Arendt 1969; Aron 1975; Bondurant [1958] 1988; Clausewitz 1966; Ellul 1969; Gandhi 1957; ISA 1957; McNeil 1965; Merton 1980). Some scholars argue that there are no root causes and that interpersonal violence is unrelated to global violence. As one of our colleagues put it, "There is no relationship between warfare and wife beating." We dispute this and similar claims.

The Micro- and Macrolinkages and Violence

Social scientists have done surprisingly little research that explores the links between interpersonal, collective, national, and global levels of violence. This volume takes on that task. We ask whether a relationship exists between the causes of violence at the microlevel and the causes at the macrolevel. Most scholars have been silent about this issue, despite the recent interest in micro/macro links within sociology (e.g., Alexander, Giesen, Munch, and Smelser 1987). While we agree that scholars must be both rigorous in analyzing violence and sensitive to the social forces at work at the micro- and macrolevels, we believe it is possible to identify the social mechanisms that link violence in the interpersonal realm to that at the global level. We contend that there are two forms of micro/macro social linkages. First, we postulate that there is a dialectic between the macro- and microlevels of violence. Second, we posit a relationship between different forms of violence that occur at the interpersonal, collective, and global levels. While the nature of those linkages and the mechanisms that sustain them are complex and difficult to ascertain, we must, nonetheless, work to identify them.

Theorizing about Violence

Theorizing about violence is not only important in itself but also because of its implication for social policy on how to change violent behavior. The nature and causes of human violence are hotly contested, and competing perspectives on violence advocate vastly different policies. The disciplinary perspectives of the various social and policy sciences have largely shaped the debates about violence, "framing" the problem in different ways. As sociologists, we emphasize the social forces at work that shape violent behavior, but we call for an integrative approach.

Human thought involves a process of framing in which comprehensive pictures or "definitions of the situation" are constructed to provide some cognitive boundaries for perceiving and defining an issue (Goffman 1974; Bateson 1972; Glaser and Strauss 1964; Berger and Luckmann 1967; Snow, Rochford, Worden, and Benford 1986). Public discourse on an issue, including debate about violence, revolves around a constellation of images and symbols. William Gamson contends that "symbols are organized into packages of harmonious elements within a common organizing frame. These packages become part of a symbolic contest in which the weapons are metaphors, catch phrases, and other condensing symbols" (1984, 3).

Conceptual frames establish boundaries around a set of issues and define how we process information, evaluate interpretive theories, and formulate policies. In general, people tend to ignore as irrelevant any data or theories that lie outside of the frames. An understanding of this process is crucial to our argument; the imposition of dominant frames and definitions on the debate creates a certain myopia. We will first examine the major disciplinary approaches to violence, to see how they ignore the micro/macro links. In our conclusion, we shall focus on the impact of the conceptual frame on policy debates.

Proponents of biological and physiological theories contend that humans behave violently because of some innate tendency or as a consequence of a genetic or physiological abnormality. These theories enjoy considerable salience among many contemporary policy makers. They investigate the relationship between violence and brain lesions, brain dysfunction, endocrinology, premenstrual syndrome, hypoglycemia, genetic composition, and hormones but fail to demonstrate that biological factors in themselves cause human violence (e.g., Moyer 1976). If one accepts biological theories of human violence, one might support attempts to alter the chemical or physical makeup of people who engage in violent behavior. Such approaches are accused of being racist, sexist, and classist; for example, a major national study allegedly targeted and drugged African American children (Stone 1992).

A biological explanation for criminal violence provides the rationale for ignoring the social causes of crime and abandoning attempts at rehabilitating offenders (Wilson and Hernnstein 1985). In addition, a biological approach reinforces the tendency in contemporary Western societies to seek "technical fixes" to solve problems, an orientation that we criticize in our conclusion. Moreover, no scientific evidence concludes either that humans are innately violent or that social factors do not exceed or override biological ones in producing violent behavior. Indeed, as the Seville Statement on Violence suggests, the opposite is more likely the case (Adams et al. 1992).

Historians have conducted numerous studies about specific violent conflicts, especially wars, from the earliest chronicles by Thucydides on the Peloponnesian War and Homer's *Iliad* to contemporary scholarship on ancient and modern conflicts (e.g., McNeill 1982, 1989; Thompson 1982, 1985, 1986). Historical surveys of violence explore trends, such as changes in the nature of warfare (e.g., Dyer 1985; Naroll, Bullough, and Naroll 1974; Wright 1971), crime, and punishment. Archaeologists, cultural anthropologists, and historians who explore broad historical trends in warfare and violence help to place the phenomenon in an important comparative perspective (e.g., Adcock 1957; Chandler 1966; Childs 1982; Corvisier 1979; Cottrell 1961, 1968; Hopkins 1978; Luttwak 1976; Mallett 1974; Richardson 1981; Rothenberg 1977; Saunders 1971; Strachan 1983; Wellard 1982; Wright 1971).

Psychologists, offering a range of approaches to the study of violence, emphasize individualistic sources of violence, particularly those resulting from abnormal psychological development. The early work of Sigmund Freud contends that aggressive, violent behavior is a result of the interaction between instinctive and environmental influences. His theory of the personality suggests that conflicting influences within an individual's unconscious shape his or her behavior, particularly conflicts between drives and instincts (the id) and the internalized social values (superego). A third aspect of the personality, the ego, mediates these two internal forces. Violent behavior can then be explained by an overdeveloped id (which contains the aggressive drive) or a weak superego that fails to counter the id.

Physical anthropologists have also developed a variant of the drive or instinct theory, contending that evolution produced humans who were naturally aggressive (Ardrey 1961; Lorenz 1966; Eibll-Eibesfeldt 1979). No scientific evidence demonstrates conclusively, however, that an aggressive drive exists apart from social conditions, nor is there evidence that aggression must take violent forms (Fromm 1973; Adams et al. 1992).

Social psychological research has focused on the processes by which social influences are likely to make individuals behave violently (Eron, Walder, and Lefkowitz 1971). For example, psychologists have demonstrated that people are willing to submit to authority and to commit grossly unjust acts, particularly when the victim of violence is distant from one who administers it (Milgram 1974). One implication of this is that the depersonalization of an enemy may make it easier to harm that person. Other social psychological research has demonstrated that when actors assume social roles that both give them power over others and encourage violence, they are likely to behave violently (Haney, Banks, and Zimbardo 1984).

Social psychologists from the behaviorist school have theorized that violence is learned. They have demonstrated that children imitate or model violent behavior in a laboratory setting (Bandura 1973). Humans may behave violently, according to social learning theory, because they learn this behavior during childhood. From this perspective, television and other forms of popular culture play a significant role in teaching violent behavior (Huesmann and Eron 1986).

Psychologists have taught us a great deal about factors that mediate violence; but, with some notable exceptions (e.g., Bramson and Goethals 1968; Fanon 1963; Fromm 1961; Kull 1988; Lifton and Falk 1982; Pear 1950; White 1968, 1984, 1986), most have focused on individual rather than collective forms of violence. Psychologists who have studied problems of genocide and war have primarily done so by addressing the internal psychological mechanisms at work when individuals inflict or suffer from violence. Others explore the internal processes leading to aggressive behavior that may be violent (Berkowitz 1962, 1969, 1986; Patterson 1989; Straus and Donnelly 1984; Tedeschi and Felson 1994). Robert Jay Lifton (1990), one of the most influential psychologists, argues in this volume and elsewhere that psychological processes such as "doubling" allow the self to split into two parts. One part may commit violent atrocities while the other functions as a loving parent and normal member of society.

Most political scientists argue that people form states to provide security, particularly against violence. Once organized, those states compete with other states for power, often using violent means. Violence among states will be checked only to the extent that power, or violence, is balanced. The international governmental system acts as a form of social control against international violence, using institutions such as the United Nations, the

World Court, and other forms of international law (Clark and Sohn 1966; Falk 1968, 1975; Morgenthau 1985; Weston, Falk, and D'Amato 1980). But in the end, according to the dominant political science perspective (the so-called realist school), international relations are governed largely by the law of the jungle. Only limited gains can be made in reducing the inevitable violence among competing states (Kissinger 1982). Accordingly, most political scientists argue that international relations are so precarious that order must be pursued ahead of justice (Bull 1977), although some recent scholarship acknowledges the role of the perception of injustice in precipitating war (Welch 1993). From this perspective, human rights and social justice are luxuries that would upset the world's delicate balance of power, thereby unleashing new violence. What most political scientists ignore, however, is the daily violence that "order" (the absence of human rights) imposes.

Some political scientists take a more flexible approach between order and justice but even so argue that only very limited gains against routine violence can be made (Hoffman 1981). Political scientists take a similarly pessimistic approach to the role of violence in political and economic development. They argue, for example, that violence is the inevitable price of modernization. Progress can be made only under the guidance of a central authority that is willing to keep the society on course and to suppress any popular interference in the development process. Likewise, austerity measures must be accepted by underdeveloped people as the appropriate path to modernization, even if such measures impose the short-term violence of lower wages, increased malnutrition, and other features of escalating poverty (Huntington 1977).

All academic endeavors suffer from materialistic biases, but political science is especially prone to this because of its close ties to the state. The intellectual consequences of this relationship are often profound, as demonstrated by theories of state violence developed by some American political scientists. They argue that the violence entailed by the development process will be lessened under certain political systems as compared to others. That is, authoritarian regimes will practice violence and deny democratic forms of government only temporarily, until they are more developed. Totalitarian regimes, however, will commit more violence and commit it continuously (Kirkpatrick 1982).

Political scientists expect formal governmental institutions to control violence. At the domestic level, for example, the criminal justice system bears the burden of curbing criminal violence. If crime continues, then political scientists argue either that a certain level of violence is inevitable or that violence could be reduced if social control institutions—such as police departments—were strengthened (Wilson 1975). As should be evident from this discussion, most political scientists make no connections between micro- and macrolevels of violence.

Sociologists and anthropologists attend to the relationship of culture and social structure (institutions and social stratification) to the lives of society's members. Thus, they are more likely to examine macro/micro links especially in the context of the social organization of conflict (e.g., Coser 1956, 1967). They have failed, however, to link violence across levels, and the few who have studied macrolevel violence are on the fringes of the discipline (Kurtz 1992).

Using a comparative perspective, cultural anthropologists have taught us that societies vary in their levels of violence (Ember and Ember 1993; Knauft 1985). They argue that it is not innate, as the "instinctivists" Konrad Lorenz (1966) and Robert Ardrey (1961) have argued. In addition, cultural anthropologists have suggested that violence does not inevitably take gendered forms (Mead 1968).

Some anthropologists and sociologists have emphasized the decline of social networks and the family as the primary precipitator of contemporary violence (e.g., Bellah, Madsen, Sullivan, Swidler, and Tipton 1985; Durkheim [1893] 1947; Etzioni 1993; Lévi-Strauss 1963), whereas conflict sociologists and cultural anthropologists often claim that violence tends to be "organized" around social cleavages or categories, such as the tribe or clan in preindustrial societies, and race, class, ethnicity, and gender in industrial societies. From this perspective, those who have power often use violence or the threat of violence to maintain their privileged status, while the powerless often see violence as the most efficacious way to improve their situation (e.g., Weber 1968; Gamson 1990). Sociologists from the symbolic interactionist school point out that, in many cases, taboo lines are situation-specific, allowing, for example, violence in self-defense but prohibiting its use against noncombatants. Through an elaborate labeling process, the same acts are defined as moral or immoral, legal or illegal, on the basis of the status of both perpetrator and victim and of the ostensible reason for the actions (Turpin 1986, 1995). Other sociologists have focused on the narratives, or rhetorical strategies, that justify violence, such as the "social construction of evil" (Kurtz 1989; Mehan and Skelly 1988; Urban 1987), or on the emotional aspects of collective action leading to violence (Scheff 1994).

Organizational sociologists suggest that the bureaucratization and institutionalization of violence also perpetuate it, even by those institutions allegedly constructed to control violence (Kurtz 1989; Mills 1963). Sociologists note that the increasing technological and bureaucratic nature of violence has made contemporary violence quite different from that in the past (Benedict 1959; Collins 1974b; Gibson 1986; Otterbein 1973). Others explore violence related to ethnic conflict, revolutions, and other forms of collective behavior (e.g., Haimson and Tilly 1989; Tilly 1978, 1993; Weber 1968).

Most sociologists and anthropologists who study war contend that war and other forms of violence are unrelated (Creighton and Shaw 1987), although some emerging perspectives claim otherwise. For example, feminist scholars have encountered resistance to their work connecting war with violence against women (Reardon 1985). While sociologists who study the military and peace are often marginalized in their discipline, they have made considerable contributions to our understanding of violence, often from an interdisciplinary perspective, which we will discuss below (Boulding, Elder, Goertzel, Jacobs, and Kriesberg 1974; Butler 1980; Etzioni 1962; Finsterbusch 1985; Gibson 1986; Janowitz 1960, 1975, 1977; Janowitz and Little 1974; Kurtz 1992; Merton and Lazarsfeld 1950; Moskos 1970; Moskos and Wood 1988; Osgood 1962; Segal 1986; Segal and Segal 1988; Shaw 1984; Shils and Janowitz 1948; Stouffer, Suchman, DeVinney, Star, and Williams 1949).

Problems with Theorizing about Violence

While there are a number of problems with current theories on violence, we have identified four particularly salient issues:

1. Traditional disciplinary approaches obscure the problem of violence even as they have also clarified parts of it. The boundaries or conceptual frames around which academic disciplines orient their work compartmentalize the study of violence. Interdisciplinary work is the most creative approach to this issue, but it is discouraged in the academy. This conclusion was also reached by a recent National Research Council panel on understanding and preventing violence (Reiss and Roth 1993).

2. Scholars neglect the micro/macro issue, tending to focus on one particular level of violence. Psychologists and biologists tend to focus on individualistic violence, while sociologists, anthropologists, and political scientists focus on collective and, especially, interstate violence.

3. Conventional social science methodologies encourage narrow approaches to the study of violence, prompting a focus on one specific form of violence that is often limited in spatial and temporal terms. This has the

unfortunate consequence of obscuring the micro/macro links. The search for root causes has been abandoned in favor of quantifying the correlates of violence. While we are sympathetic to empirical studies of violence, we also believe that the obsessive drive within social science to emulate the natural sciences has given us tunnel vision, narrowing our view of complex problems.

4. We lack a diversity of approaches to the study of violence in part because we disregard work by women, non-Westerners, and people of color. While this has been a result of the lack of diversity in academia generally, it is also a consequence of the marginalization of scholarship representing alternative theoretical and methodological approaches.

Interdisciplinary Approaches

The academy has marginalized interdisciplinary approaches that reframe the problem of violence. Nonetheless, such approaches offer a more convincing explanation of the links. Several interdisciplinary perspectives address the problem of violence in a more holistic manner: critical criminology, gender studies, peace and conflict studies, and public health.[2] Not all scholars in critical criminology, gender studies, peace studies, or public health make the micro/macro links; indeed, many of them would disagree with our argument. Still, it is in these four fields that we see significant forward movement on the micro/macro question in the study of violence.

The most widely studied and well-funded research on violence in the social sciences (outside of the Bureau of Army Research) is in the field of criminology. Criminologists focus on criminal violence and have compiled a significant database for the study of illegal violence, especially in North America, Australia, and Western Europe. Of particular interest to them are the crimes defined as most serious by law enforcement agencies: sexual assault, robbery, aggravated assault, and especially homicide.

The important contribution of mainstream criminology to the study of violence is the collection and interpretation of statistics regarding crime rates and the consequences of crime for its victims as well as for the larger society in which it occurs. Criminologists are active in the construction of theories and models to analyze such data (especially quantitative) and to discern patterns and trends, particularly in the kind of violence defined as illegitimate by criminal justice systems (e.g., Hirschi 1994; Reiss 1993). Although much of this work has been on specific countries, especially the United States, comparative studies contribute more fully to our understanding of this phenomenon (e.g., Archer and Gartner 1984).

Some scholars in the field link crime rates to social structure and demographic variables (Blau and Blau 1982; Messner 1989) and to corporate crime (e.g., Clinard and Yeager 1980). Others focus on the issue of delinquency and criminal subcultures (Cloward and Ohlin 1960; Hirschi 1969), the impact of crime on victims (Strauss, Gelles, and Steinmetz 1980), and the effects of different efforts to mitigate crime (Kellerman, Rivara, Rushforth, Banton, Reay, Francisco, Locci, Prodzinski, Hackman, and Somes 1993; Wheeler, Weisburd, and Bode 1982).

The most useful theorizing about violence in criminology comes from the work of "critical criminologists," who explicitly link macrostructures and culture to violent crime. In their definition, crime is broadened to include not only those acts officially outlawed by the state but also acts that are committed by the state and by organizations and elites that typically go unpunished. These researchers have thus developed social justice approaches to the study of crime, which link micro- and macroissues, arguing that undemocratic and unequal social arrangements, rather than insufficient social control, lead to criminal violence (e.g., Chambliss and Mankoff 1976; Elias 1986, 1993; Pepinsky 1991; Pepinsky and Quinney 1991; Hanmer, Radford, and Stanko 1989; Reiman 1986; Messerschmidt 1986).

One of the most striking facts about the phenomenon of violence is that it is committed mostly by men. Violence, especially violence against women, has been a central concern among gender scholars. Many of these scholars have been in the forefront of attempts to make micro/macro links, arguing that patriarchal culture, in which masculine dominates feminine, creates both microlevel violence against women and children and macrolevel violence such as war. Sexist ideology, they argue, perpetuates systemic violence from the household to the global political order. Betty Reardon, for example, articulated this perspective in her book, *Sexism and the War System* (1985). Others have demonstrated the gendered nature of violence, from interpersonal to global, and its relationship to gender socialization and to the gendered division of resources at all levels of society (e.g., Brock-Utne 1985; Hutchings 1992; Enloe 1993; Boulding 1992b; Peterson and Sisson-Runyon 1993; Dworkin 1993; Faludi 1991; Schwendinger and Schwendinger 1983; Vickers 1993; Tomasevski 1993). Gender studies scholars have also argued that there are alternatives to both sexism and the war system (e.g., Eisler 1987; Boulding 1992b; Kimmel 1987) and have examined the important role of women in peacemaking (Alonso 1989; Cooke and Woollacott 1993; Swerdlow 1993).

This emerging interdisciplinary field has focused primarily on critiquing approaches to the study of war and developing alternatives to war

(Barash 1991; Cancian and Gibson 1990; Elias and Turpin 1994; Lopez 1989). Many scholars who might not teach in peace studies programs nonetheless contribute to the field through their critical scholarship and integrative work. Unlike conventional social scientists, critical scholars in social science fields have developed alternative models to address the problems of violence and war, emphasizing justice rather than order (e.g., Falk, Kim, and Mendlovitz 1982).

Increasingly, peace studies research attends to the problem Johan Galtung calls "structural violence" (1975, 116–30). Galtung developed the concept to account for the violence that occurs when people are harmed because of inequitable social arrangements rather than by overt physical violence. This concept has proven useful to feminist researchers and other social scientists concerned with the structural arrangements that produce harm in the absence of direct violence (e.g., Boulding 1978; Brock-Utne 1985; Elias 1993; Goulet 1971; Lappe, Collins, and Kinley 1980). A number of peace studies scholars have examined peace movements (Benford 1993a, 1993b; Bess 1993; Epstein 1991; Howlett 1991; Jamison and Eyerman 1994; Hunt, Benford, and Snow 1994; Kleidman 1993; Lofland 1993; Swerdlow 1993; Wittner 1993), as well as the various conditions that promote war or peace, violence or nonviolence (Ackermann and Kruegler 1994; Dajani 1995; Elias and Turpin 1994; Herngren 1993; Joseph 1993; Kellner 1992; Kurtz 1992; Kurtz and Asher forthcoming; Marullo 1993; Paige 1993; Schwartz, Derber, Fellman, Gamson, Schwartz, and Withen 1990; Sharp 1973; Weston 1984).

Other peace studies scholars have examined conflict resolution processes in creative ways, applied innovative approaches to the conventional topics of social sciences (Dumas 1986; Fisher and Ury 1981; Fogg 1985; Janis 1982; Kriesberg 1992; Paige 1993; Smock 1993), examined the efficacy of transnational organizations and civic culture (Boulding 1990), or studied systems of international law (Clark and Sohn 1966; Falk 1968, 1975).

Physicians and other scholars doing research on public health issues also address problems of violence across micro- and macrolevels.[3] Many of these researchers identify environmental degradation and war as threats to human health. For example, Physicians for Social Responsibility (PSR) and International Physicians for the Prevention of Nuclear War (IPPNW) were founded in response to the threat of nuclear war. Moreover, through its Center for Environmental Health and Injury Control, the CDC has implemented programs to study the public health consequences of violence.

In addition to studying problems of interpersonal violence, public health researchers also examine the consequences of structural violence such as unequal development, racism, food policy, nutrition, sanitation, and health care (Prothrow-Stith 1991; Prothrow-Stith and Weisman 1991). Educators concerned with public health believe that "the probability of man killing his fellow humans in unheard-of numbers, and destroying the globe in the near future, is dramatically increasing" and that "keeping that from happening is the greatest health priority of this century" (Leviton 1991, 4).

Those health educators who emphasize what they call "horrendous-type deaths" focus on violence caused by conventional and nuclear war (e.g., Leviton 1991; Caldicott 1986; Robock 1991; Stillion 1991; Pacholski 1991), the destruction of the environment (e.g., Caldicott 1993; Bertell 1991), homicide (e.g., Schuetz 1991; Stark 1991), genocide (e.g., Charny 1994), terrorism (e.g., Fleming and Schuetz 1991), racism, malnutrition, and poverty (e.g., Gorlick 1991; Foster 1991), and the effects of war and violence on health care and the welfare of children (Zwi, Macrae, and Ugalde 1992). Thus, they are concerned with both direct and structural violence as well as micro- and macrosocial forms of violence. They emphasize the interdependence of life, integrate these issues as "global community health problems" (Leviton 1991, 6), and advocate alternatives to violence (Cohen 1991; Jenkins 1991; Ostos 1991; Mason 1991).

Conclusion

We see these interdisciplinary developments as the most promising venues for understanding violence. In fact, the most exciting developments, in our view, result from interactions among these interdisciplinary lines of thought. While we are heartened by the fact that so much attention is accorded to problems of violence, simply imposing the old frameworks for understanding will not produce solutions.

We conceptualize problems of violence as a "web," because the causes of violence, from interpersonal to global, are connected, as are the consequences. Discourse about violence from interpersonal to global also frames violence in a parallel fashion. Finally, solutions to violence, from interpersonal to global, are generally framed in the same way.

There are a number of assumptions underlying our approach to violence. First, we assume that conflict is endemic to social life. We do not see conflict as either positive or negative but rather as given. Second, we assume that there are alternative means for addressing social conflict. Third, we believe that effectively addressing the problem of violence requires changing our social organization, as well as changing individuals. Fourth, we see the problem of violence as one of the central problems of modern life. Fifth, we believe that micro/macro linkages exist and that the effective resolution of the problem of global violence necessitates dealing with interpersonal violence, and vice versa. Finally, we believe that academic specialization obscures the problem by neglecting holistic approaches and encouraging "technical fix" solutions. Finding solutions to the problems of violence requires a more holistic approach.

Organization and Contributors

In this volume, we hope to reframe and broaden our analysis of violence, giving special attention to the micro/macro issues. We assert that there are links, but we do not presume to know what all those linkages are, nor do we wish to make facile connections. We see this as an exploratory project in which we may begin to unravel the intricacies of some of the mechanisms.

We believe there are several areas that may link micro- and macrolevels of violence that we should explore. The authors in this book are critical social science thinkers who theorize in these areas. First, we should explore the psychological mechanisms that work within individuals, allowing or encouraging them to commit violence at the macrolevel. Robert Jay Lifton addresses such microlevel processes, arguing that Nazi doctors experienced "doubling," which allowed them to commit gross acts of violence. Lifton delves into the psychological processes within individuals who contribute to macroforms of violence, such as genocide and war.

Second, we should examine socialization processes, especially gender socialization and socialization around "military" values, which may form a basis for gendered violence at both the micro- and macrolevels. Two essays by leading feminist scholars call for reconceptualizing our approach to the study of violence to assess the gendered nature of micro- and macrolevel violence. Birgit Brock-Utne offers a new model for conceptualizing both violence and development problems, to incorporate the micro- and macroissues. Without greater attention to the microlevel violence occurring in households, she argues, we will be unable to understand macrolevel violence. Riane Eisler argues that scholarship on human rights has failed to recognize human rights in the private sphere, which includes much of both women's activity and microlevel human rights violations.

Third, we should analyze the role of language (and the categories of thought it provides) in legitimating violence. Two essays focus on language, conventional solutions, and rationalizing violence. Philip Smith discusses the role of narratives in the legitimation of violence and argues that narratives have changed over time to rationalize increasing violence. Robert Elias demonstrates that the United States is a culture of "violent solutions" that responds to violence at both the micro- and macrolevels with more violence, thus perpetuating the problem.

Fourth, we should explore the role of culture in mobilizing violence. Two chapters focus on the relationship of culture to violence at both the micro- and macrolevels. Christopher G. Ellison and John P. Bartkowski discuss the relationship between conservative Protestantism and corporal punishment, arguing that this religious perspective provides a rationale for violence against children by parents. Yuan-Horng Chu shows how violence was mobilized and legitimated during the Chinese cultural revolution, as well as in the more recent Tiananmen Square incident.

Finally, we should consider the role of the macrostructure of societies and the global system in violence at the microlevel. Johan Galtung analyzes the relationship between what he terms "cosmologies" and violence at all levels. Galtung offers a therapeutic, yet macroapproach to understanding violence, exploring the question of whether there is a therapy for "pathological cosmologies."

We provide a short introduction to each contribution, pointing to some significant questions raised by the authors. We hope that by exploring each of these areas we will gain insights into the nature of violence and the micro- and macrolinkages. In our conclusion, we will argue for alternative approaches to understanding and preventing violence.

Notes

1. In this introduction, we do not intend to review the vast literature on violence but rather to discuss various disciplinary approaches to the problem. A review of the literature on violence would amount to an encyclopedia, a fact that underscores our point regarding so much research yielding so little in the way of solutions.
2. Of course, scholars may identify with more than one field.
3. While only a small fraction of the scholars in public health are researching violence, they are making important contributions to both academic and public debates.

Bibliography

Ackermann, Peter, and Christopher Kruegler. 1994. *Strategic Nonviolent Conflict: The Dynamics of People Power in the Twentieth Century.* New York: Praeger.

Adams, David, et al. 1992. "The Seville Statement on Violence." *Peace Review* 4(3): 20–22.

Adcock, F. E. 1957. *The Greek and Macedonian Art of War.* Berkeley: University of California Press.

Alexander, Jeffrey C., Bernhard Giesen, Richard Munch, and Neil J. Smelser, eds. 1987. *The Micro-Macro Link.* Berkeley: University of California Press.

Alger, Chadwick, and Michael Stohl, eds. 1988. *A Just Peace through Transformation.* Boulder, Colo.: Westview Press.

Alonso, Harriet Hyman. 1989. *The Women's Peace Union and the Outlawry of War, 1921–1942.* Knoxville: University of Tennessee Press.

Archer, Dane, and Rosemary Gartner. 1984. *Violence and Crime in Cross-National Perspective.* New Haven, Conn.: Yale University Press.

Ardrey, Robert. 1961. *African Genesis: A Personal Investigation into the Animal Origins and Nature of Man.* New York: Dell.

Arendt, Hannah. 1969. *On Violence.* New York: Harcourt, Brace, and World.

Aron, Raymond. 1966. *Peace and War: A Theory of International Relations.* Trans. R. Howard and A. B. Fox. Garden City, N.Y.: Doubleday.

———. 1975. *History and the Dialectic of Violence.* Trans. Barry Cooper. Oxford: Blackwell.

Bandura, Albert. 1973. *Aggression: A Social Learning Analysis.* New York: Atheneum.

Barash, David P. 1991. *Introduction to Peace Studies.* Belmont, Calif.: Wadsworth.

Bateson, Gregory. 1972. *Steps to an Ecology of Mind.* New York: Ballantine Books.

Beitz, Charles. 1979. *Political Theory and International Relations.* Princeton: Princeton University Press.

Bellah, Robert N., Richard Madsen, William M. Sullivan, Ann Swidler, and Steven M. Tipton. 1985. *Habits of the Heart: Individualism and Commitment in American Life.* Berkeley: University of California Press.

Benedict, R. F. 1959. "The Natural History of War." In *An Anthropologist at Work.* Ed. Margaret Mead. Pp. 369–82. Boston: Houghton Mifflin.

Benford, Robert D. 1993a. "Frame Disputes within the Nuclear Disarmament Movement." *Social Forces* 71:677–701.

———. 1993b. "You Could Be the Hundredth Monkey: Collective Action Frames and Vocabularies of Motive within the Nuclear Disarmament Movement." *Sociological Quarterly* 34:195–216.

Berger, Peter, and Thomas Luckman. 1967. *The Social Construction of Reality.* New York: St. Martin's Press.

Berkowitz, Bruce D. 1962. *Aggression: A Social Psychological Analysis.* New York: McGraw-Hill.

———. 1969. *Roots of Aggression: A Re-examination of the Frustration-Aggression Hypothesis.* New York: Atherton Press.

———. 1986. *American Security: Dilemmas for a Modern Democracy.* New Haven, Conn.: Yale University Press.

———. 1987. *Calculated Risks: A Century of Arms Control, Why It Has Failed and How It Can Be Made to Work.* New York: Simon and Schuster.

Bertell, Rosalie. 1991. "Destruction of the Environment, a Living Biosphere." Pp. 177–89 in *Horrendous Death, Health, and Well-Being,* ed. Leviton.

Bess, Michael. 1993. *Realism, Utopia, and the Mushroom Cloud: Four Activist Intellectuals and Their Strategies for Peace, 1945–1989.* Chicago: University of Chicago Press.

Blau, Judith, and Peter Blau. 1982. "The Cost of Inequality: Metropolitan Structure and Violent Crime." *American Sociological Review* 47:114–29.

Blumenthal, Monica D., Letha B. Chadiha, Gerald A. Cole, and Toby Epstein Jayaratne. 1975. *More about Justifying Violence: Methodological Studies of Attitudes and Behavior.* Ann Arbor, Mich.: Institute for Social Research.

Bondurant, Joan. [1958] 1988. *Conquest of Violence: The Gandhian Philosophy of Conflict.* Rev. ed. Princeton: Princeton University Press.

Boulding, Elise. 1990. *Building a Global Civic Culture: Education for an Interdependent World.* Syracuse, N.Y.: Syracuse University Press.

———. 1992a. *New Agendas for Peace Research: Conflict and Security Reexamined.* Boulder, Colo.: Lynne Rienner Publishers.

———. 1992b. *The Underside of History: A View of Women through Time.* Newbury Park, Calif.: Sage.

Boulding, Elise, Joseph W. Elder, Ted Goertzel, Ruth Harriet Jacobs, and Louis Kriesberg. 1974. "Teaching the Sociology of World Conflicts: A Review of the State of the Field." *American Sociologist* 9:187–93.

Boulding, Kenneth. 1978. *Stable Peace.* Austin: University of Texas Press.

Bramson, Leon, and George W. Goethals. 1968. *War: Studies from Psychology, Sociology, and Anthropology.* Rev. ed. New York: Basic Books.

Brock-Utne, Birgit. 1985. *Educating for Peace: A Feminist Perspective.* New York: Pergamon.

Brownmiller, Susan. 1975. *Against Our Will: Men, Women, and Rape.* New York: Simon and Schuster.

Bull, Hedley. 1977. *The Anarchical Society: A Study of Order in World Politics.* New York: Columbia University Press.

Burt, Martha R. 1980. "Cultural Myths and Supports for Rape." *Journal of Personality and Social Psychology* 38:217–30.

Butler, John Sibley. 1980. *Inequality in the Military: The Black Experience.* Saratoga, Calif.: Century Twenty-One.

Caldicott, Helen. 1986. *Missile Envy: The Arms Race and Nuclear War.* New York: Bantam.

———. 1993. *If You Love This Planet.* New York: Norton.

Cancian, Francesca M., and James William Gibson. 1990. *Making War/Making Peace: The Social Foundations of Violent Conflict.* Belmont, Calif.: Wadsworth.

Chambliss, William, and Milton Mankoff. 1976. *Whose Law? Whose Order?* New York: John Wiley.

Chandler, David. 1966. *The Campaigns of Napoleon.* London: Weidenfeld and Nicholson.

Charny, Israel W. 1994. *The Widening Circle of Genocide.* New Brunswick, N.J.: Transaction.
Childs, John. 1982. *Armies and Warfare in Europe, 1648–1789.* Manchester: Manchester University Press.
Chomsky, Noam. 1982. *Towards a New Cold War.* New York: Pantheon.
———. 1988. *The Culture of Terrorism.* Boston: South End Press.
Clark, Grenville, and Louis Sohn. 1966. *World Peace through World Law: Two Alternative Plans.* Cambridge, Mass.: Harvard University Press.
Clausewitz, Carl von. 1966. *On War.* Trans. J. J. Graham. Rev. ed. London: Routledge and Kegan Paul.
Clinard, Marshall B., and Peter Yeager. 1980. *Corporate Crime.* New York: Free Press.
Cloward, Richard, and Lloyd Ohlin. 1960. *Delinquency and Opportunity: A Theory of Delinquent Gangs.* New York: Free Press.
Cohen, Larry. 1991. "The Coalition for Alternatives to Violence and Abuse." *Public Health Reports* 106(3): 239–40.
Collins, Randall. 1974a. *Conflict Sociology.* New York: Academic Press.
———. 1974b. "Three Faces of Cruelty: Toward a Comparative Sociology of Violence." *Theory and Society* 1:415–40.
Cooke, Miriam, and Angela Woollacott, eds. 1993. *Gendering War Talk.* Princeton: Princeton University Press.
Corvisier, Andre. 1979. *Armies and Societies in Europe, 1494–1789.* Bloomington: Indiana University Press.
Coser, Lewis A. 1956. *The Functions of Social Conflict.* Glencoe, Ill.: Free Press.
———. 1967. *Continuities in the Study of Social Conflict.* New York: Free Press.
Cottrell, Leonard. 1961. *The Great Invasion.* London: Pan.
———. 1968. *The Warrior Pharaohs.* London: Evans Brothers.
Creighton, Colin, and Martin Shaw, eds. 1987. *The Sociology of War and Peace.* Dobbs Ferry: Sheridan House.
Dajani, Souad. 1995. *Eyes without a Country: Searching for a Palestinian Strategy of Liberation.* Philadelphia: Temple University Press.
Dumas, Lloyd J. 1986. *The Overburdened Economy.* Berkeley: University of California Press.
Durkheim, Émile. [1893] 1947. *The Division of Labor in Society.* Glencoe, Ill.: Free Press.
Durkheim, Émile, and E. Denis. 1915. *Who Wanted War? The Origins of the War according to Diplomatic Documents.* Paris: A. Colin.
Dworkin, Andrea. 1993. *Letters from a War Zone.* Brooklyn: Lawrence Hill.
Dyer, Gwyn. 1985. *War.* New York: Crown.
Eibll-Eibesfeldt, Irenaus. 1979. *The Biology of War and Peace: Men, Animals and Aggression.* New York: Viking.
———. 1992. *Bonding Behavior and Aggression Control in the !Ko Bushmen.* Munich: R. Piper.

Eisler, Riane. 1987. *The Chalice and the Blade: Our History, Our Future.* San Francisco: Harper and Row.

Elias, Robert. 1986. *The Politics of Victimization: Victims, Victimology, and Human Rights.* New York: Oxford University Press.

———. 1993. *Victims Still: The Political Manipulation of Crime Victims.* Newbury Park, Calif.: Sage.

Elias, Robert, and Jennifer Turpin, eds. 1994. *Rethinking Peace.* Boulder, Colo.: Lynne Rienner Publishers.

Ellul, Jacques. 1969. *Violence.* New York: Seabury Press.

Ember, Carol R., and Melvin Ember. 1993. *Anthropology.* 7th ed. Englewood Cliffs, N.J.: Prentice-Hall.

Enloe, Cynthia. 1993. *The Morning After: Sexual Politics at the End of the Cold War.* Berkeley: University of California Press.

Epstein, Barbara. 1991. *Political Protest and Cultural Revolution: Nonviolent Direct Action in the 1970s and 1980s.* Berkeley: University of California Press.

Erikson, Kai. 1966. *Wayward Puritans: A Study in the Sociology of Deviance.* New York: John Wiley.

———. 1976. *Everything in Its Path.* New York: Simon and Schuster.

Eron, Leonard D., Leopold O. Walder, and Monroe M. Lefkowitz. 1971. *Learning of Aggression in Children.* Boston: Little, Brown.

Etzioni, Amitai. 1962. *The Hard Way to Peace: A New Strategy.* New York: Collier.

———. 1993. *The Spirit of Community: The Reinvention of American Society.* New York: Crown.

Fahey, Joseph J. 1992. "Columbus and the Catholic Crusades." *Peace Review* 4(3): 36–40.

Falk, Richard A. 1968. *Legal Order in a Violent World.* Princeton: Princeton University Press.

———. 1975. *A Study of Future Worlds.* New York: Free Press.

Falk, Richard, Samuel Kim, and Saul Mendlovitz. 1982. *Toward a Just World Order.* Boulder, Colo.: Westview Press.

Faludi, Susan. 1991. *Backlash: The Undeclared War against American Women.* New York: Crown.

Fanon, Franz. 1963. *The Wretched of the Earth.* New York: Grove Press.

Finsterbusch, Kurt. 1985. "Nuclear Issues in Social Research." *Society* 22:2–3.

Fisher, Roger, and William Ury. 1981. *Getting to Yes.* Boston: Houghton Mifflin.

Fleming, Dan B., and Arnold Schuetz. 1991. "Terrorism, Assassination, and Political Torture." Pp. 157–74 in *Horrendous Death, Health, and Well-Being,* ed. Leviton.

Fogg, Richard Wendell. 1985. "Dealing with Conflict: A Repertoire of Creative, Peaceful Approaches." *Journal of Conflict Resolution* 29(June): 330–58.

Forcey, Linda. 1989. *Peace: Meanings, Politics, Strategies.* New York: Praeger.

———. 1991. "Women as Peacemakers." *Peace and Change* 16(4): 331–54.

Foster, Phillips. 1991. "Malnutrition, Starvation, and Death." Pp. 205–18 in *Horrendous Death, Health, and Well-Being,* ed. Leviton.

Freud, Sigmund. 1950. *Totem and Taboo.* Trans. J. Strachey. New York: Norton.

Fromm, Eric. 1961. *Man for Himself: An Inquiry into the Psychology of Ethics.* New York: Holt, Rinehart, and Winston.

———. 1973. *The Anatomy of Human Destructiveness.* New York: Holt, Rinehart, and Winston.

Galtung, Johan. 1975. *Peace: Research, Education, Action.* Vol. 1: *Essays in Peace Research.* Copenhagen: Christian Ejlers.

———. 1980. *The True Worlds: A Transnational Perspective.* New York: Free Press.

———. 1984. *There Are Alternatives.* Nottingham: Russell Press.

Gamson, William. 1984. "Political Symbolism and Nuclear Arms Policy." Paper presented at the annual meeting of the American Sociological Association, August, San Antonio, Tex.

———. 1990. *The Strategy of Social Protest.* Belmont, Calif.: Wadsworth.

Gandhi, Mohandas K. 1957. *An Autobiography: The Story of My Experiments with Truth.* 2d ed. Trans. Mahadev Desai. Boston: Beacon.

Gerson, Joseph, ed. 1986. *The Deadly Connection: Nuclear War and U.S. Intervention.* Philadelphia: New Society Publishers.

Gibson, James William. 1986. *The Perfect War: Technowar in Vietnam.* New York: Atlantic Monthly Press.

———. 1989. "Paramilitary Culture." *Critical Studies in Mass Communication* 6(March): 90–95.

———. 1994. *Warrior Dreams: Paramilitary Culture in Post-Vietnam America.* New York: Hill and Wang.

Givens, R. Dale, and Martin A. Nettleship. 1976. *Discussions on War and Human Aggression.* The Hague: Mouton.

Glaser, Barney, and Anselm Strauss. 1964. "Awareness Contexts and Social Interaction." *American Sociological Review* 29:669–79.

Goffman, Erving. 1974. *Frame Analysis.* New York: HarperCollins.

Gorlick, Carolyne. 1991. "Unemployment and Poverty." Pp. 191–204 in *Horrendous Death, Health, and Well-Being,* ed. Leviton.

Goulet, Denis. 1971. *The Cruel Choice.* New York: Atheneum.

Gurr, Ted R. 1993. *Minorities at Risk: A Global View of Ethnopolitical Conflicts.* Washington, D.C.: U.S. Institute of Peace.

Haimson, Leopold, and Charles Tilly, eds. 1989. *Strikes, Wars, and Revolutions in an International Perspective.* Cambridge: Cambridge University Press.

Haney, Craig, Curtis Banks, and Philip Zimbardo. 1984. "A Study of Prisoners and Guards in a Simulated Prison." In *Readings about the Social Animal.* Ed. E. Aronson. Pp. 52–67. New York: W. H. Freeman.

Hanmer, J., J. Radford, and E. Stanko. 1989. *Women, Policing and Male Violence.* New York: Routledge.

Herman, Edward. 1982. *The Real Terror Network.* Boston: South End Press.
Herngren, Per. 1993. *Path of Resistance: The Practice of Civil Disobedience.* Trans. Margaret Rainey. Philadelphia: New Society Publishers.
Hirschi, Travis. 1969. *Causes of Delinquency.* Berkeley: University of California Press.
———. 1994. *Towards a General Theory of Crime.* Berkeley: University of California Press.
Hoefnagels, Marjo. 1977. *Repression and Repressive Violence.* New Brunswick, N.J.: Transaction.
Hoffman, Stanley. 1981. *Duties beyond Borders.* Syracuse, N.Y.: Syracuse University Press.
Hopkins, Keith. 1978. *Conquerors and Slaves: Sociological Studies in Roman History.* Vol. 1. Cambridge: Cambridge University Press.
Howlett, Charles F. 1991. *The American Peace Movement: References and Resources.* New York: G. K. Hall.
Huesmann, L. Rowell, and Leonard D. Eron. 1986. *Television and the Aggressive Child: A Cross-National Comparison.* Hillsdale, N.J.: L. Erlbaum Associates.
Hunger Project. 1984. *Ending Hunger—An Idea Whose Time Has Come.* New York: Praeger.
Hunt, Scott A., Robert D. Benford, and David A. Snow. 1994. "Identity Fields: Framing Processes and the Social Construction of Movement Identities." In *New Social Movements: From Ideology to Identity.* Ed. Enrique Larana, Hank Johnston, and Joseph R. Gusfield. Pp. 185–208. Philadelphia: Temple University Press.
Huntington, Samuel. 1977. *Political Order in Changing Societies.* New Haven, Conn.: Yale University Press.
Hutchings, Nancy. 1992. "Family Violence." *Peace Review* 4(3): 24–27.
International Sociological Association (ISA), ed. 1957. *The Nature of Conflict: Studies on the Sociology of Aspects of International Tensions.* Paris: UNESCO.
Jamison, Andrew, and Ron Eyerman. 1994. *Seeds of the Sixties.* Berkeley: University of California Press.
Janis, Irving. 1982. *Groupthink: Psychological Studies of Policy Decisions and Fiascoes.* 2d ed. Boston: Houghton Mifflin.
Janowitz, Morris. 1960. *The Professional Soldier.* New York: Free Press.
———. 1975. *Military Conflict.* Beverly Hills, Calif.: Sage.
———. 1977. *The Military in the Political Development of New Nations.* Rev. and expanded ed. Chicago: University of Chicago Press.
Janowitz, Morris, and R. W. Little. 1974. *Sociology and the Military Establishment.* Beverly Hills, Calif.: Sage.
Jenkins, Ronnie. 1991. "New Way of Fighting." *Public Health Reports* 106(3): 240–41.
Joseph, Paul. 1993. *Peace Politics.* Philadelphia: Temple University Press.
Kaufman, Michael, ed. 1987. *Beyond Patriarchy: Essays by Men on Pleasure, Power, and Change.* New York: Oxford University Press.

Kellerman, Arthur L., Frederick P. Rivara, Norman B. Rushforth, Joyce G. Banton, Donald T. Reay, Jerry T. Francisco, Ana B. Locci, Janice Prodzinski, Bela Hackman, and Grant Somes. 1993. "Gun Ownership as a Risk Factor for Homicide in the Home." *New England Journal of Medicine* 329(15): 1084–91.

Kellner, Douglas. 1992. *The Persian Gulf TV War.* Boulder, Colo.: Westview Press.

Kimmel, Michael, ed. 1987. *Changing Men: New Directions on Men and Masculinity.* Newbury Park, Calif.: Sage.

Kirkpatrick, Jeanne. 1982. *Dictators and Double Standards.* New York: Simon and Schuster.

Kissinger, Henry. 1982. *Years of Upheaval.* Boston: Little, Brown.

Klare, Michael, and Cynthia Arnson. 1981. *Supplying Repression: U.S. Support for Authoritarian Regimes Abroad.* Washington, D.C.: Institute for Policy Studies.

Kleidman, Robert. 1993. *Organizing for Peace: Neutrality, the Test Ban, and the Freeze.* Syracuse, N.Y.: Syracuse University Press.

Knauft, Bruce M. 1985. *Good Company and Violence: Sorcery and Social Action in a Lowland New Guinea Society.* Berkeley: University of California Press.

Kriesberg, Louis. 1982. *Social Conflicts.* Englewood Cliffs, N.J.: Prentice-Hall.

———. 1986. "Consequences of Efforts at Deescalating the American-Soviet Conflict." *Journal of Political and Military Sociology* 14(Fall): 215–34.

———. 1992. *International Conflict Resolution.* New Haven, Conn.: Yale University Press.

Kull, Stephen. 1988. *Minds at War.* New York: Basic Books.

Kurtz, Lester R. 1989. *The Nuclear Cage: A Sociology of the Arms Race.* Englewood Cliffs, N.J.: Prentice-Hall.

———. 1992. "War and Peace on the Sociological Agenda." In *Sociology and Its Publics: The Forms and Fates of Disciplinary Organization,* ed. Terence Halliday and Morris Janowitz. Pp. 61–98. Chicago: University of Chicago Press.

Kurtz, Lester R., and Sarah Beth Asher, eds. Forthcoming. *The Geography of Nonviolence.* Oxford: Blackwell.

Kurtz, Lester R., and Jennifer E. Turpin. 1989. "The Social Psychology of Warfare." Pp. 77–89 in *The Nuclear Cage,* Kurtz.

Kwitny, Jonathan. 1984. *Endless Enemies: The Making of an Unfriendly World.* New York: Congdon and Weed.

Lappe, Frances Moore, Joseph Collins, and David Kinley. 1980. *Aid as Obstacle.* San Francisco: Institute for Food and Development Policy.

Lévi-Strauss, Claude. 1963. *Structural Anthropology.* New York: Basic Books.

Leviton, Daniel, ed. 1991. *Horrendous Death, Health, and Well-Being.* New York: Hemisphere Publishing.

Lifton, Robert Jay. 1990. *The Genocidal Mentality: Nazi Holocaust and Nuclear Threat.* New York: Basic Books.

Lifton, Robert Jay, and Richard Falk. 1982. *Indefensible Weapons: The Political and Psychological Case against Nuclearism.* New York: Basic Books.

Lofland, John. 1993. *Polite Protesters: The American Peace Movement of the 1980s.* Syracuse, N.Y.: Syracuse University Press.

Lopez, George A., ed. 1989. "Peace Studies: Past and Future." *Annals of the American Academy of Political and Social Science* 504 (July).

Lorenz, Konrad. 1966. *On Aggression.* New York: Harcourt, Brace, and World.

Luttwak, Edward N. 1976. *The Grand Strategy of the Roman Empire from the First Century A.D. to the Third Century A.D.* Baltimore: Johns Hopkins University Press.

Mallett, Malcolm. 1974. *Mercenaries and Their Masters.* London: Bodley Head.

Marullo, Sam. 1993. *Ending the Cold War at Home.* Lexington, Mass.: Lexington Books.

Mason, James O. 1991. "Prevention of Violence: A Public Health Commitment." *Public Health Reports* 106(3): 265–68.

McNeil, Elton B. 1965. *The Nature of Human Conflict.* Englewood Cliffs, N.J.: Prentice-Hall.

McNeill, William. 1982. *The Pursuit of Power: Technology, Armed Force, and Society since A.D. 1000.* Chicago: University of Chicago Press.

———. 1989. *The Age of Gunpowder Empires, 1450–1800.* Washington, D.C.: American Historical Association.

Mead, Margaret. 1968. "Alternatives to War." In *War: The Anthropology of Armed Conflict and Aggression.* Ed. M. Fried, M. Harris, and R. Murphy. Pp. 215–28. Garden City, N.Y.: Natural History Press.

Mehan, Hugh, and James M. Skelly. 1988. "Reykjavik: The Breach and Repair of the Pure War Script." La Jolla, Calif.: Institute on Global Conflict and Cooperation.

Merton, Robert, and Paul Lazarsfeld, eds. 1950. *Studies in the Scope and Method of "The American Soldier."* Glencoe, Ill.: Free Press.

Merton, Thomas. 1980. *The Nonviolent Alternative.* New York: Farrar, Straus, Giroux.

Messerschmidt, James. 1986. *Capitalism, Patriarchy, and Crime.* Totowa, N.J.: Rowman and Allanheld.

Messner, Michael, and Don Sabo, eds. 1990. *Sport, Men and the Gender Order.* Champaign, Ill.: Human Kinetics.

Messner, Steven F. 1989. "Economic Discrimination and Societal Homicide Rates: Further Evidence on the Cost of Inequality." *American Sociological Review* 54:597–611.

Miedzian, Miriam. 1991. *Boys Will Be Boys: Breaking the Link between Masculinity and Violence.* New York: Doubleday.

Milgram, Stanley. 1974. *Obedience to Authority.* New York: Harper and Row.

Mills, C. Wright. 1958. *The Causes of World War Three.* New York: Simon and Schuster.

———. 1963. *Power, Politics and People.* New York: Ballantine.

Morgenthau, Hans. 1985. *Politics among Nations: The Struggle for Power and for Peace.* New York: Alfred A. Knopf.
Moskos, Charles C. 1970. *The American Enlisted Man.* New York: Russell Sage Foundation.
Moskos, Charles C., and Frank R. Wood. 1988. *The Military: More than Just a Job?* Washington, D.C.: Pergamon-Brassey.
Moyer, K. E. 1976. *The Psychobiology of Aggression.* New York: Harper and Row.
Naroll, Raoul, Vern L. Bullough, and Frada Naroll. 1974. *Military Deterrence in History: A Pilot Cross-Historical Survey.* Albany: State University of New York Press.
Osgood, Charles E. 1962. *An Alternative to War or Surrender.* Urbana: University of Illinois Press.
Ostos, Tony. 1991. "Alternatives to Gang Membership: The Paramount Plan." *Public Health Reports* 106(3): 241.
Otterbein, K. F. 1973. "The Anthropology of War." In *Handbook of Social and Cultural Anthropology.* Ed. J. Honigmann. Pp. 923–58. New York: Columbia University Press.
Pacholski, Richard. 1991. "Nuclear Weapons and Nuclear War." Pp. 341–58 in *Horrendous Death, Health, and Well-Being,* ed. Leviton.
Paige, Glenn D. 1993. *To Nonviolent Political Science: From Seasons of Violence.* Honolulu: Center for Global Nonviolence Planning Project, Matsunaga Institute for Peace, University of Hawaii.
Parenti, Michael. 1989. *The Sword and the Dollar: Imperialism, Revolution, and the Arms Race.* New York: St. Martin's Press.
Patterson, Gerald R. 1989. *Depression and Aggression in Family Interaction.* Hillsdale, N.J.: Lawrence Erlbaum Associates.
Pear, Tom Hatherley. 1950. *Psychological Factors of Peace and War.* New York: Philosophical Library.
Pearce, Jenny. 1982. *Under the Eagle: U.S. Intervention in Central America and the Caribbean.* Boston: South End Press.
Pepinsky, Harold E. 1991. *The Geometry of Violence and Democracy.* Bloomington: Indiana University Press.
Pepinsky, Harold E., and Richard Quinney, eds. 1991. *Criminology as Peacemaking.* Bloomington: Indiana University Press.
Peterson, V. Spike, and Anne Sisson-Runyon. 1993. *Global Gender Issues.* Boulder, Colo.: Westview Press.
Prothrow-Stith, Deborah. 1991. "Needed: A New Pathway to the Prevention of Violence." *Public Health Reports* 106:263–65.
Prothrow-Stith, Deborah, with Michaele Weisman. 1991. *Deadly Consequences.* New York: HarperCollins.
Reardon, Betty A. 1985. *Sexism and the War System.* New York: Teachers College Press.

Reiman, Jeffrey. 1986. *The Rich Get Richer and the Poor Get Prison.* New York: John Wiley.

Reiss, Albert J. 1993. "Whither the Craft of Criminology." *Journal of Research in Crime and Delinquency* 30(November): 505–14.

Reiss, Albert J., and Jeffrey A. Roth, eds. 1993. *Understanding and Preventing Violence.* Washington, D.C.: National Academy Press.

Richardson, Frank. 1981. *The Public and the Bomb.* Edinburgh: William Blackwood.

Rieder, Jonathan. 1984. "The Social Organization of Vengeance." In *Toward a General Theory of Social Control.* Ed. Donald Black. Pp. 131–62. Orlando, Fla.: Academic Press.

Robock, Alan. 1991. "Nuclear Winter: Global Horrendous Death." Pp. 241–63 in *Horrendous Death, Health, and Well-Being,* ed. Leviton.

Rothenberg, Gunther. 1977. *The Art of Warfare in the Age of Napoleon.* London: Batsford.

Sanders, Jerry W. 1983. "Empire at Bay: Containment Strategies and American Politics at the Crossroads." World Policy Institute paper, no. 25.

Saunders, J. J. 1971. *The History of the Mongol Conquests.* London: Routledge and Kegan Paul.

Scheff, Thomas J. 1994. *Bloody Revenge: Emotion, Nationalism, and War.* Boulder, Colo.: Westview Press.

Schuetz, Arnold. 1991. "Casualties in Future Wars." Pp. 83–108 in *Horrendous Death, Health, and Well-Being,* ed. Leviton.

Schwartz, William, and Charles Derber, with Gordon Fellman, William Gamson, Morris Schwartz, and Patrick Withen. 1990. *The Nuclear Seduction: Why the Arms Race Doesn't Matter—and What Does.* Berkeley: University of California Press.

Schwendinger, Julia R., and Herman Schwendinger. 1983. *Rape and Inequality.* Beverly Hills, Calif.: Sage.

Segal, David R. 1986. "Measuring the Institutional Occupational Change Thesis." *Armed Forces and Society* 12:351–76.

Segal, David, and Mady Wechsler Segal. 1988. "Military Sociology." *International Military and Defense Encyclopedia.* 5:2449–55. Washington, D.C.: Brassey's.

Sharp, Gene. 1973. *The Politics of Nonviolent Action.* 3 vols. Boston: Porter Sargent.

Shaw, Martin, ed. 1984. *War, State, and Society.* New York: St. Martin's Press.

———. 1991. *Post-Military Society: Militarism, Demilitarization, and War at the End of the Twentieth Century.* Philadelphia: Temple University Press.

Shils, Edward, and Morris Janowitz. 1948. "Cohesion and Disintegration in the German Wehrmacht in World War II." *Public Opinion Quarterly* 21:281–315.

Singer, J. David. 1965. *Human Behavior and International Politics.* Chicago: Rand McNally.

Singer, J. David, and Melvin Small. 1972. *The Wages of War, 1816–1965: A Statistical Handbook.* New York: John Wiley.

Slater, Philip. 1991. *A Dream Deferred: America's Discontent and the Search for a New Democratic Ideal.* Boston: Beacon.

Smock, David R. 1993. *Making War and Waging Peace: Foreign Intervention in Africa.* Washington, D.C.: U.S. Institute of Peace.

Snow, David A., E. Burke Rochford Jr., Steven K. Worden, and Robert D. Benford. 1986. "Frame Alignment Process, Micromobilization, and Movement Participation." *American Sociological Review* 51:464–81.

Sorel, Georges. [1950] 1961. *Reflections on Violence.* Trans. T. E. Hulme and J. Roth. New York: Collier.

Sorokin, Pitirim. 1937–41. *Social and Cultural Dynamics.* 4 vols. New York: American.

Stanko, Elizabeth. 1985. *Intimate Intrusions: Women's Experience of Male Violence.* London: Routledge and Kegan Paul.

Stark, Evan. 1991. "Preventing Primary Homicide." Pp. 109–36 in *Horrendous Death, Health, and Well-Being,* ed. Leviton.

Stillion, Judith. 1991. "Growing Up in the Shadows." Pp. 265–90 in *Horrendous Death, Health, and Well-Being,* ed. Leviton.

Stockholm International Peace Research Institute (SIPRI). 1993. *SIPRI Yearbook 1993: World Armaments and Disarmament.* New York: Oxford University Press.

Stockwell, John. 1978. *In Search of Enemies: A CIA Story.* New York: Norton.

Stohl, Michael, and George Lopez, eds. 1986. *Government Violence and Repression.* New York: Greenwood Press.

Store, Richard. 1992. "HHS Violence Initiative Caught in a Crossfire." *Science* 258(9 October): 212–13.

Stouffer, Samuel A., Edward A. Suchman, Leland C. DeVinney, Shirley A. Star, and Robin M. Williams Jr. 1949. *The American Soldier.* Vol. 1: *Adjustment during Army Life;* Vol. 2: *Combat and Its Aftermath.* Princeton: Princeton University Press.

Strachan, Hew. 1983. *European Armies and the Conduct of War.* London: George Allen and Unwin.

Strauss, Murray A., Richard J. Gelles, and Suzanne K. Steinmetz. 1980. *Behind Closed Doors: Violence in the American Family.* New York: Doubleday/Anchor.

Strauss, Murray A., and Denise A. Donnelly. 1984. *Beating the Devil Out of Them: Corporal Punishment in American Families.* New York: Lexington.

Swerdlow, Amy. 1993. *Women Strike for Peace: Traditional Motherhood and Radical Politics in the 1960s.* Chicago: University of Chicago Press.

Tedeschi, James T., and Richard B. Felson. 1994. *Violence, Aggression and Coercive Actions.* Washington, D.C.: American Psychological Association.

Thompson, E. P. 1982. *Exterminism and the Cold War.* London: New Left Books.

———. 1985. *The Heavy Dancers.* New York: Pantheon.

———. 1986. *Mad Dogs: The U.S. Raids on Libya.* Ed. Mary Kaldor and Paul Anderson. London: Pluto Press, in association with European Nuclear Disarmament.

Tilly, Charles. 1978. *From Mobilization to Revolution.* Reading, Mass.: Addison-Wesley.

———. 1993. *European Revolutions, 1492–1992.* Oxford: Blackwell.

Tomasevki, Katarina. 1993. *Women and Human Rights.* London: Zed Books.

Turpin, Jennifer. 1986. "Rape as a Social Problem." In *The Austin Rape Crisis Center Training Manual.* Pp. 1–35. Austin, Tex.: Austin Rape Crisis Center.

———. 1995. *Reinventing the Soviet Self: Media and Social Change in the Former Soviet Union.* Westport, Conn.: Praeger.

U.S. Dept. of Justice. 1992. *Criminal Victimization in the United States, 1990.* Washington, D.C.: Government Printing Office.

Urban, Gregory. 1987. "Rhetoric of a War Chief." Paper presented to the Violence Study Group, University of Texas, Austin, October 1989.

Vickers, Jeanne. 1993. *Women and War.* London: Zed Books.

Wachtel, Paul. 1983. *The Poverty of Affluence.* New York: Free Press.

Wallerstein, Emmanuel. 1983. *The Politics of the World Economy.* Cambridge: Cambridge University Press.

Weber, Max. 1947. *The Theory of Social and Economic Organization.* New York: Oxford University Press.

———. 1968. *Economy and Society.* 3 vols. New York: Bedminster Press.

Weiner, Neil A., Margaret Zahn, and Rita Sagi, eds. 1990. *Violence: Patterns, Causes, Public Policy.* San Diego: Harcourt Brace Jovanovich.

Welch, David A. 1993. *Justice and the Genesis of War.* Cambridge: Cambridge University Press.

Wellard, James. 1982. *By the Waters of Babylon.* London: Hutchinson.

Weston, Burns H., ed. 1984. *Toward Nuclear Disarmament and Global Security.* Boulder, Colo.: Westview Press.

Weston, Burns H., Richard A. Falk, and Anthony D'Amato, eds. 1980. *International Law and World Order.* St. Paul, Minn.: West.

Wheeler, Stanton, David Weisburd, and Nancy Bode. 1982. "Sentencing the White Collar Offender: Rhetoric and Reality." *American Sociological Review* 47:641–59.

White, Ralph. [1968] 1970. *Nobody Wanted War: Misperception in Vietnam and Other Wars.* Rev. ed. Garden City, N.Y.: Anchor.

———. 1984. *Fearful Warriors: A Psychological Profile of U.S.-Soviet Relations.* New York: Free Press.

———, ed. 1986. *Psychology and the Prevention of Nuclear War.* New York: New York University Press.

Wilson, James Q. 1975. *Thinking about Crime.* New York: Vintage.

Wilson, James Q., and Richard Hernnstein. 1985. *Crime and Human Nature.* Cambridge, Mass.: Harvard University Press.

Wittner, Lawrence S. 1993. *One World or None: A History of the World Nuclear Disarmament Movement through 1953.* Stanford, Calif.: Stanford University Press.

Wright, John B. 1971. *Bushman Raiders of the Drakarsberg, 1840–1870.* Pietermarizburg: University of Natal Press.

Wright, Quincy. 1942. *A Study of War.* 2 vols. Chicago: University of Chicago Press.

Zwi, Anthony, Joanne Macrae, and Antonio Ugalde. 1992. "Children and War." *Kangaroo* 1(December): 46–50.

1

Doubling: The Faustian Bargain

Robert Jay Lifton

[In this chapter, Lifton connects microprocesses with macrolevel violence, arguing that psychological processes occur within the self in order for ordinary people to commit horrendous acts of violence. Using the Nazi doctors as a case study, Lifton argues that the doctors experienced "doubling," or "the psychological means by which one invokes the evil potential of the self."

Lifton shows how the social environment, in this case Auschwitz, demands that individuals adapt in order to function in that environment. The Auschwitz self fit in with the broader Auschwitz environment, which altered the meaning of murder, thus legitimating formerly illegitimate killing. In this way, a political movement demanded individual psychological change, and "normal" people participated in genocide.]

> Not only will you break through the paralyzing difficulties of the time—you will break through time itself . . . and dare to be barbaric, twice barbaric indeed.
>
> *Thomas Mann*

> Any of us could be the man who encounters his double.
>
> *Friedrich Durrenmat*

The key to understanding how Nazi doctors came to do the work of Auschwitz is the psychological principle I call "doubling": the division of the self into two functioning wholes, so that a part-self acts as an entire self. An Auschwitz doctor could, through doubling, not only kill and contribute to killing but organize silently, on behalf of that evil project, an entire self-structure (or self-process) encompassing virtually all aspects of his behavior.

Doubling, then, was the psychological vehicle for the Nazi doctor's Faustian bargain with the diabolical environment in exchange for his contribution to the killing; he was offered various psychological and material benefits on behalf of privileged adaptation. Beyond Auschwitz was the larger Faustian temptation offered to German doctors in general: that of becoming the theorists and implementers of a cosmic scheme of racial cure by means of victimization and mass murder.

One is always ethically responsible for Faustian bargains—a responsibility in no way abrogated by the fact that much doubling takes place outside of awareness. In exploring doubling, I engage in psychological probing on behalf of illuminating evil. For the individual Nazi doctor in Auschwitz, doubling was likely to mean a choice for evil.

Generally speaking, doubling involves five characteristics. There is, first, a dialectic between two selves in terms of autonomy and connection. The individual Nazi doctor needed his Auschwitz self to function psychologically in an environment so antithetical to his previous ethical standards. At the same time, he needed his prior self to continue to see himself as humane physician, husband, father. The Auschwitz self had to be both autonomous and connected to the prior self that gave rise to it. Second, doubling follows a holistic principle. The Auschwitz self "succeeded" because it was inclusive and could connect with the entire Auschwitz environment: it rendered coherent, and gave form to, various themes and mechanisms, which I shall discuss shortly. Third, doubling has a life-death dimension: the Auschwitz self was perceived by the perpetrator as a form of psychological survival in a death-dominated environment; in other words, we have the paradox of a "killing self" being created on behalf of what one perceives as one's own healing or survival. Fourth, a major function of doubling, as in Auschwitz, is likely to be the avoidance of guilt: the second self tends to be the one performing the "dirty work." And, finally, doubling involves both an unconscious dimension—taking place, as stated, largely outside of awareness—and a significant change in moral consciousness. These five characteristics frame and pervade all else that goes on psychologically in doubling.

For instance, the holistic principle differentiates doubling from the traditional psychoanalytic concept of "splitting." This latter has had several meanings but tends to suggest a sequestering off of a portion of the self so that the "split off" element ceases to respond to the environment (as in what I have been calling "psychic numbing"), or is otherwise at odds with the remainder of the self. Splitting in this sense resembles what Pierre Janet (1907), Freud's nineteenth-century contemporary, originally called "dissociation," and Freud himself tended to equate the two terms. But in regards to sustained forms of adaptation, there has been confusion about how to explain the autonomy of that separated "piece" of the self—confusion over (as one thoughtful commentator has put it) "What splits in splitting?" (Pruyser 1975).[1]

"Splitting" or "dissociation" can thus denote something about Nazi doctors' suppression of feeling, or psychic numbing, in relation to their participation in murder.[2] But to chart their involvement in a continuous routine of killing, over a year or two or more, one needs an explanatory principle that draws upon the entire, functioning self. (The same principle applies in sustained psychiatric disturbance, and my stress on doubling is consistent with the increasing contemporary focus on the holistic function of the self.) (Erikson 1968; Kohut 1977; Guntrip 1971; Lifton 1983)

Doubling is part of the universal potential for what William James called the "divided self": that is, for opposing tendencies in the self. James quoted the nineteenth-century French writer Alphonse Duadet's despairing cry "Homo duplex, homo duplex!" in noting his "horrible duality"—as, in the face of his brother Henri's death, Daudet's "first self wept" while his "second self" sat back and somewhat mockingly staged the scene for an imagined theatrical performance (James 1961). To James and Daudet the potential for doubling is part of being human, and the process is likely to take place in extremity, in relation to death.

But that "opposing self" can become dangerously unrestrained, as it did in the Nazi doctors. And when it becomes so, as Otto Rank discovered in his extensive studies of the "double" in literature and folklore, that opposing self can become the usurper from within and replace the original self until it "speaks" for the entire person (Rank 1958, 1971). Rank's work also suggests that the potential for an opposing self, in effect the potential for evil, is necessary to the human psyche: the loss of one's shadow or soul or "double" means death.

In general psychological terms, the adaptive potential for doubling is integral to the human psyche and can at times be life saving: for a soldier in combat, for instance; or for a victim of brutality such as an Auschwitz inmate, who must also undergo a form of doubling in order to survive. Clearly, the "opposing self" can be life enhancing. But under certain conditions it can embrace evil with an extreme lack of restraint.

The Nazi doctor's situation resembles that of one of Rank's examples (taken from a 1913 German film, *The Student of Prague*): a student fencing champion accepts an evil magician's offer of great wealth and the chance for marriage with his beloved in return for anything the old magician wishes to take from the room; what he takes is the student's mirror image, a frequent representation of the double. That double eventually becomes a killer by making use of the student's fencing skills in a duel with his beloved's suitor, despite the fact that the student (his original self) has promised the woman's father that he will not engage in such a duel. This variation on the Faust legend parallels the Nazi doctor's "bargain" with Auschwitz and the regime: to do the killing, he offered an opposing self (the evolving Auschwitz self)—a self that, in violating his own moral standards, met with no effective resistance and in fact used his original skills (in this case, medical-scientific) (Rank 1958, 1971; Kracauer 1947).[3]

Rank stressed the death symbolism of the double as "symptomatic of the disintegration of the modern personality type." That disintegration leads to a need for "self-perpetuation in one's own image" (Rank 1958)—what I would call a literalized form of immortality—as compared with "the perpetuation of the self in work reflecting one's personality" or a creative symbolic form of immortality. Rank saw the Narcissus legend as depicting both the danger of the literalized mode and the necessity of the shift to the creative mode (as embodied by the "artist-hero").[4] But the Nazi movement encouraged its would-be artist-hero, the physician, to remain, like Narcissus, in thralldom to his own image. Here Mengele comes immediately to mind, his extreme narcissism in the service of his quest for omnipotence, and his exemplification to the point of caricature of the general situation of Nazi doctors in Auschwitz (Rank 1958).

The way in which doubling allowed Nazi doctors to avoid guilt was not by the elimination of conscience but by what can be called the *transfer of conscience.* The requirements of conscience were transferred to the Auschwitz self, which placed it within its own criteria for good (duty, loyalty to group, "improving" Auschwitz conditions, etc.), thereby freeing the original self from responsibility for actions there. Rank spoke similarly of guilt "which forces the hero no longer to accept the responsibility for certain actions of his ego, but place it upon another ego, a double, who is either personified by the devil himself or is created by making a diabolical pact" (Rank 1971): that is, the Faustian bargain of Nazi doctors mentioned earlier. Rank spoke of a "powerful consciousness of guilt" as initiating the transfer (Rank 1971), but for most Nazi doctors, the doubling maneuver seemed to fend off that sense of guilt prior to its developing, or to its reaching conscious dimensions.

There is an inevitable connection between death and guilt. Rank equates the opposing self with a "form of evil which represents the perishable and mortal part of the personality" (Rank 1958). The double is evil in that it represents one's own death. The Auschwitz self of the Nazi doctor similarly assumed the death issue for him but at the same time used its evil project as a way of staving off awareness of his own "perishable and mortal part." It does the "dirty work" for the entire self by rendering that work "proper" and in that way protects the entire self from awareness of its own guilt and its own death.

In doubling, one part of the self "disavows" another part. What is repudiated is not reality itself—the individual Nazi doctor was aware of what he was doing via the Auschwitz self—but the meaning of that reality. The Nazi doctor knew that he selected, but did not interpret selections as murder. One level of disavowal, then, was the Auschwitz self's altering of the meaning of murder; and on another, the repudiation by the original self of *anything* done by the Auschwitz self. From the moment of its formation, the Auschwitz self so violated the Nazi doctor's previous self-concept as to require more or less permanent disavowal. Indeed, disavowal was the lifeblood of the Auschwitz self.[5]

Doubling, Splitting, and Evil

Doubling is an active psychological process, a means of *adaptation to extremity.* That is why I use the verb form, as opposed to the more usual noun form, "the double." The adaptation requires a dissolving of "psychic glue" (Allison 1977) as an alternative to a radical breakdown of the self. In Auschwitz, the pattern was established under the duress of the individual doctor's transition period. At that time the Nazi doctor experienced his own death anxiety as well as such death equivalents as fear of disintegration, separation, and stasis. He needed a functional Auschwitz self to still his anxiety. And that Auschwitz self had to assume hegemony on an everyday basis, reducing expressions of the prior self to odd moments and to contacts with family and friends outside the camp. Nor did most Nazi doctors resist that usurpation as long as they remained in the camp. Rather they welcomed it as the only means of psychological function. If an environment is sufficiently extreme, and one chooses to remain in it, one may be able to do so *only* by means of doubling.

Yet doubling does not include the radical dissociation and sustained separateness characteristic of multiple or "dual personality." In the latter condition, the two selves are more profoundly distinct and autonomous, and tend either not to know about each other or else to see each other as alien. The pattern for dual or multiple personality, moreover, is thought to begin early in childhood, and to solidify and maintain itself more or less indefinitely. Yet in the development of multiple personality, there are likely to be such influences as intense psychic or physical trauma, an atmosphere of extreme ambivalence, and severe conflict and confusion over identifications[6]—all of which can be instrumental in doubling. Also relevant to both conditions is Janet's principle that "once baptized"—that is, named or confirmed by someone in authority—a particular self is likely to become more clear and definite (Ellenberger 1970). Though never as stable as a self in multiple personality, the Auschwitz self nonetheless underwent a similar baptism when the Nazi doctor conducted his first selections.

A recent writer has employed the metaphor of a tree to delineate the depth of "splitting" in schizophrenia and multiple personality—a metaphor that could be expanded to include doubling. In schizophrenia, the rent in the self is "like the crumbling and breaking of a tree that has deteriorated generally, at least in some important course of the trunk, down toward or to the roots." In multiple personality, that rent is specific and limited, "as in an essentially sound tree that does not split very far down" (Bowers et al. 1971). Doubling takes place still higher on a tree whose roots, trunk, and larger branches have previously experienced no impairment; of the two branches artificially separated, one grows fetid bark and leaves in a way that enables the other to maintain ordinary growth, and the two intertwine sufficiently to merge again should external conditions favor that merging.

Was the doubling of Nazi doctors an antisocial "character disorder"? Not in the classical sense, in that the process tended to be more a form of adaptation than a lifelong pattern. But doubling can include elements considered characteristic of "sociopathic" character impairment: these include a disorder of feeling (swings between numbing and rage), pathological avoidance of a sense of guilt, and resort to violence to overcome "masked depression" (related to repressed guilt and numbing) and maintain a sense of vitality (Lifton 1983; King 1975). Similarly, in both situations, destructive or even murderous behavior may cover over feared disintegration of the self.

The disorder in the type of doubling I have described is more focused and temporary and occurs as part of a larger institutional structure which encourages or even demands it. In that sense, Nazi doctors' behavior resembles that of certain terrorists—and members of the Mafia, of "death squads" organized by dictators, or even of delinquent gangs. In all these situations, profound ideological, family, ethnic, and sometimes age-specific ties help shape criminal behavior. Doubling may well be an important psychological mechanism for individuals living within any criminal sub-culture: the Mafia or "death squad" chief who coldly orders (or himself carries out) the murder of a rival while remaining a loving husband, father, and churchgoer. The doubling is adaptive to the extreme conditions created by the subculture, but additional influences, some of which can begin early in life, always contribute to the process.[7] That, too, was the case with the Nazi doctors.

In sum, doubling is the psychological means by which one invokes the evil potential of the self. That evil is neither inherent in the self nor foreign to it. To live out the doubling and call forth the evil is a moral choice for which one is responsible, whatever the level of consciousness involved.[8] By means of doubling, Nazi doctors made a Faustian choice for evil: in the process of doubling, in fact, lies an overall key to human evil.

Varieties of Doubling

While individual Nazi doctors in Auschwitz doubled in different ways, all of them doubled. Ernst B., for instance, limited his doubling; in avoiding selections, he was resisting a full-blown Auschwitz self. Yet his conscious desire to adapt to Auschwitz was an accession to at least a certain amount of doubling: it was he, after all, who said that "one could react like a normal human being in Auschwitz only for the first few hours"; after that "you were caught and had to go along," which meant that you had to double. His own doubling was evident in his sympathy for Mengele and, at least to some extent, for the most extreme expressions of the Nazi ethos (the image of the Nazis as a "world blessing" and of Jews as the world's "fundamental evil"). And despite the limit to his doubling, he retains aspects of his Auschwitz self to this day in his way of judging Auschwitz behavior.

In contrast, Josef Mengele's embrace of the Auschwitz self gave the impression of a quick adaptive affinity, causing one to wonder whether he required any doubling at all. But doubling was indeed required in a man who befriended children to an unusual degree and then drove some of them personally to the gas chamber; or by a man so "collegial" in his relationship to prisoner doctors and so ruthlessly flamboyant in his conduct of selections. Whatever his affinity for Auschwitz, a man who could be pictured under ordinary conditions as "a slightly sadistic German professor" had to form a new self to become an energetic killer. The point about Mengele's doubling was that his prior self could be readily absorbed into the Auschwitz self; and his continuing allegiance to the Nazi ideology and project probably enabled his Auschwitz self, more than in the case of other Nazi doctors, to remain active over the years after the Second World War.

The doubling of Eduard Wirths, the chief Auschwitz doctor, was neither limited (like Dr. B.'s) nor harmonious (like Mengele's): it was both strong and conflicted. We see him as a "divided self" because both selves retained their power: the prior self enabling him to be humane and thoughtful with many individual prisoners; his Auschwitz self enabling him to function as an efficient Nazi bureaucrat in setting up and maintaining the structure of Auschwitz medicalized killing. Yet his doubling was the most successful of all from the standpoint of maintaining the Auschwitz institution and the Nazi project. Even his suicide was a mark of that success: while the Nazi defeat enabled him to equate his Auschwitz self more clearly with evil, he nonetheless retained responsibility to that Auschwitz self sufficiently to remain inwardly divided and unable to imagine any possibility of resolution and renewal—either legally, morally, or psychologically.

Within the Auschwitz structure, significant doubling included future goals and even a sense of hope. Styles of doubling varied because each Nazi doctor created his Auschwitz self out of his prior self, with its particular history, and with his own psychological mechanisms. But in all Nazi doctors, prior self and Auschwitz self were connected by the overall Nazi ethos and the general authority of the regime. Doubling was a shared theme among them.

Doubling and Institutions

Indeed, Auschwitz as an *institution*—as an atrocity-producing situation—ran on doubling. An atrocity-producing situation is one so structured externally (in this case, institutionally) that the average person entering it (in this case, as part of the German authority) will commit or become associated with atrocities. Always important to an atrocity-producing situation is its capacity to motivate individuals psychologically toward engaging in atrocity (Lifton 1984).

In an institution as powerful as Auschwitz, the external environment could set the tone for much of an individual doctor's "internal environment." The demand for doubling was a part of the environmental message immediately perceived by Nazi doctors, the implicit command to bring forth a self that could adapt to killing without one's feeling oneself a murderer. Doubling became not just an individual enterprise but a shared psychological process, the group norm, part of the Auschwitz "weather." And that group process was intensified by the general awareness that, whatever went on in other camps, Auschwitz was the great technical center of the Final Solution. One had to double in order that one's life and work there not be interfered with either by the corpses one helped to produce or by those "living dead" (the *Muselmänner*) all around one.

Inevitably, the Auschwitz pressure toward doubling extended to prisoner doctors, the most flagrant examples of whom were those few who came to work closely with the Nazis. Even those prisoner doctors who held strongly to their healing ethos, and underwent minimal doubling, inadvertently contributed to Nazi doctors' doubling simply by working with them, as they had to, and thereby in some degree confirmed a Nazi doctor's Auschwitz self.

Doubling undoubtedly occurred extensively in nonmedical Auschwitz personnel as well. Rudolf Höss, commandant of Auschwitz, told how noncommissioned officers regularly involved in selections "pour[ed] out their hearts" to him about the difficulty of their work (their prior self speaking)—but went on doing that work (their Auschwitz self directing behavior). Höss described the Auschwitz choices: "either to become cruel, to become heartless and no longer to respect human life [that is, to develop a highly functional Auschwitz self] or to be weak and to get to the point of a nervous breakdown [that is, to hold on to one's prior self, which in Auschwitz was nonfunctional]" (Buchheim 1968). But in the Nazi doctor, the doubling was particularly stark in that a prior healing self gave rise to a killing self that should have been, but functionally was not, in direct opposition to it. And as in any atrocity-producing situation, Nazi doctors found themselves in a psychological climate where they were virtually certain to choose evil: they were propelled, that is, toward murder.

Doubling—Nazi and Medical

Beyond Auschwitz, there was much in the Nazi movement that promoted doubling. The overall Nazi project, replete with cruelty, required constant doubling in the service of carrying out that cruelty. The doubling could take the form of a gradual process of "slippery slope" compromises: the slow emergence of a functional "Nazi self" via a series of destructive actions, at first agreed to grudgingly, followed by a sequence of assigned tasks each more incriminating, if not more murderous, than the previous ones.

Doubling could also be more dramatic, infused with transcendence, the sense (described by a French fascist who joined the SS) of being someone entering a religious order "who must now divest himself of his past" and of being "reborn into a new European race" (de La Mazière 1974). That new Nazi self could take on a sense of mystical fusion with the German *Volk*, with "destiny," and with immortalizing powers. Always there was the combination noted earlier of idealism and terror, imagery of destruction and renewal, so that "gods . . . appear as both destroyers and culture-heroes, just as the Führer could appear as front comrade and master builder" (Hanson 1981). Heinrich Himmler, especially in his speeches to his SS leaders within their "oath-bound community" (as sociologist Werner Picht has phrased it) (Hohne 1970), called for the kind of doubling necessary to engage in what he considered to be heroic cruelty, especially in the killing of Jews.

The degree of doubling was not necessarily equivalent to Nazi party membership; thus, the German playwright Rolf Hochhuth (1980) could claim that "the great divide was between Nazis [meaning those with well-developed Nazi selves] and decent people, not between Party members and other Germans." But probably never has a political movement demanded doubling with the intensity and scale of the Nazis.

Doctors as a group may be more susceptible to doubling than others. For example, a former Nazi doctor claimed that the anatomist's insensitivity toward skeletons and corpses accounted for his friend August Hirt's grotesque "anthropological" collection of Jewish skulls. While hardly a satisfactory explanation, this doctor was referring to a genuine pattern not just of numbing but of medical doubling. That doubling usually begins with the student's encounter with the corpse he or she must dissect, often enough on the first day of medical school. One feels it necessary to develop a "medical self," which enables one not only to be relatively inured to death but to function reasonably efficiently in relation to the many-sided demands of the work. The ideal doctor, to be sure, remains warm and humane by keeping that doubling to a minimum. But few doctors meet that ideal standard. Since studies have suggested that a psychological motivation for entering the medical profession can be the overcoming of an unusually great fear of death, it is possible that this fear in doctors propels them in the direction of doubling when encountering deadly environments. Doctors drawn to the Nazi movement in general, and to SS or concentration-camp medicine in particular, were likely to be those with the greatest previous medical doubling. But even doctors without outstanding Nazi sympathies could well have had a certain experience with doubling and a proclivity for its further manifestations.

Certainly the tendency toward doubling was particularly strong among *Nazi* doctors. Given the heroic vision held out to them—as cultivators of the genes and as physicians to the *Volk,* and as militarized healers combining the life-death power of shaman and general—any cruelty they might perpetrate was all too readily drowned in hubris. And their medical hubris was furthered by their role in the sterilization and "euthanasia" projects within a vision of curing the ills of the Nordic race and the German people.

Doctors who ended up undergoing the extreme doubling necessitated by the "euthanasia" killing centers and the death camps were probably unusually susceptible to doubling. There was, of course, an element of chance in where one was sent, but doctors assigned either to the killing centers or to the death camps tended to be strongly committed to Nazi ideology. They may well have also had greater schizoid tendencies, or been particularly prone to numbing and omnipotence-sadism, all of which also enhance doubling. Since, even under extreme conditions, people have a way of finding and staying in situations they connect with psychologically, we can suspect a certain degree of self-selection there too. In these ways, previous psychological characteristics of a doctor's self had considerable significance—but significance in respect to tendency or susceptibility, and no more. Considerable doubling occurred in people with the most varied psychological characteristics.

We thus find ourselves returning to the recognition that most of what Nazi doctors did would be within the potential capability—at least under certain conditions—of most doctors and of most people. But once embarked on doubling in Auschwitz, a Nazi doctor did indeed separate himself from other physicians and from other human beings. Doubling was the mechanism by which a doctor, in his actions, moved from the ordinary to the demonic.

Doubling as German?

Is there something especially German in doubling? Germany, after all, is the land of the *Doppelgänger*, the double as formalized in literature and humor. Otto Rank, while tracing the theme back to Greek mythology and drama, stresses its special prominence in German literary and philosophical romanticism, and refers to the "inner split personality, characteristic of the romantic type" (Rank 1958). That characterization, not only in literature but in political and social thought, is consistent with such images as the "torn condition" (*Zerrissenheit*), or "cleavage," and the "passages and galleries" of the German soul (Pinson 1966). Nietzsche asserted that duality in a personal way by depicting himself as both "the antichrist" and "the crucified"; and similar principles of "duality-in-unity" can be traced to earlier German writers and poets such as Hölderlin, Heine, and Kleist (Gray 1965).

Indeed, Goethe's treatment of the Faust legend is a story of German doubling: "Two souls, alas, reside within my breast / And each withdraws from and repels its brother" (Pinson 1966). And the original Faust, that doctor of magic, bears more than a passing resemblance to his Nazi countrymen in Auschwitz. In Goethe's hands, Faust is inwardly divided into a prior self, responsible to worldly commitments, including those of love, and a second self characterized by hubris in its quest for the supernatural power of "the higher ancestral places."[9] In a still earlier version of the legend, Faust acknowledges the hegemony of his evil self by telling a would-be spiritual rescuer, "I have gone further than you think and have pledged myself to the devil with my own blood, to be his in eternity, body, and soul" (Kaufman 1961). Here his attitude resembles the Auschwitz self's fidelity to evil. And Thomas Mann's specific application of the Faust legend to the Nazi historical experience captures, through a musician protagonist, the diabolical quest of the Auschwitz self for unlimited "creative power": the promise of absolute breakthrough, of conquering time and therefore death; if the new self will "dare to be barbaric, twice barbaric indeed" (Mann 1948).[10]

Within German psychological and cultural experience, the theme of doubling is powerful and persistent. Moreover, German vulnerability to doubling was undoubtedly intensified by the historical dislocations and fragmentations of cultural symbols following the First World War. Who can deny the Germanic "feel" of so much of the doubling process, as best described by a brilliant product of German culture, Otto Rank?

Yet the first great poet to take up Faust as a theme was not Goethe but the English playwright Christopher Marlowe. And there has been a series of celebrated English and American expressions of the general theme of the double, running through Edgar Allan Poe's "William Wilson," Robert Louis Stevenson's *The Strange Case of Dr. Jekyll and Mr. Hyde,* Oscar Wilde's *Picture of Dorian Gray,* and the comic strip *Superman.* Indeed, the theme penetrates the work of writers of all nationalities: for instance, Guy de Maupassant's *Le Horla* and Dostoevski's novel *The Double* (Rank 1971; Rogers 1970).

Clearly, the Nazis took hold of a universal phenomenon, if one given special emphasis by their own culture and history. But they could not have brought about widespread doubling without the existence of certain additional psychological patterns that dominated Auschwitz behavior. These eternalized expressions of the environment of the death camp came to characterize the Auschwitz self, and have significance beyond that place and time.

Notes

This chapter first appeared in Robert Jay Lifton's *The Future of Immortality and Other Essays for a Nuclear Age* (New York: Basic Books, 1987), 195–208. Copyright © 1987 by Robert Jay Lifton. Reprinted by permission of Basic Books, a division of HarperCollins Publishers, Inc.

1. This writer seemed to react against the idea of a separated-off piece of the self when he ended the article by asking, "Why should we invent a special intrapsychic act of splitting to account for those phenomena as if some internal chopper were at work to produce them?" (Pruyser 1975; Lustman 1977; Rycroft 1968). Janet meant by "dissociation" the hysteric's tendency to "sacrifice" or "abandon" certain psychological functions, so that these become "dissociated" from the rest of the mind and give rise to "automatisms," or segmented-off symptom complexes (Janet 1907, 1923; Havens 1973; Ellenberger 1970). Freud spoke, in his early work with Josef Breuer, of "splitting of consciousness," "splitting of the mind," and "splitting of personality" as important mechanisms in hysteria (Freud and Breuer 1955). Edward Glover referred to the psychic components of splitting or dissociation as "ego nuclei" (Glover 1956). And, beginning with the

work of Maxine Klein, splitting has been associated with polarization of "all good" and "all bad" imagery within the self, a process that can be consistent with normal development but, where exaggerated, can become associated with severe personality disorders now spoken of as "borderline states" (Klein 1946; Kernberg 1973).

2. Henry V. Dicks (1972) invokes this concept in his study of Nazi killers.

3. Rank's viewing of *The Student of Prague,* during a revival in the mid-1920s, was the original stimulus for a lifelong preoccupation with the theme of the double. Rank noted that the screenplay's author, Hanns Heinz Ewers, had drawn heavily on E. T. A. Hoffmann's (1952) "Story of the Lost Reflection."

4. In his earlier work, Rank followed Freud in connecting the legend with the concept of "narcissism," of libido directed toward one's own self. But Rank gave the impression that he did so uneasily, always stressing the issue of death and immortality as lurking beneath the narcissism. In his later adaptation, he boldly embraced the death theme as the earlier and more fundamental one in the Narcissus legend and spoke somewhat disdainfully of "some modern psychologists [who] claimed to have found a symbolization of their self-love principle" in it (Rank 1958). By then he had broken with Freud and established his own intellectual position.

5. Michael Franz Basch (1982) speaks of an interference with the "union of affect with percept without, however, blocking the percept from consciousness." In that sense, disavowal resembles psychic numbing, as it alters the *valencing* or emotional charge of the symbolizing process.

6. The first two influences are described in George B. Greaves (1977). Freud (1955) emphasized the third.

7. Robert W. Rieber (n.d.) uses the term "pseudopsychopathy" for what he describes as "selective joint criminal behavior" within the kinds of subculture mentioned here.

8. James S. Grotstein (1979) speaks of the development of "a separate being living within one that has been preconsciously split off and has an independent existence with independent motivation, separate agenda, etc.," and from which can emanate "evil, sadism, and destructiveness" or even "demoniacal possession." He calls this aspect of the self a "mind parasite" (after Colin Wilson) and attributes its development to those elements of the self that have been artificially suppressed and disavowed early in life.

9. The passage concerning the "two souls" continues: "One with tenacious organs holds in love / And clinging lust the world within its embraces. / The other strongly sweeps this dust above / Into the higher ancestral places."

The historian of German literature Ronald Gray (1965) finds patterns of "polarity and synthesis" in various spheres of German culture; Luther's concept of a God who "works by contraries," the Hegelian principle of thesis and antithesis, and the Marxist dialectic emerging from Hegel. In all of these, there is the "fusion of opposites," the rending of the individual as well as the collective self, and the passionate quest for unity. One could almost say that the German apocalyptic tradition—the Wagnerian "twilight of the gods" and the general theme of the death-haunted collective end—may be the "torn condition" extended into the realm of larger human connectedness and disconnectedness.

10. Mann (1948) also captures the continuity in doubling by speaking of the "implicit Satanism" in German psychology, and by having the devil make clear to the Faust figure that "we lay upon you nothing new . . . [but] only ingeniously strengthen and exaggerate all that you already are."

References

Allison, Ralph D. 1977. "When the Psychic Glue Dissolves." *HYPNOS-NOTT* (December).

Basch, Michael Franz. 1982. "The Perception of Reality and the Disavowal of Meaning." *Annual of Psychoanalysis* 11:147. New York: International Universities Press.

Bowers, Margaretta K., et al. 1971. "Theory of Multiple Personality." *International Journal of Clinical and Experimental Hypnosis* 19:60.

Buchheim, Karl. 1968. "Command and Compliance." In *Anatomy of the SS State.* Ed. Helmut Krausnick et al. P. 374. New York: Walker.

de la Mazière, Christian. 1974. *The Captive Dreamer.* Pp. 14, 34. New York: Saturday Review Press.

Dicks, Henry V. 1972. *Licensed Mass Murder: A Socio-Psychological Study of Some SS Killers.* New York: Basic Books.

Ellenberger, Henri F. 1970. *The Discovery of the Unconscious.* Pp. 364–417. New York: Basic Books.

Erikson, Erik H. 1968. *Identity: Youth and Crisis.* New York: W. W. Norton.

Freud, Sigmund. 1955. "The Ego and the Id." In *Standard Edition of the Works of Sigmund Freud.* Ed. James Strachey. Vol. 19. Pp. 30–31. London: Hogarth Press.

Freud, Sigmund, and Josef Breuer. 1955. "Studies on Hysteria." In *Standard Edition of the Works of Sigmund Freud.* Ed. James Strachey. Vol. 2. Pp. 3–305. London: Hogarth Press.

Glover, Edward. 1956. *On the Early Development of Mind: Selected Papers on Psychoanalysis.* Vol. 1. Pp. 307–23. New York: International Universities Press.

Gray, Ronald. 1965. *The German Tradition in Literature, 1871–1945.* Pp. 3, 79. Cambridge: Cambridge University Press.

Greaves, George B. 1977. "Multiple Personality: 165 Years After Mary Reynolds." *Journal of Nervous and Mental Disease* 168:577–96.

Grotstein, James S. 1979. "The Soul in Torment: An Older and Newer View of Psychopathology." *Bulletin of the National Council of Catholic Psychologists* 25:36–52.

Guntrip, Henry. 1971. *Psychoanalytic Theory, Therapy and the Self.* New York: Basic Books.

Hanson, John H. 1981. "Nazi Aesthetics." *Psychohistory Review* 9:276.

Havens, Leston. 1973. *Approaches to the Mind.* Pp. 34–62. Boston: Little, Brown.
Hochhuth, Rolf. 1980. *A German Love Story.* P. 220. Boston: Little, Brown.
Hoffmann, E. T. A. 1952. "Story of the Lost Reflection." In *Eight Tales of Hoffmann.* Ed. J. M. Cohen. London: Macmillan.
Hohne, Heinz. 1970. *The Order of Death's Hand: The Story of Hitler's S.S.* Pp. 460–61. New York: Coward-McCann.
James, William. 1961. *The Varieties of Religious Experience: A Study in Human Nature.* P. 144. New York: Collier.
Janet, Pierre. 1907. *The Major Symptoms of Hysteria.* New York: Macmillan.
———. 1923. *Psychological Healing.* New York: Macmillan.
Kaufmann, Walter. 1961. *Goethe's Faust.* P. 17. New York: Doubleday.
Kernberg, Otto F. 1973. "The Syndrome." In *Borderline Conditions and Pathological Narcissism.* Pp. 3–47. New York: Jason Aronson.
King, Charles H. 1975. "The Ego and the Integration of Violence in Homicidal Youth." *American Journal of Orthopsychiatry* 45:142.
Klein, Melanie. 1946. "Notes on Some Schizoid Mechanisms." *International Journal of Psychoanalysis* 27:99–110.
Kohut, Heinz. 1977. *The Restoration of the Self.* New York: International Universities Press.
Kracauer, Siegfried. 1947. *From Caligari to Hitler: A Psychological History of the German Film.* Pp. 28–30. Princeton: Princeton University Press.
Lifton, Robert Jay. 1983. *The Broken Connection: On Death and the Continuity of Life.* New York: Basic Books.
———. 1984. *Home from the War: Vietnam Veterans, Neither Victims nor Executioners.* New York: Basic Books.
Lustman, Jeffrey. 1977. "On Splitting." In *The Psychoanalytic Study of the Child.* Ed. Kurt Eissler et al. Pp. 19–54. New York: Harper and Row.
Mann, Thomas. 1948. *Doctor Faustus: The Life of the German Composer Adrian Leverkuhn as Told by a Friend.* P. 243. New York: Alfred A. Knopf.
Pinson, Koppel S. 1966. *Modern Germany: Its History and Civilization.* 2d ed. Pp. 1–3. New York: Macmillan.
Pruyser, Paul W. 1975. "What Splits in Splitting?" *Bulletin of the Menninger Clinic* 39:1–46.
Rank, Otto. 1958. "The Double as Immortal Self." In *Beyond Psychology.* Pp. 62–101. New York: Dover.
———. 1971. *The Double: A Psychoanalytic Study.* Chapel Hill: University of North Carolina Press.
Rieber, Robert W. n.d. "The Psychopathy of Everyday Life." Unpublished manuscript.
Rogers, Robert. 1970. *A Psychoanalytic Study of the Double in Literature.* Detroit: Wayne State University Press.
Rycroft, Charles. 1968. *A Critical Dictionary of Psychoanalysis.* Pp. 156–57. New York: Basic Books.

2

Religion and the Legitimation of Violence: Conservative Protestantism and Corporal Punishment

Christopher G. Ellison and John P. Bartkowski

[The process of socializing individuals into religious and cultural traditions provides one of the major links between personal attitudes and behavior, on the one hand, and large-scale social phenomena such as violence, on the other. In this chapter, Ellison and Bartkowski explore a case study in the legitimation of violence: the use of corporal punishment among conservative U.S. Protestants. This subculture, they argue, not only legitimates a restricted use of force by parents to enforce their authority in the family but also teaches children to view the world in a way that may result in a "cultural spillover" that legitimizes other forms of violence. They conclude, however, that further research is necessary to determine if corporal punishment produces either long-term insensitivity to various types of violence or the intergenerational transmission of violent attitudes and behaviors.]

In recent years, a new crescendo of alarm about the dangers of corporal punishment[1] has risen within popular and academic circles (Straus, Gelles, and Steinmetz 1980; LeShan 1985; Balter and Shreve 1989; Leach 1989; Kersey 1991; Levine 1991; Straus 1994). A growing number of scholars (e.g., Gelles and Straus 1988; Poole, Ushkow, Nader, Bradford, Asbury, Worthington, Sanabria, and Carruth 1991) have called on U.S. policymakers to follow the lead of other advanced industrial societies and restrict or ban the use of corporal punishment by teachers and parents alike. Several broad critiques have attacked the practice of physical punishment. For instance, some charge that this disciplinary strategy is ineffective, that it results in a variety of negative developmental outcomes (e.g., delinquency, psychopathology, academic failure, substance abuse, and social difficulties), and that it can cause serious injuries to young children (Taylor and Maurer 1985; Hotaling, Finkelhor, Kirkpatrick, and Straus 1988; Simons, Whitbeck, Conger, and Wu 1991; Simons, Johnson, and Conger 1994; Straus 1994).

In addition to these concerns, opponents of corporal punishment argue that the experience of physical punishment trains youngsters in violence in several ways: (1) by establishing an association between love and violence, (2) by encouraging the view that "might makes right" and that powerful people should be able to subordinate less powerful others by force, and (3) by teaching that feelings of anger and frustration justify the use of violence (Straus 1991). This general line of criticism has gained considerable credibility with many popular parenting experts (e.g., LeShan 1985; Leach 1989; Balter and Shreve 1989; Kersey 1991). Its widespread popularity is exemplified in this comment by Dr. Benjamin Spock, perhaps the best-known parenting expert in America:

> In earlier decades . . . I avoided a flat statement of disapproval of physical punishment. . . . What made me [reverse myself] was my growing concern over the sky-high and ever-rising figures for murders within the family, wife abuse, and child abuse in America, and our government's enthusiasm for the nuclear arms race and for an aggressive foreign policy. It's not that physical punishment creates these alarming conditions by itself, but it certainly plays a role in our acceptance of violence. If we are ever to turn toward a kindlier society and a safer world, a revulsion against the physical punishment of children would be a good place to start. (1988, 151–52)

Given these various arguments regarding the negative consequences of corporal punishment, a growing body of research explores the social and cultural bases of the continued support for corporal punishment. Several studies have linked conservative Protestantism (fundamentalism and conservative evangelicalism) with support for the use of physical force in the discipline of youngsters (Greven 1977, 1990; Maurer 1982; Wiehe 1990; Grasmick, Bursik, and Kimpel 1991; Ellison and Sherkat 1993a; Bartkowski 1995; Ellison et al. 1996). Nevertheless, efforts to understand the religious factors underlying support for corporal punishment in the United States remain in their very early stages.

Our goal is to clarify the role of contemporary conservative Protestant religious values in legitimating the practice of corporal punishment. A multidisciplinary literature on the religious legitimation of various types of violence demonstrates that religious rhetoric is often used to imbue violent conduct with particular meaning and purpose, thus *sacralizing* violence by linking it with matters of ultimate concern (e.g., salvation or divine will). Given the widespread ambivalence of societies toward violence, however, religious values are also deployed to *delimit* violence—that is, to establish boundaries or "taboo lines" that distinguish acceptable (even desirable) forms of violence from unacceptable violence (Kurtz 1995, 120–45; Turpin and Kurtz, this volume). In these ways, religion is implicated in processes that make certain uses of coercive physical force seem natural, appropriate, and unavoidable. By sustaining "ground rules" that are frequently well understood by both perpetrator and victim as well as by others in society, religious legitimation can redefine certain acts of physical force as something other (and less serious) than "violence."

While religious perspectives have helped to legitimize state-sanctioned acts of violence, such as the execution of convicted murderers and the prosecution of "just" warfare (NCCB 1983; Knelman 1985; Walters 1986; Kurtz 1988; Runyon 1989), they have also justified the corporal punishment of children by parents and other authority figures.[2] In examining this issue, we draw extensively on parenting literature that is produced and distributed primarily within conservative Protestant communities. This will allow us to explore their use of religious values and symbols to support the use of corporal punishment.

First, we investigate the sacralization of corporal punishment by elucidating the theological rationales for physical discipline promoted by conservative Protestant writers. In their view, physical punishment is much more than a means to elicit compliance from children. Rather, physical punishment is considered a vital part of a child's spiritual development, communicating lessons about the essential nature of God, the centrality of scriptural guidance over human affairs, and the importance of obedience to structures of authority over the life course. Second, we focus on the efforts of conservative Protestant parenting authors to delimit the use of physical force in the discipline of children. A careful review of that literature reveals detailed consideration of the conditions under which corporal punishment is appropriate and the methods of administering physical discipline that are acceptable, often with explicit recourse to religious scripture.

Sacralizing Violence: Theology and Support for Corporal Punishment

Biblical Inerrancy, Epistemology, and the Problem of Interpretive Community

The various critiques leveled at corporal punishment provoked a number of sharply polemical responses from fundamentalists and conservative evangelicals during the 1970s and 1980s (Christenson 1970; Dobson 1970, 1976; LaHaye 1977; Meier 1977; Lessin 1979; Fugate 1980; see Greven 1990; Bartkowski and Ellison 1995; Bartkowski 1995).[3] While this dispute surely involves a number of issues, we trace the roots of this conflict over corporal punishment to the divergent epistemological commitments of popular experts and academic specialists, on the one hand, and conservative Protestants on the other (Ellison and Sherkat 1993a). Compared to their secular counterparts, conservative Protestant parenting writers downplay or ignore the findings and fashions of social science researchers investigating disciplinary techniques and their consequences. Instead, their beliefs about the right and responsibility of parents (and other authority figures) to discipline children with physical force begin with their belief that the Bible should be interpreted as the inerrant Word of God. Thus, the usefulness of scientific research and new information gained from other nonscriptural sources must ultimately be gauged by its compatibility with biblical principles.

Although many conservative Protestants would disagree, many observers argue that the Bible, like any text, contains passages that permit multiple readings. Thus, it is important to note that understandings of scripture—"inerrant" or otherwise—do not emerge in a mechanical fashion from the solitary study and reflection of individuals (Boone 1989). Rather, scriptural readings are *social* products, generated and disseminated within interpretive communities. Members of interpretive communities make certain a priori assumptions about a given text, and they adopt certain ground rules to define the boundaries of acceptable interpretive practice. These assumptions and conventions shape their subsequent readings of concrete passages, ruling out alternative understandings.

Inerrantists generally consider the Bible to be divine communication, the absolute Word of God purposively conveyed to humankind (Lindsell 1976; Achtemeier 1980; Barr 1981; Boone 1989). Consequently, the Bible is believed to provide reliable, empirically verifiable, and sufficient truths to guide the conduct of human affairs (e.g., Fugate 1980, 262–63). Echoing the claims of the deuteronomic writers of the Old Testament (e.g., Deut. 28:1–2, 15, 30:19), many conservative religious commentators insist that there are predictable, fixed consequences (i.e., blessings and curses) that result from observing or violating biblical guidelines. Building on these core interpretive assumptions, with the aid of a handful of accepted scriptural commentaries, networks of conservative Protestant theologians and pastors shape the scriptural readings that often prevail among most lay adherents (Boone 1989, 77–84).

Families and Authority Relations

The preoccupation with the legitimacy of biblical authority is one facet of a broader conservative Protestant worldview that Kenneth D. Wald, Dennis E. Owen, and Samuel S. Hill (1989) have termed "authority-mindedness." Some suggest that the implications of this worldview can be seen in the workings of the conservative evangelical congregation itself. For instance, based on her lengthy participant observation in one fundamentalist congregation, Nancy T. Ammerman concludes:

> The preaching situation thus provides the model for authority: A biblically legitimated expert provides unquestioned and respected leadership for those less able to care for themselves. Because this model of social relationships involves

> an unequal division of authority and status, believers come to see such a division as valued and right—both inside and outside the church. They come to expect groups to be divided between sheep and shepherds. The shepherds are entitled to deference and rewards, while the sheep are entitled to love and care. (1987, 128)

Indeed, many commentators maintain that the general concerns of authority and obedience permeate virtually every aspect of conservative Protestant life (Schaeffer 1981; McNamara 1985; Peshkin 1986; Hunter 1987; Rose 1988; Wald, Owen, and Hill 1989). They suggest that two types of hierarchical relationships in conservative Christian thought and practice—(1) between God and His creation and (2) between pastor and congregants—establish a paradigm for social relationships that is generalized to other spheres, particularly the school and home. In the conservative Protestant view, families are characterized by specific, divinely ordained patterns of authority relations—that is, sets of superordinate and subordinate roles (Christenson 1970, 17–18; Fugate 1980, 21–27). Conservative evangelicals cite numerous passages from Old and New Testament sources conveying the sense that children should honor and obey parental authority (Exod. 20:12; Eph. 6:2; 1 Tim. 3:4–5). They also call attention to Old Testament writings that threaten disobedient children with social and familial ostracism, and even death (Exod. 21:15–17; Deut. 21:18–21, 27:16; Prov. 30:17), thus underscoring the imperative of intergenerational hierarchy within the family (Ellison and Sherkat 1993b). Most religious conservatives reject emphatically the image—popular among bestselling parenting experts and academic childrearing specialists—of the family as a training ground for democratic or egalitarian values and practices (Bartkowski and Ellison 1995). As James Dobson puts it, "I find no place in the Bible where our little ones are installed as co-discussants at a conference table, deciding what they will and will not accept from the older generation" (1976, 170). In addition, many conservatve religious commentators also emphasize that parents are held strictly accountable for any deviations from biblical parenting guidelines (Christenson 1970, 91; Dobson 1976, 199–200; Fugate 1980, 30–31).

In the conservative Protestant literature on family life, it is especially important for parents to transmit their religious values to their offspring (Deut. 6:6–7; Prov. 22:6; Eph. 6:4). The most important lesson that parents must impart to their children is that Christian salvation depends upon subordinating one's selfish desires to the will and influence of God's ultimate authority. For the members of fundamentalist and conservative evangelical communities, successful parenting also involves raising youngsters who are comfortable with hierarchy and authority relations. This involves (1) submitting willingly to legitimate authorities (e.g., employers, teachers, government officials) when situated in a subordinate role and (2) exercising responsible, biblically based leadership when occupying a superordinate role.

Original Sin, Divine Judgment, and "Shaping the Will"

As we have discussed elsewhere, in addition to this affinity between biblical inerrancy and "authority-mindedness," it is also important to recognize the link between inerrantist interpretations of scripture and basic conceptions of human nature (Ellison and Sherkat 1993a; Ellison et al. 1996). Conservative Protestants accord particular significance to the doctrine of original sin, reflected in the fall of Adam and Eve from the garden of Eden (Gen. 2–5). According to this view, all individuals are born sinful (Ps. 51:5, 58:3)—that is, predisposed toward selfish, egocentric conduct and inclined toward rebellion against authority in all forms (Dobson 1976, 17–18; LaHaye 1977, 2–3; Meier 1977, 122; Fugate 1980, 49–50; Swindoll 1991, 73–77). Indeed, Dobson believes that it is this view of human nature that distinguishes the disciplinary proclivities of religious conservatives from those of secularists and popular writers: "Parents who believe all toddlers are infused with goodness and sunshine are urged to get out of the way and let their pleasant nature unfold. On the other hand, parents who recognize the inevitable internal war between good and evil will do their best to influence the child's choices—to shape his will and provide a solid spiritual foundation. They recognize the dangers of willful defiance" (Dobson 1976, 174).

The inerrantist view of scripture sustained by conservative Protestants also underscores the disastrous consequences of sin (Ellison and Sherkat 1993a; Ellison et al. 1996). Conservative religious writers maintain that, unless the tendency toward rebellion is reversed, such children grow up unwilling to obey parents and other authority figures (Dobson 1970, 14–15; LaHaye 1977, 131–32; Swindoll 1991, 74–75). They nurture lifelong antiauthority tendencies that will impede their occupational success and undermine their marital and family relationships (Dobson 1976, 24–25; Fugate 1980, 14–15).

More important, however, conservative Protestants worry that this rebelliousness could leave children unwilling to accept parental values, including religious values, and unable to accept the guidance and dictates of God, who for religious conservatives constitutes the supreme authority in the universe (Dobson 1976, 26; Fugate 1980, 190; Daugherty 1991, 72). Beverly LaHaye, founder of Concerned Women for America, remarks: "Society now has a generation of children raised in a spirit of permissiveness who have been allowed to act disrespectfully to their parents and others in authority. . . . The young child who is permitted without correction to raise his fist in defiance to his parents will probably never be able to raise his face to Jesus Christ and say, 'Dear Lord, what would you have me do?'" (1977, 128).

Such concerns make discipline in general, and the elimination of willful defiance in particular, an urgent priority for "Christian" (i.e., conservative Protestant) parents (Ellison and Sherkat 1993a). Until the rebellious, selfish nature of a child is constrained via external controls, conservative Protestant parenting specialists believe that little positive training can take place. Further, given their assumptions regarding the sinful nature of all children, it is not surprising that these authors advise parents to abandon any hope of avoiding family conflicts (Fugate 1980, 80–81); willful defiance is believed to be all but inevitable among youngsters.

These religious writers argue forcefully that physical "chastisement" with the "rod" is the biblically ordained response to overt challenges to parental authority (Christenson 1970, 98; LaHaye 1977, 145; Lessin 1979, 30; Fugate 1980, 137; Daugherty 1991, 67–68). According to the Christian pediatrician Paul D. Meier, "The only means of discipline for young children mentioned in the Bible . . . are the rod and reproof" (1977, 166). A number of biblical passages—primarily passages from Old Testament sources, with only a few exceptions (e.g., Heb. 12:5–11)—are commonly marshaled to support corporal punishment (e.g., Prov. 13:24, 19:18, 22:15, 23:13–14).

While fundamentalist and conservative evangelical parenting specialists clearly endorse corporal punishment as a means of inducing behavioral conformity, they are separated from their secular counterparts by yet another conviction: they believe that physical discipline communicates a positive spiritual lesson to children (Ellison and Sherkat 1993a). They argue that many children develop and express their understanding of God through parental images and therefore that children may infer God's view of them based on the treatment they receive from their parents (Dobson 1976, 171; LaHaye 1977, 69; Meier 1977, 93). Consequently, they maintain that parents should teach their children by example that God is loving and merciful. Because God's punishment of sin is understood as both inevitable and consistent, however, they argue that parental discipline must embody these characteristics as well (Christenson 1970, 100; Dobson 1976, 184;

Fugate 1980, 41–42). For instance, according to Dobson, "To show our little ones love without authority is as serious a distortion of God's nature as to reveal an iron-fisted authority without love" (1976, 172). Given these convictions, conservative Protestants maintain that the experience of loving discipline helps the child to develop an appropriate, accurate image of God and underscores the importance of obedience to God's authority. From this perspective, it is scarcely an exaggeration to say that corporal punishment lays the foundation for salvation through the establishment of a personal relationship with God (Ellison et al. 1996).

In sum, the doctrine of biblical inerrancy is one of the defining features of contemporary conservative Protestantism, and the social and theological meanings now associated with this doctrine incline many fundamentalists and evangelicals to embrace the principle of corporal punishment. Certainly, the Bible contains a number of passages that extol the virtues of physical punishment. In addition, however, a careful reading of the contemporary conservative Protestant parenting literature reveals an affinity between inerrancy and (1) beliefs regarding the spiritual significance of hierarchy and traditional authority relations within human institutions, including the family, (2) well-defined conceptions of human nature as sinful and egoistic, and (3) a general preoccupation with the pervasiveness of human sinfulness and the certainty of divine judgment. For conservative Protestants, then, chastisement with the rod is sacralized—that is, linked explicitly with matters of ultimate concern and explained in terms of its "higher purpose"—and defined as something other than ordinary violence. They perceive corporal punishment as a moral corrective aimed at fostering the child's well-being in this world and, ultimately, in the next.

Taboo Lines: Delimiting the Use of Corporal Punishment

While conservative Protestant writers use religious rhetoric and values to sacralize corporal punishment, they also employ religious discourse to address the inevitable ambivalence toward the use of coercive physical force. They struggle to *delimit* the acceptable use of physical force in disciplining youngsters (Green 1990; Ellison 1996). In identifying taboo lines, they attempt to specify the conditions under which force—rather than nonviolent disciplinary strategies—can and should be used, and several of these writers debate appropriate methodologies for administering corporal punishment (Bartkowski 1995). To simplify the presentation of these issues, our discussion centers on the ideas of James Dobson, perhaps the most popular, respected, and explicit of the conservative Protestant parenting writers—although we also consider other writers at certain points.

Willful Defiance and the Conditionality of Punishment

No responsible conservative Protestant author supports indiscriminate violence against children (Bartkowski 1995). Virtually all of these commentators acknowledge certain limits on the legitimate use of corporal punishment, and most are careful to restrict their advocacy of corporal punishment to instances of willful defiance (Dobson 1987, 92; Swindoll 1991, 85–88). According to Dobson and others, physical force should be used only to root out rebellion against parental authority, not to punish unintentional transgressions such as childish forgetfulness or irresponsibility. When rebellion surfaces, however, they insist that corporal punishment be used *exclusively.* Its regular, predictable use in such circumstances is viewed as an essential part of good parenting, partly because of the dire implications of unchecked revolt by children:

> In a moment of rebellion, a little child will consider his parents' wishes and defiantly choose to disobey. . . . When that nose-to-nose confrontation occurs between generations, it is *extremely* important for the adult to win decisively and confidently. . . . *Nothing* is more destructive to parental leadership than for a mother or father to disintegrate during that struggle. When the parent consistently loses those battles . . . some dramatic changes take place in the way they are "seen" by their children. (Dobson 1976, 31–32)

The importance of defending and reinforcing parental authority notwithstanding, at several points Dobson also highlights the complexity of children and the difficulty of distinguishing in practice between willful defiance and other types of youthful transgressions (e.g., 1970, 22). Dobson exhorts parents to "get behind the eyes of your child, seeing what he sees and feeling what he feels" (1976, 121).[4] He hastens to point out that not all incidents of disobedience stem from rebellion; some may reflect deep-seated feelings of rejection or frustration, and Dobson warns that these should not be met with physical force.[5] In sum, according to Dobson, the decision of the parent to employ corporal punishment rests entirely on his/her determination of the child's *intention.* Good parents must be sure that their child is both fully aware of the rules and fully capable of complying with parental directives. Dobson emphasizes that corporal punishment should be avoided if there is any doubt about the intentionality of disobedience (1976, 31, 33; cf. Fugate 1980, 195–98).

While Dobson is more emphatic than others about using corporal punishment *only* in response to willful defiance, most other conservative Protestant authors agree with this proposition. A rare exception is Pat Fabrizio (1969), who recommends spanking children for almost any offense, because in her view virtually all disciplinary problems ultimately boil down to matters of (dis)obedience, even forgetfulness. Dobson challenges her counsel, for noteworthy reasons (1976, 119–20): he argues that Fabrizio's indiscriminate use of physical force would be likely to make it more difficult for children to understand the reasons and purpose behind the punishment and hence more difficult for them to understand the paramount lessons of authority and obedience that are integral to conservative Protestant socialization.

Against Out-of-Control Parenting: The Negative Consequences of Anger

Dobson and other religious conservatives strongly concur with popular experts that corporal punishment—or *any* punishment—meted out in anger or rage is inappropriate and likely to be ineffective as well (e.g., LaHaye 1977, 71–72; Fugate 1980, 145–46): "It is possible for parents to create hostility and aggressiveness in their children by behaving violently themselves. If they scream and yell, lashing out emotionally and flailing the children for their accidents and mistakes, they serve as models for their children to imitate. *That kind of parental violence is worlds apart from the proper disciplinary approach*" (Dobson 1970, 40, emphasis added). There are several reasons for this admonition. First, many religious conservatives tend to share the concerns of popular experts about the potential for negative modeling. Second, parents who exhibit frustration are showing their loss of control, thus eroding the child's respect for parental leadership and confidence in parental justice (Dobson 1976, 99–101). Third, recall the conservative Protestant conviction that children base their images of God on parental demeanor. The experience of angry, erratic punishment rather than loving discipline may also have undesirable spiritual consequences, leading children to believe that divine justice is equally fickle and unpredictable. Finally, spontaneous, emotional physical punishment is often more violent and involves hitting the child in vulnerable, unprotected places (e.g., the head and face). This may increase youthful resentment—and the possibility of eventual rejection of parental beliefs and lifestyle—and increase the chances of injuring the child (e.g., LaHaye 1977, 146–47).[6]

Developmental Stage and Punishment

Motivated by their distinctive views of a child's inherent nature and their long-term goals of instilling obedience and promoting salvation, conservative Protestant parenting experts generally consider the age and developmental stage of children when prescribing discipline. Dobson offers the most detailed discussion of this topic (1976, 39–62; 1970, 46–47; 1987, 92). In his view, children should not be punished at all during their first seven months. The initial challenge to parental authority usually surfaces at eight to fourteen months of age, but he recommends handling these mostly with diversionary tactics, directing the child's attention away from potential violations and toward fresh objects or activities. Dobson suggests that mild spankings can begin between fifteen months and two years but that they should be infrequent. He warns parents that excessively authoritarian discipline during this early stage of development can be psychologically damaging, particularly when it impedes a child's natural tendency to explore the physical environment.

After this age, however, Dobson advises that parents will see a marked increase in the number of direct confrontations over authority-related issues, and he suggests that spankings generally become more frequent when the child reaches two to three years of age. For children between ages four and eight, Dobson recommends that parents subtly shift their disciplinary emphasis, from constraining undesirable (and dangerous) behaviors to shaping the attitudes that motivate behavior. Nevertheless, in Dobson's view the inclination toward willful disobedience will remain prominent, and he advises that the use of corporal punishment to curb rebellion should continue throughout this period.

By the time the youngster reaches nine to twelve years of age, Dobson recommends that parents devote greater attention to linking behavior with consequences, moving from an emphasis on external controls to a focus on internal controls (self-discipline). He foresees a decreasing need for physical punishment during this developmental stage, particularly if earlier disciplinary efforts were successful. After the child reaches adolescence, Dobson argues that corporal punishment is inappropriate. Parental use of physical force is humiliating, and self-esteem is especially fragile among adolescents. Thus, in his view, continued use of physical punishment could result in long-term psychological damage and resentment, undermining the parent-child relationship and the child's openness to the parents' religious convictions (cf. Meier 1977, 169–70).[7]

Targets and Instruments in the Administration of Corporal Punishment

Besides trying to qualify their support for corporal punishment, conservative Protestant writers have frequently deliberated the merits of various techniques for administering physical punishment (e.g., Greven 1990, 72–81). It is important to note that most religious conservatives criticize the application of any force beyond the minimum necessary to elicit willing obedience. Writers in this tradition agree that the central objective is to cause sufficient short-term pain to make an impression on the youngster's consciousness *without risking damage or serious injury,* and most of these commentators are careful to caution that small amounts of surface pain are ample for small children (e.g., Dobson 1976, 47; Fugate 1980, 138–39).

What, then, are the appropriate instruments of corporal punishment, or "chastisement"? Conservative Protestants often cite biblical references to the "rod" (e.g., 2 Sam. 7:14; Prov. 13:24, 19:18, 22:15, 23:13–14, 29:15; Heb. 12:6–7), and many have quite specific ideas about which objects are suitable for this end. For instance, there is virtual unanimity that parents should not use parts of their body, such as their hands, for punishment: "I have always felt that the hand should be seen by the child as an object of love rather than as an instrument of punishment. Furthermore, if a parent commonly slaps a youngster when he is not expecting to be hit, then he will probably duck and flinch whenever Father suddenly scratches his ear. And, of course, a slap in the face can reposition the nose or do permanent damage to the ears or jaw" (Dobson 1976, 46). Religious conservatives generally agree that neutral objects should be used instead (e.g., Fugate 1980, 137–38). While some write approvingly of the use of paddles (e.g., LaHaye 1977, 145–46), many criticize the use of hard, unyielding surfaces out of concern for the physical safety of youngsters. Apparently for this reason, Dobson recommends belts, leather straps, and supple wooden switches for administering corporal punishment. Roy Lessin (1979, 67–68) and others (e.g., Fugate 1980, 141) maintain that a literal understanding of the biblical concept "rod" requires the use of a young, flexible stick (i.e., a switch) that is capable of producing considerable short-term surface pain without lasting injury (Greven 1990, 74–75).

These authors also consider certain body parts ideal for the administration of corporal punishment or chastisement. In particular, they cite biblical passages (e.g., Prov. 10:13, 19:29, 26:3) that direct parents to strike the bare back of the youngster, by which they usually mean the buttocks area. This part of the anatomy is viewed as an ideal site for this purpose for at least two reasons: (1) it is highly sensitive, thereby ensuring that even a brief spanking will make a painful impression on a disobedient youngster (Lessin 1979, 74–75; Fugate 1980, 143)—by contrast, striking children in the face or about the head is unacceptable (e.g., Meier 1977, 169)—and (2) it is also well-cushioned, thus minimizing the risk of injury to the child (e.g., La-Haye 1977, 147). Indeed, some have suggested—only somewhat facetiously—that the buttocks area was conceived by God precisely with corporal punishment in mind (Greven 1990, 76–77)!

Promptness, Ritual, and Reconciliation

Most conservative Protestant authors emphasize the importance of prompt and consistent punishment. Promptness and consistency have both pragmatic and spiritual implications for fundamentalists as they work to develop a child's notions of justice (Dobson 1970, 44). These considerations are especially important in the case of toddlers, who have very limited memories and attention spans (Dobson 1976, 45–47). Delayed and erratic disciplinary behavior by parents frustrates the establishment of a cognitive link in young minds between behavior and consequence, and it undermines the very sense of certain justice prized by fundamentalists: "What better way is there to give a child nightmares than never to know when the Lord will send Daddy in to spank him for some behavior that was tolerated yesterday?" (Dobson 1976, 120). In addition to these concerns, there is also another reason for prompt punishment: the moderate use of corporal punishment early in the episode of willful defiance, "while the parent's emotional apparatus is still under control," helps to ensure that parents do not explode into abusive violence after a protracted and frustrating conflict (Dobson 1976, 36, 104; LaHaye 1977, 147).

Concerns about promptness must be balanced, however, against the need to administer corporal punishment as a *ritual* that both conveys a sense of the seriousness and ultimate meaning of the punishment and involves a period of dreaded anticipation that should, over time, serve as an additional deterrent (e.g., LaHaye 1977, 146; Fugate 1980, 145). This protracted ritual also permits parents time to gain control over their tempers and emotions prior to administering physical force, thereby reducing the risk of harsh or abusive punishment.

This ritualization of the punitive act itself is mirrored by a focus on post-punishment reconciliation. For instance, Dobson recommends this practice following an episode of corporal punishment: "Hold him close and tell him of your love. Rock him gently and let him know, again, why he was punished and how he can avoid the trouble next time. . . . For the Christian family, it is extremely important to pray with the child at this time, admitting to God that we have *all* sinned and no one is perfect. Divine forgiveness is a marvelous experience, even for a very young child" (Dobson 1976, 33). Thus, in this setting the parent should demonstrate to the child that it was the offending behavior—not the child—that the parent has rejected (Dobson 1970, 24; Swindoll 1991, 94). The intimate parent-child communication that occurs following an episode of corporal punishment is as important as the act of chastisement itself. Indeed, in contrast to the claims of many secular parenting specialists, who maintain that corporal punishment erodes youthful self-esteem and psychological well-being, Dobson argues that this loving conclusion to the disciplinary session may actually bolster the self-worth and security of the youngster. He pointedly observes that "this kind of communication is not made possible by any other disciplinary measures, including standing the child in the corner or taking away his firetruck" (1970, 23). Further, Dobson suggests that this post-punishment ritual—especially when combined with family prayer—turns the unpleasant occasion into a spiritual lesson by reaffirming the dual nature of God as both just and loving.

Conclusion

This study has explored the role of conservative Protestantism in the legitimation of corporal punishment. A broad multidisciplinary literature focusing primarily on state-sanctioned violence demonstrates that religious symbols, institutions, and rhetorics are often deployed to both sacralize and delimit the use of coercive physical force. We have argued that analogous processes of religious legitimation are at work in the case of microlevel violence—in this case, the corporal punishment of children.

While we have focused on the ways in which religious writers legitimate the use of physical force to discipline children, the outcomes of such legitimation also deserve brief mention. First, it is often the case that the participants—perpetrator and victim alike—understand, or *feel* that they understand, the "ground rules" that govern the use of coercive force. Further, they come to see these as natural and even universal. Dobson illustrates this by recounting an episode in which he spanked his defiant young son in a public place. His son protested and cried loudly. When an angry passerby accused Dobson of child abuse and threatened to bring the authorities, his son ceased to cry and, puzzled, asked his father: "Gee, Dad, what's wrong with her?" Dobson concludes from this incident that, the loud public protests notwithstanding, his son understood that he was being punished for willful disobedience and he expected physical force to be used. Dobson contends that *all* children really crave the security of firm parental guidelines and confident parental leadership, as exemplified by this incident.

A second outcome of the religious legitimation of violence is the (re)definition of violence. The role of religious symbolism and rhetoric in sacralizing violence and establishing clear taboo lines leads perpetrators, victims, and others in society to define the "approved" use of force as something other than—and something *less serious than*—"real" violence:

> [One argument against] corporal punishment . . . assumes that spankings teach children to hit and hurt others. It depicts corporal punishment as a hostile physical attack by an angry parent whose purpose is to damage or inflict harm on his little victim. . . . However, corporal punishment in the hands of a loving parent is *altogether different in purpose and practice.* It is a teaching tool by which harmful behavior is inhibited, rather than a wrathful attempt by one person to damage another. *One is an act of love; the other is an act of hostility, and they are as different as night and day.* (Dobson 1976, 35, emphasis added)

Thus, the deployment of religious rhetoric in sacralizing and delimiting the use of physical force promotes a redefinition of corporal punishment, such that it is seen as dramatically, qualitatively different from other types of violence against children.

We have focused exclusively on the advice given by conservative Protestant authors regarding child discipline. Although it is clear that rank-and-file conservative Protestants support corporal punishment more strongly, and employ it more frequently, than other parents (Ellison and Sherkat 1993a; Ellison et al. 1996), we have no solid data on how their implementation of this punishment differs from that of other parents. A number of child development specialists are engaged in ongoing research programs designed to identify (1) the circumstances under which corporal punishment is deemed appropriate by parents and (2) the impact of situational or contextual information (e.g., nature of the offense, public versus private setting of offense, child temperament) that is processed by parents as they select disciplinary tactics (Holden 1983, 1989; Holden and West 1989). Future research on these issues might benefit from closer attention to the role of religious factors in such parental decision making (Ellison 1996).

For instance, conservative Protestant writers have argued strongly for the *principled* use of corporal punishment, as the *exclusive* response to willful disobedience by children (e.g., Dobson 1976; LaHaye 1977). In disciplinary situations that do not involve youthful rebellion, however, they propose more flexible, nonviolent responses. These and other distinctive conservative Protestant recommendations raise important and provocative questions. Do conservative religious parents actually employ corporal punishment consistently in response to the defiance of their children? Do they actually consider the reservations and qualifications of Dobson and other authors when implementing corporal punishment? If so, how closely does their behavior "in the heat of the moment" correspond to that recommended by leading religious specialists on these issues?[8]

It remains conceivable that, despite conscientious warnings by Dobson and other authors, some conservative Protestant parents may administer corporal punishment relatively indiscriminantly in the home. It is also possible that religious legitimation of the principle of physical force within the family, however carefully circumscribed in print, may facilitate other, more severe forms of violence. These possibilities also seem to haunt Dobson himself, who repeatedly denounces parental harshness: "Let it never be said that I favor the 'slap 'em across the mouth' approach to authoritarianism. . . . No subject distresses me more than the phenomenon of child abuse which is so prevalent in America today. . . . *The last thing on earth that I want to do is to provide a rationalization and justification for such parental oppression.* Let me say it again: I don't believe in harsh, inflexible discipline, even when it is well-intentioned" (1976, 73–75, emphasis added).

As we noted at the beginning of this chapter, concern over the use of corporal punishment has resulted partly from research claiming that children who are exposed to harsh or abusive parenting are at risk for a number of negative developmental outcomes. Moreover, according to the well-known "cultural spillover" theory developed by Murray Straus and his associates, the use of corporal punishment may legitimize other forms of violence: "Since physical punishment is used by authority figures who tend to be loved or respected and since it is almost always used for a morally correct end when other methods fail, physical punishment teaches that violence can and should be used under similar circumstances" (Straus 1991, 134).

Some evidence suggests that children who experience harsh physical punishment are more likely to assault their siblings and peers as youngsters and to assault their children and/or spouses as adults (Larzelere 1986; Simons et al. 1991). Further, Straus and his colleagues perceive connections among "spheres" of violence (e.g., interpersonal and societal, legal and illegal), and they argue that the message conveyed by legal family violence, such as corporal punishment of children, may also dispose individuals to engage in illegal societal violence, such as assault, rape, and even murder (Straus 1991).

Such claims directly contradict conservative Protestant parenting specialists, who argue that the use of corporal punishment—under the conditions they propose—will contribute to positive outcomes for youngsters. It is conceivable, of course, that the distinctive cultural meanings associated with corporal punishment, and the distinctive strategies for implementing this form of discipline, result in different outcomes among conservative Protestants than in the general population.

Researchers should explore the effectiveness of corporal punishment, as administered by these conservative Christians, in producing short-term behavioral compliance. Moreover, they should investigate whether these experiences of physical punishment yield various negative developmental outcomes among conservative Protestant children and adolescents: a long-term insensitivity to various types of violence, an inclination toward violence against peers and family members, the intergenerational transmission of violent attitudes and behaviors, undesirable psychological consequences (e.g., impeded creativity, self-esteem, and self-confidence), and stunted development of internal controls, to name but a few. Research along these lines should also be sensitive to variations in the severity of discipline—for example, the difference between "spanking" and "slapping" and harsher forms of punishment—as well as age variations in the effects of such punishments. Such studies could shed new light on the individual and societal implications of corporal punishment and on its legitimation and practice within conservative Protestant families and communities.

Notes

Portions of this study were presented at the 1992 meetings of the Association for the Sociology of Religion, Pittsburgh, the 1992 meetings of the Southern Sociological Society, New Orleans, and an informal luncheon seminar sponsored by the Religious Studies Program at the University of Texas. The authors thank George Holden, Lester Kurtz, Paula Nesbitt, Richard Schoenherr, and Christine Williams for helpful comments and suggestions on earlier versions. The authors are responsible for any errors of fact or interpretation that remain.

1. Throughout this essay, we use several terms interchangeably: "corporal punishment," "physical punishment," "physical discipline," and "chastisement." We do so out of stylistic convenience, recognizing that not all fundamentalist authors would agree. Some argue that discipline refers to a positive process of developing internal controls in children (LaHaye 1977). Others reserve the term "chastisement" for the use of physical force with the rod, while using punishment to refer to other parental responses to youthful transgressions (Fugate 1980).

2. While we focus on physical punishment in the home, it is important to note that conservative Protestants also seem willing to extend their support for cor-

poral punishment into other institutional settings, particularly the school (Grasmick, Morgan, and Kennedy 1992). Several of the ideas presented here may help to explain this pattern as well. First, although few if any biblical passages extol the use of physical discipline by extra-parental authority figures, the notion that teachers and administrators have responsibility for their students in loco parentis may make the practice of corporal punishment in the schools seem a natural extension of parental discipline. Second, in the eyes of many fundamentalists, just as salvation requires submission to divine will, worldly attainment requires obedience to divinely ordained authority structures within human institutions (e.g., government, school, workplace). In their view, children who are not accustomed to the principles of obedience and submission at an early age will be disinclined to accept and embrace divine authority.

3. Most of the books and manuals discussed in this study have been bestsellers in Christian bookstores (additional information is available upon request; see also, Bartkowski and Ellison 1995; Bartkowski 1995). We do not assume that the arguments made by these authors have influenced the opinions of conservative Protestants in the general population. Instead, we analyze these "insider documents" (McNamara 1985) to gain a clearer sense of the worldview that animates the childrearing ideologies and practices of conservative Protestants. In identifying general themes shared by most conservative Protestant childrearing specialists, we necessarily downplay the heterogeneity within this camp. For an example of one evangelical writer who defies several of the generalizations developed in this chapter, see Campbell and Likes, *Kids Who Follow, Kids Who Don't* (1989).

4. In addition, Dobson emphasizes the need for parents to respect their children and to take their feelings seriously: "Respect is unsuccessful as a unilateral affair; it must operate on a two-way street. A mother cannot require her child to treat her with dignity if she will not do the same for him. She should be gentle with his ego, never belittling him or embarassing him in front of his friends. Punishment should usually be administered away from the curious eyes of gloating onlookers. The child should not be laughed at unmercifully. His strong feelings and requests, even if foolish, should be given an honest appraisal" (1970, 19).

5. These attempts by specialists to recommend limits on the practice of corporal punishment underscores the tension between the parental imperative of ensuring the safety and well-being of the child and the freedom of parents as divinely ordained authorities to administer their families as they feel necessary, responsible only to God. To be sure, Dobson's restriction of corporal punishment to instances of willful disobedience makes him somewhat more moderate than other conservative Protestant authors (LaHaye 1977, 145; Fugate 1980, 196). Some conservative religious parenting specialists also worry about the pitfalls of "excessive" parental empathy and the unfettered expression of anger and other youthful emotions. For instance, Fugate discourages parents from focusing on

the reasons for children's behavior, warning that children can perceive this empathy as a sign of parental weakness and/or as an opportunity to manipulate or deceive parents (1980, 79–80). Further, Fugate suggests that parental interest in the reasons behind youthful misconduct may have the potential to communicate undesirable and unintended lessons about escaping personal responsibility for one's actions.

6. There are, of course, differing views of the specific ways in which developmental considerations impinge on the disciplinary process. Some authors advise parents to begin the use of corporal punishment well before fifteen months of age (e.g., Fugate 1980). Meier suggests that the use of corporal punishment by parents peaks ideally when the child is between fifteen and thirty-six months of age (1977, 123–24, 129). Further, a few conservative Protestant authors hold out the possibility of the continued use of corporal punishment with teenagers if they persist in defying authority (Christenson 1970; Lessin 1979; Fugate 1980).

7. LaHaye (1977) argues that children with certain personality types—she calls them "choleric" youngsters—may require a steady diet of corporal punishment as toddlers, while others may not.

8. This advocacy of consistent physical punishment in response to "willful disobedience" contrasts with the stance of some more moderate religious writers, who would use corporal punishment only as a pragmatic "last resort," after other tactics have failed (e.g., Campbell and Likes 1989). According to Dobson, the use of corporal punishment as a last resort may allow parental frustration and anger to build, heightening the risk of child abuse.

References

Achtemeier, Paul J. 1980. *The Inspiration of Scripture.* Philadelphia: Westminster.

Ammerman, Nancy T. 1987. *Bible Believers.* New Brunswick, N.J.: Rutgers University Press.

Balter, Lawrence, with Anita Shreve. 1989. *Who's in Control? Dr. Balter's Guide to Discipline without Combat.* New York: Poseidon.

Barr, James. 1981. *The Scope and Authority of the Bible.* Atlanta, Ga.: John Knox.

Bartkowski, John P. 1995. "Spare the Rod . . . or Spare the Child? Divergent Perspectives on Conservative Protestant Child Discipline." *Review of Religious Research* 37:97–116.

Bartkowski, John P., and Christopher G. Ellison. 1995. "Divergent Models of Childrearing in Popular Advice Manuals: Conservative Protestants versus the Mainstream Experts." *Sociology of Religion* 56:21–34.

Boone, Kathleen C. 1989. *The Bible Tells Them So: The Discourse of Protestant Fundamentalism.* Albany: State University of New York Press.

Campbell, Ross, with Pat Likes. 1989. *Kids Who Follow, Kids Who Don't.* Wheaton, Ill.: Victor Books.

Christenson, Larry. 1970. *The Christian Family.* Minneapolis, Minn.: Bethany House.

Daugherty, Billy Joe. 1991. *Building Stronger Marriages and Families: Making Your House a Home.* Tulsa, Okla.: Harrison House.

Dobson, James. 1970. *Dare to Discipline.* Wheaton, Ill.: Living Books/Tyndale House.

———. 1976. *The Strong-Willed Child: Birth through Adolescence.* Wheaton, Ill.: Living Books/Tyndale House.

———. 1987. *Parenting Isn't for Cowards.* Dallas: Word.

Ellison, Christopher G. 1996. "Conservative Protestantism and the Corporal Punishment of Children: Clarifying the Issues." *Journal for the Scientific Study of Religion* 35:1–16.

Ellison, Christopher G., John P. Bartkowski, and Michelle L. Segal. 1996. "Conservative Protestantism and the Parental Use of Corporal Punishment." *Social Forces* 74(March): 1003–28.

Ellison, Christopher G., and Darren E. Sherkat. 1993a. "Conservative Protestantism and Support for Corporal Punishment." *American Sociological Review* 58:131–44.

———. 1993b. "Obedience and Autonomy: Religion and Parental Childrearing Values Reconsidered." *Journal for the Scientific Study of Religion* 32:313–29.

Fabrizio, Pat. 1969. *Children—Fun or Frenzy?* Palo Alto, Calif.: By the author.

Fish, Stanley. 1980. *Is There a Text in This Class? The Authority of Interpretive Communities.* Cambridge, Mass.: Harvard University Press.

Fugate, J. Richard. 1980. *What the Bible Says about . . . Child Training.* Tempe, Ariz.: Alpha Omega.

Gelles, Richard J., and Murray A. Straus. 1988. *Intimate Violence.* New York: Simon and Schuster.

Grasmick, Harold G., Robert J. Bursik, and M'Lou Kimpel. 1991. "Protestant Fundamentalism and Attitudes toward Corporal Punishment." *Violence and Victims* 6:283–99.

Grasmick, Harold G., Carole Morgan, and M. Kennedy. 1992. "Support for Corporal Punishment in the Schools: A Comparison of the Effects of Socioeconomic Status and Religion." *Social Science Quarterly* 73:177–89.

Greven, Philip. 1977. *The Protestant Temperament: Patterns of Child-Rearing, Religious Experience, and the Self in Early America.* New York: Alfred A. Knopf.

———. 1990. *Spare the Child: The Religious Roots of Punishment and the Psychological Impact of Physical Abuse.* New York: Alfred A. Knopf.

Holden, George W. 1983. "Avoiding Conflict: Mothers as Tacticians in the Supermarket." *Child Development* 54:233–40.

———. 1989. "Parental Selection of Responses to Misbehavior: The Case of Physical Punishment." Paper presented at the biennial meeting of the Society for Research in Child Development, Kansas City, Mo.

Holden, George W., and Meredith J. West. 1989. "Proximate Regulation by Mothers: A Demonstration of How Differing Styles Affect Young Children's Behavior." *Child Development* 60:64–69.

Hotaling, Gerald T., David Finkelhor, J. T. Kirkpatrick, and Murray A. Straus, eds. 1988. *Family Abuse and Its Consequences: New Directions in Research.* Beverly Hills, Calif.: Sage.

Hunter, James Davison. 1987. *Evangelicalism: The Coming Generation.* Chicago: University of Chicago Press.

Kersey, Katharine C. 1991. *Don't Take It Out on Your Kids.* Washington, D.C.: Acropolis.

Knelman, F. H. 1985. *Reagan, God, and the Bomb.* New York: McClelland and Stewart.

Kurtz, Lester R., ed. 1988. *The Nuclear Cage: A Sociology of the Arms Race.* Englewood Cliffs, N.J.: Prentice-Hall.

———. 1995. *Gods in the Global Village: The World's Religions in Sociological Perspective.* Thousand Oaks, Calif.: Pine Forge Press.

LaHaye, Beverly. 1977. *How to Develop Your Child's Temperament.* Eugene, Ore.: Harvest House.

Larzelere, Robert E. 1986. "Moderate Spanking: Model or Deterrent of Children's Aggression in the Family?" *Journal of Family Violence* 1:27–36.

Leach, Penelope. 1989. *Your Baby and Child: From Birth to Age Five.* New York: Alfred A. Knopf.

LeShan, Eda. 1985. *When Your Child Drives You Crazy.* New York: St. Martin's Press.

Lessin, Roy. 1979. *Spanking: Why, When, How?* Minneapolis, Minn.: Bethany House.

Levine, Katherine Gordy. 1991. *When Good Kids Do Bad Things.* New York: W. W. Norton.

Lindsell, Harold. 1976. *The Battle for the Bible.* Grand Rapids, Mich.: Zondervan.

Maurer, Adah. 1982. "Religious Values and Child Abuse." In *Institutional Abuse of Children and Youth.* Ed. Ranae Hanson. Pp. 57–63. New York: Haworth Press.

McNamara, Patrick H. 1985. "The New Christian Right's View of the Family and Its Social Science Critics: A Study in Differing Presuppositions." *Journal of Marriage and the Family* 47:449–58.

Meier, Paul D. 1977. *Christian Child-Rearing and Personality Development.* Grand Rapids, Mich.: Baker House.

National Conference of Catholic Bishops (NCCB). 1983. *The Challenge of Peace: God's Promise and Our Response.* Washington, D.C.: U.S. Catholic Conference.

Peshkin, Alan. 1986. *God's Choice: The Total World of a Fundamentalist Christian School.* Chicago: University of Chicago Press.

Poole, Steven R., Martin C. Ushkow, Philip R. Nader, Bradley J. Bradford, John R. Asbury, Daniel C. Worthington, Kathleen Sanabria, and Thea Carruth. 1991. "The Role of the Pediatrician in Abolishing Corporal Punishment in Schools." *Pediatrics* 88:162–67.

Rose, Susan D. 1988. *Keeping Them Out of the Hands of Satan: Evangelical Schooling in America.* New York: Routledge, Chapman, and Hall.

Runyon, Theodore, ed. 1989. *Theology, Politics, and Peace.* Maryknoll, N.Y.: Orbis.

Schaeffer, Francis A. 1981. *A Christian Manifesto.* Westchester, Ill.: Crossway Books.

Simons, Ronald L., Christine Johnson, and Rand D. Conger. 1994. "Harsh Corporal Punishment versus Quality of Parental Involvement as an Explanation of Adolescent Maladjustment." *Journal of Marriage and the Family* 56:591–607.

Simons, Ronald L., Les B. Whitbeck, Rand D. Conger, and Wu Chyi-In. 1991. "Intergenerational Transmission of Harsh Parenting." *Developmental Psychology* 27:159–71.

Spock, Benjamin. 1988. *Dr. Spock on Parenting: Sensible Advice from America's Most Trusted Child-Care Expert.* New York: Simon and Schuster.

Straus, Murray A. 1991. "Discipline and Deviance: Physical Punishment of Children and Violence and Other Crime in Adulthood." *Social Problems* 38:133–54.

———. 1994. *Beating the Devil Out of Them: Corporal Punishment in American Families and Its Effects on Children.* Boston: Lexington Books.

Straus, Murray A., Richard J. Gelles, and Suzanne K. Steinmetz. 1980. *Behind Closed Doors: Violence in the American Family.* Garden City, N.Y.: Doubleday.

Swindoll, Chuck. 1991. *The Strong Family: Growing Wise in Family Life.* Portland, Ore.: Multnomah.

Taylor, Leslie, and Adah Maurer. 1985. *Think Twice: The Medical Effects of Physical Punishment.* Berkeley, Calif.: Generation Books.

Wald, Kenneth D., Dennis E. Owen, and Samuel S. Hill. 1989. "Habits of the Mind? The Problem of Authority in the New Christian Right." In *Religion and Political Behavior in the United States.* Ed. Ted G. Jelen. Pp. 93–108. New York: Praeger.

Walters, Leroy. 1986. "The Simple Structure of 'Just-War' Theory." In *Peace, Politics, and the People of God.* Ed. Paul Peachey. Pp. 135–48. Philadelphia: Fortress Press.

Wiehe, Vernon R. 1990. "Religious Influence on Parental Attitudes toward the Use of Corporal Punishment." *Journal of Family Violence* 5:173–86.

3

The Counterrevolution—A Family of Crimes: Chinese Communist Revolutionary Rhetoric, 1929–89

Yuan-Horng Chu

[Just as the conservative Protestant parents studied by Ellison and Bartkowski used violence to enforce their authority in the family, so Chinese communist officials engaged in widespread spectacles of violence against "counterrevolutionaries," or "enemies of the people," to mobilize popular support for their revolution. In this chapter, Yuan-Horng Chu explores the ways in which a nation-state and political movements can use rituals of violence and the rhetorics of denunciation and popular mobilization not merely to eliminate "enemies" but also to create a political culture in which violence is taken for granted. Violence was used to instill a widespread perception of an "operational crisis" in an attempt to prove "the real by the imaginary," just as the Nazis legitimated their view of reality by pointing to an alleged Jewish world conspiracy. Violence thus becomes a tool not so much for seizing power but for staging events that convince people to confer power on those who promise protection from alleged threats. It is a ubiquitous pattern in the modern world from the gangs in the neighborhood to superpower politics.]

> The revolution made progress, forged ahead, not by its immediate tragicomic achievements, but on the contrary by the creation of a powerful, united counterrevolution, by the creation of an opponent in combat with whom, only, the party of overthrow ripened into a really revolutionary party.
>
> *Karl Marx,* The Class Struggles in France, 1848–50

> Everything is metamorphosed into its inverse in order to be perpetuated in its purged form. Every form of power, every situation speaks of itself by denial, in order to attempt to escape, by simulation of death, its real agony. Power can stage its own murder to rediscover a glimmer of existence and legitimacy.
>
> *Jean Baudrillard,* Simulations

The term "counterrevolution" was coined during the French Revolution by Marie Jean Condorcet, who had defined it as "*une revolution en sens contraire*" (Condorcet 1849). Although it may be interpreted as having several meanings, "a revolution in reverse" is apparently not a category "opposite" to revolution. Rather, it is a derivative that shares in the revolutionary course of events.

In the historical context of the French Revolution, both conservative thought and reactionary movements derived not only their most telling points but their very existence from the event of the revolution (Arendt 1963). As Jacques Godechot (1972) has shown, the doctrinaires of the French counterrevolution were for the most part revolutionaries in their own way; very few of them wanted to restore the Old Regime, an order that no longer existed. Distinct from a mere turning back of the historical clock, counterrevolutionaries are committed to a fight for change; their target is the new, revolutionary order. Counterrevolution is thus a program fed by the revolutionary momentum and, at the same time, is itself another revolution (Meisel 1966).

Such a theoretical discourse of historical dialectics is impossible, however, within a venerated tradition of revolution. To a revolutionary regime, in which the rhetoric of revolution has established itself as a law, counterrevolution is simply a category of "crimes" against the revolution. Due to the effective state control of the propaganda and publishing apparatuses in the postrevolutionary Soviet Union and China, in these nations there is nothing comparable to the vigor of French counterrevolutionary activities, nor is there anyone equivalent in influence to the foreign counterrevolutionaries of the French period, such as a Burk, Mallet du Pan, or von Schlotzer. Yet in the postrevolutionary Soviet Union and China, counterrevolution has been the most notorious and frequently used category of crimes pursued by both nations. In addition to extensive legal codes for punishing counterrevolutionaries (Cohen 1968), the semantic ambiguity of the category allows a very broad scope for enforcement. As Adam Michnik characterizes it, "in Soviet semantics the word socialism means the total domination of the Communist Party, whereas the word counterrevolution denotes all actions that subvert the totality of this domination" (1985, 157).

In the Bolshevik and Maoist context, there is an operational dialectic between revolution and counterrevolution. Unlike what the rhetoric of revolution has attributed to it, the question of counterrevolution has never been that of stripping the mask off the "hidden enemy" or "disguised traitor"; instead, counterrevolution is the mask to be put on a selected people in order to prove the revolutionary reality (Arendt 1963).[1] It is always a matter of proving the real by the imaginary. Like proving the Nazi reality by the Jewish world conspiracy, counterrevolution is an "operational crisis," imperative for proving the power of revolution.

The Latest Mug Shot

Who are the counterrevolutionaries? We can begin with China's recent portrayal of them. From April to June 1989, a group of rioters, agitated by a handful of hooligans, occupied Tiananmen Square, at the heart of the great capital of socialist China. Although the real size of the "riot" was not known (because of the media blackout), tens of thousands of armed soldiers of the People's Liberation Army were called to drive the demonstrators out of the square.

In the early morning hours of June 4, army troops moving toward Tiananmen were viciously attacked by rioters brandishing firebombs and guns financed by "overseas reactionary political forces." The reluctant soldiers exercised maximum self-restraint but were finally compelled to open fire. Even then, as a general insisted at a press conference, "Soldiers never fired directly at the people." In the end, civilian casualties numbered no more than the soldiers and policemen killed, which totaled nearly one hundred ("Deng's" 1989). Such is the official story of the Tiananmen Square episode that was broadcast repeatedly through every national media to China's 1.1 billion people: it was touted as a victory in suppressing counterrevolutionaries.

Outside China, the world marveled at the remarkable restraint of the seven-week peaceful demonstration, in which several million Chinese civilians participated. Then, in the morning of June 4, the whole world watched the dark night massacre of Tiananmen. The People's Liberation Army, ten thousand strong, mounted a deliberate and vicious assault. Soldiers leveled their AK-47 assault rifles and fired into the unarmed crowd; tanks and armored personnel carriers sped into the square, chasing the panic-stricken people and crushing their tents indiscriminately. After a long bloody night, thousands of dead were reported ("Despair" 1989).[2]

At a later press conference, when Yuan Mu, speaker of the Chinese government, was confronted with the reports of international journalists, he said: "Well, modern technology allows foreign reporters to fabricate whatever they like their audience to hear." Photographs depicting bloodied faces and battered bodies, news footage documenting the clatter of gunfire and the crunch of army tanks, foreign press reports detailing the piles of dead bodies at hospitals—none of this happened. In Tiananmen, as the headline of the *Liberation Daily* proclaimed on June 4, 1989, there occurred "a great victory over a counterrevolutionary insurrection." The massacre never took place ("Deng's" 1989).

The Orwellian Ministry of Truth does not solely rely on a careful whitewash. The tactics for constructing reality involve judicial and ritual performances. On the one hand, the regime launched a campaign to glorify the army troops as heroes, repeatedly televising the scene of the "martyred" soldiers. Top leaders visited the hospitals to salute the wounded soldiers for a job well done. Citizens who had turned in the wanted "criminals," especially their own family and acquaintances, were honored at a public ceremony. On the other hand, the regime broadcasted mug shots of wanted "hooligans" and in front of cameras paraded arrested students with their heads shaved and bowed, their wrists cuffed, and signs detailing their crimes strapped around their necks. Hour after hour, their "confessions" of crime were run on national television ("Deng's" 1989). The court procedure and punishment were swift. Only one week after the Tiananmen incident, the regime began a wave of executions. The convicted counterrevolutionary rioters were paraded in front of crowds and cameras on the way to the execution site, where they were shot by a single pistol bullet into the base of their skulls ("Face" 1989).

There is nothing stunning about the cruel treatment of the counterrevolutionaries. The 1989 suppression was no more cruel than many previous operations against "counterrevolutionaries" in the regime's history. In a sketch of its history, however, the frequency and ever changing face of the counterrevolutionary crimes are indeed breathtaking.

Portrait One: After the Liberation

In the first two decades of the communist movement, counterrevolution had already served three practical functions: (1) as the object of uncontrolled violence perpetrated through a controlled political maneuver, (2) as a camouflage for the communist intraparty power struggle, and (3) as a morality play for the edification of the masses. All three basic functions were ingrained in communist practices before their rise to power in 1949. But the pre-1949 practices only prepared the stage for more elaborate performances after liberation. In 1950, the regime launched the Suppression of Counterrevolutionaries campaign (*Cheng fan*), which lasted through most of 1951 and produced a massive wave of executions. In refuting a Hong Kong news report that the communist regime had capriciously killed twenty million people in its first three years, Mao Tse-Tung maintained that only seven to eight hundred thousand people were killed; he justified the killing: "Have there been any people unjustly killed? Yes, there were. But basically there were no errors; that group of people should have been killed. . . . If they had not been killed, the people would not have been able to raise their heads. The people demanded the killing in order to liberate the productive forces. They [those killed] were fetters on the productive forces . . . the backbone elements of the five types of counterrevolutionaries" (Mao 1989, 142).

A segment of the population classified as counterrevolutionaries by the regime's revolutionary People's Tribunals had been liquidated. Actually, as A. Doak Barnett observed in the early years of the communist rule, the vagueness of the "Regulations on the Punishment of Counterrevolutionaries" and of the whole approach to law made it possible in effect for the state to arrest anyone it wanted to (Barnett 1964). In addition to mass executions, several million "counterrevolutionary criminals" were sent to labor camps. According to Article 7 of the Common Program:

> The People's Republic of China must suppress all counterrevolutionary activities, severely punish all Kuomintang counterrevolutionary war criminals and other obdurate arch-counterrevolutionary elements who collude with imperialism, commit treason against the fatherland, and oppose the cause of People's Democracy. Reactionary elements, feudal landlords, and bureaucratic capitalists in general must, according to law, also be deprived of their political rights within a necessary period after they have been disarmed and their special po-

> litical rights abolished; but at the same time they shall be given a means of living and compelled to reform themselves through labor to become new men. (Barnett 1964, 62)

After the Suppression of Counterrevolutionaries in 1950–51 came the Three-Anti and Five-Anti campaigns of 1952, in which the urban bourgeoisie was the primary target. Within a year, about five hundred were executed and thirty-four thousand imprisoned; another two thousand committed suicide. In 1955, the regime launched a second campaign against counterrevolutionaries, the *Su fan* (Elimination of Hidden Counterrevolutionaries), in the course of which, according to the *People's Daily,* eighty-one thousand intellectuals were "unmasked and punished," and more than three hundred thousand lost their civil rights because of "political unreliability" (Dittmer 1987, 47–48).

The search-and-destroy operation against counterrevolutionaries was an effective tactic for consolidating the regime's power. Yet what if, after years of campaigns, the real enemies had already been eliminated or completely put under control? What if the operation had eliminated its valid target? Could the revolutionary regime then adopt and adhere to the rules of normal life and government?

This shift in focus has not occurred in China. In fact, in one campaign after another, new target groups have been systematically selected to symbolize opposition to specific regime policies. Sometimes a national model would be chosen as a new target, such as Kao Kang and Hu Feng, and various local authorities would in turn discover their own exemplars, leading to the exposure of a Kao Kang or Hu Feng of their localities. (As later in the Cultural Revolution, the same logic applied to the definition of Khrushchev as the model of a revisionist traitor, leading to the exposure of Liu Shao-ch'i as the "Khrushchev of China [Dittmer 1987].)

The central idea of the operation against counterrevolutionaries is the notion of "objective enemies," as Hannah Arendt has characterized it. The identity of objective enemies changes according to prevailing circumstances, so that as soon as one category is liquidated, war may be declared on another, corresponding to the "factual" situation reiterated over and over again by those in power (Arendt [1951] 1968, 123). Considering the cases of Nazi Germany and Soviet Russia, Arendt argues that "only after the extermination of real enemies has been completed and the hunt for 'objective enemies' begins does terror become the actual content of totalitarian regimes" (Arendt [1951] 1968, 120–22).[3]

"There are still counterrevolutionaries, but not many. . . . Ninety-five percent of the people must be mobilized to struggle against the 5 percent who are enemies." This was one of Mao's most consistent principles proclaimed throughout the 1950s and 1960s (Mao 1989; Barnett 1967). Yet a Chinese interviewee, who felt cheated by Mao's principles after many years of devotion, put forth his own calculation: "Chairman Mao said that 95 percent of the people had to be united and that only 5 percent were bad. But there had been so many movements, and every time it was a different 5 percent that were bad, so really the 'bad' people were much more than 5 percent" (Thurston 1987, 284). These two statements illustrate the nature of objective enemies. They are always a manageable minority; the official definitions of them are ever changing; and they always exist.

Thus, it is clear why the party began to set fixed quotas for investigations in the early 1950s (Dittmer 1987, 48). The search for targets in response to administrative quotas produced a certain ritualization of the campaign against counterrevolutionaries. During the investigation and forced self-criticism, the accused must provide "subjective" proof for the "objective" crimes. The arrest and punishment of the selected target are not based on any act that has been committed, nor because he or she is considered capable of committing a crime that more or less fits the suspected personality.

Rather, arrest and punishment are based on what Arendt has termed "possible crimes": acts and thoughts that, according to the logical anticipation of objective developments, lead to the absurd and terrible consequences anticipated by the rulers. The accused is a "carrier of tendencies," like the carrier of a dormant disease. The possible crime is beyond the competence of the police, who can neither discover, invent, nor provoke it; the task of the police is simply to be on hand when the possible crimes and the objective enemies have been specified by the political authorities (Arendt 1968).[4]

Moreover, the operation against counterrevolutionaries fulfills a function far more important than ferreting out and eliminating possible deviates. The method of the nationwide campaign is aimed at mobilizing the entire population into the movement. During the Suppression of Counterrevolutionaries campaign, articles in the youth magazine emphatically encouraged the youth to resolutely reject their friends and relatives who were so classified (Townsend 1969). In the 1952 Five-Anti campaign, the media described it as a movement for "one denunciation per man" (Gardner 1969, 510).

The collaboration of the population in denouncing political opponents and in voluntary surveillance has made the specialty of police agents an everyday method of dealing with people, in which everybody, willingly or not, is forced to participate. It creates a pervasive atmosphere in which mutual suspicion permeates all social relationships. In such a system of ubiquitous spying, anyone may be a police agent and all individuals feel as if they are under constant surveillance (Arendt 1968).

In each movement, according to Mao's formula, 95 percent of the people must be united in hunting down the 5 percent of hidden enemies. But before each campaign, the enemy of the people is both unknown and unpredictable; those who belong to the category of "people" are thus as indeterminate as those who belong to the category of "enemy." As Claude Lefort has suggested, the hunted enemy is the other of the people-as-one, and the definition of the enemy constitutes the identity of the people (1986, 287). Yet the always changing circle of the prescribed enemy reveals that the image of the people-as-one and of its enemy are two mirrors of the same illusion.

This illusion is the foundation of revolutionary totalitarianism. The socialist revolution in particular, as in Lefort's analysis, is supposed to produce a classless society; yet after the revolution, a new dominant stratum seizes the state apparatus, separates itself from the rest of the society, and thus contradicts the principle of homogeneity. This real division, however, is denied by affirming a division, on the level of illusion, between the people-as-one and the other as enemy (Lefort 1986). The evil other could be the remaining forces of the old society, such as landlords and the bourgeoisie. But after their extermination, the enemy becomes their descendants or the agents of the imperialist world, such as spies, Chinese Christians, or foreign-educated intellectuals.

The constitution of the people-as-one requires the incessant production of enemies. Thus, we can understand why the totalitarian regime must be, as Arendt has termed it, a "movement regime" (Arendt [1951] 1968, 21). As long as the new division (in terms of power, economic opportunity, or political point of view) emerges to contradict the revolutionary ideology of homogeneity, the contradiction has to be converted into the unceasing pursuit of the enemies of the people. The campaigns of exclusion, persecution, and terror not only produce the image of a united people but also ensure that power will remain concentrated within the limits of the ruling apparatus that "embodies" the unity and will of the people.

Portrait Two: President as Traitor

The real divisions that threaten the purity and integrity of the revolution certainly involve the intraparty factional conflicts, which reflect conceptual dissonance among the leaders about the revolutionary reality. In the first decade of communist rule in China, the consensus among the revolutionary leaders was remarkable. But the debacle of the Great Leap Forward in 1959 shattered that consensus, and since then the policy differences have grown steadily. On one side are economic administrators, technical bureaucrats, and all sorts of specialists who seemingly favor relatively pragmatic, realistic, and moderate policies for national administration and development. On the other side are those who still strongly believe in the effectiveness of ideological mobilization and insist that sustaining revolutionary momentum and ensuring rapid change can only be achieved through a high level of ideological fervor.

After 1962, the second group, represented by Mao, renewed a struggle for "the continuation of the revolution" and launched a series of major campaigns to indoctrinate the entire population into Maoist dogma: the nationwide movements for the emulation of model heroes in 1963 and the "socialist education" movement in 1964, both of which prepared the ground for the Great Proletariat Cultural Revolution and Red Guard campaign in 1966. Meanwhile, there had been a steady rise in the rate of party purges, which culminated in the massive purge of the Cultural Revolution.

During the ten-year Cultural Revolution, a whole range of party functionaries, government bureaucrats, intellectuals, writers, and artists—at both central and provincial levels—were persecuted on the charge of having opposed Mao's "proletarian revolutionary line." According to the figures produced during the 1980 Trial of the Gang of Four, 727,000 were persecuted, among whom 425 were leading cadres in the party, army, and government. Those who had been executed numbered 34,274 ("Verdict" 1980).[5]

The typical ritual of persecution begins with an intensive nationwide media denunciation. The official newspapers and Red Guard tabloids listed in detail the "crimes" of the denounced. Usually the victims were accused of antiparty, antisocialist, and counterrevolutionary crimes and then denigrated as "traitors," "spies," or "ox demons, snake spirits." The Red Guards, following the instruction of the Cultural Revolution Group, raided the victims' homes, confiscated their properties, and searched for evidence of crimes in their personal diaries and letters. The victims were then arrested and brought to trial, either in a mass struggle meeting or by a secret court set up by the Red Guards. Torturous interrogations and wringing confessions on fabricated charges were common.

The most notorious example is the persecution of Liu Shao-ch'i, chairman of the People's Republic and vice chairman of the Communist Party. On December 25, 1966, about five thousand Red Guards, incited by the

Central Cultural Revolution Group, demonstrated in Peking, shouted the slogans "Down with Liu Shao-ch'i," pasted the city with big character posters, and passed out thousands of leaflets vilifying Liu. This was followed by a nationwide campaign that attacked Liu as "a big counterrevolutionary, hidden traitor, renegade and enemy agent."

On the night of July 18, 1967, a horde of people broke into Liu's home and dragged him and his wife to two separate halls in Chungnanhai where they were subjected to insults and humiliation. Liu, in his late sixties, was forced to stand for two hours and twenty minutes bent forward from the waist, head bowed, prohibited from responding to the accusations hurled against him. At the same time, his home was searched and ransacked. Following this, numerous innocent people were labeled "agents" or "lackeys" of Liu and were arrested and tortured to try to extract confessions that would implicate Liu's family. Many relatives and family friends were tortured to death in the process (*Li-shih* 1981).

On August 5, Liu's family was subjected to another confrontation in the courtyard of their home. The children were forced to watch the Red Guards humiliate their parents—pushing down their heads, twisting their arms, poking their bodies, jabbing their knees, dragging Liu Shao-ch'i by his thinning white hair, forcing him to raise his head to be photographed and forcing it down again. At the end of this struggle, Liu could no longer stand upright; his leg was crippled and his face swollen and bruised. He was then separated from his family, imprisoned for another two years, during which the paralyzed old man was kept alive only to suffer. He was fed with stale and coarse food; his medications were suspended. His body grew weak and developed numerous illnesses. On November 12, 1969, he was found dead lying naked on the concrete floor of the prison basement. The hair of his body was over a foot long. Liu Shao-ch'i was cremated under a pseudonym; his family was not informed for another three years, the people of China not for another ten (Thurston 1987, 124, 151–53).

The man who had joined the Chinese Communist Party at its inception and led it in China's struggle for liberation, who had risen to the vice chair of the party and become the chief of the People's Republic, had been transformed overnight into a "big counterrevolutionary and hidden traitor." Moreover, his fate was shared by tens of thousands of party cadres, government officials, intellectuals, and veteran revolutionaries who had been faithful to the communist cause for decades. As Georg Simmel observes, the inner enemies are those who are most bitter. The close relationship between the accusers and the condemned increases the violence of the antagonism and therefore also the possibility of mobilization (Simmel 1971, 90–92).

The mental and physical torture Liu suffered was by no means exceptional. The methods of mass persecution, such as false charges, frame-ups, ransacking homes, extorting confessions, torturous interrogations, street parades, and incited struggle sessions, were everyday nationwide practices during the Cultural Revolution. Since 1978, much literature has documented the atrocities and cruelties of the Cultural Revolution, which remain beyond the comprehension of outsiders. At the Fourth Congress of Writers and Artists, held in fall 1979, Yang Han-sheng read the names of over a hundred writers and artists who had died by murder, beating, torture, or engineered suicide during the Cultural Revolution (Thurston 1987, 132).

These bloodcurdling, horrendous atrocities were staged as part of the struggle for continuing the revolution, as a war against counterrevolution. The life of the counterrevolutionary was cheap. At the very moment he was so designated, his rights as a human being were destroyed. Following the home searches and street parades, the dehumanizing sessions were usually held in the workplace of the accused—in classrooms, offices, auditoriums—and colleagues, students, friends, and sometimes even relatives, people one knew and saw everyday, participated in the attacks.

Subordinates were pitted against superiors, students against teachers, friends against friends, colleagues against colleagues, and, often, children against parents and spouse against spouse. When children and spouses refused to join as persecutors, they were often forced to accompany the accused (Thurston 1987, 121). Those who survived these attacks lived as social pariahs. They were often given some kind of visible stigma, such as the yin-yang haircut with half their heads shaved. They were avoided by friends and relatives, ostracized by all. They were refused all social services, including food and medical treatment.

Suicide was common. From fear or despair, people hanged, electrocuted, or drowned themselves, jumped from buildings, drank insecticide, lay across the railway tracks, or threw themselves in front of cars (Thurston 1987, 138). But when all human solidarity has been destroyed, when social ostracism assured that no one belonged to him and that he belonged to no one, death lost its social meaning. It was thus impossible to be a martyr, to act beyond one's death (Arendt 1968, 149–50). One's suicide merely proved the fact that one was guilty or had something to hide. Suicide showed the reality of counterrevolutionary crimes.

Portrait Three: A Mutant Play after Mao

To reiterate a Maoist saying, "So long as it is revolutionary, no action is a crime." But the rule of the game is that revolutionaries and counterrevolutionaries are reversible categories. The revolutionaries of one stage become the counterrevolutionaries of the next. The persecutors of yesterday become the victims of today. Many party cadres who were pulled down during the Cultural Revolution were the people who had victimized the intellectuals during the antirightist movement.

In turn, the early Red Guards who were the persecutors in the Cultural Revolution were put into the "cowshed" (*niu-p'eng*). Then, after a while, a second wave of revolutionary rebels were condemned. This comic strip of the power play reached its apex between the death of Mao in 1976 and the Trial of the Gang of Four in 1980, during which the persecutors and victims reversed completely their role.

In early April 1976, five months before Mao's death, tens of thousands of Peking's citizens turned out in Tiananmen Square carrying wreaths, memorial photographs, and posters to mourn the recently dead Premier Chou En-lai. In speeches and poems, the demonstrators criticized Mao and his closest associates. On April 5, armed police and militia brutally broke up the demonstration. The Politburo condemned the demonstrators as counterrevolutionaries and arrested hundreds of them; Deng Xiaoping was accused for the upheaval and purged from all his official posts.

On October 6, four weeks after Mao's death, the Gang of Four, Mao's collaborators, were arrested. Nine months later, the twice-purged Deng returned to office as the vice premier and the party vice chairman. When the Eleventh Central Committee convened in August 1977, more than half of its 201 members were people who, like Deng, had been persecuted in the Cultural Revolution and were later restored to office (Nathan 1985). The campaign against the Gang of Four and its supporters began.

The third plenum of the Eleventh Central Committee (December 18–22, 1978) marked Deng's ascent to full power. At the same time, the verdict on the Tiananmen Square incident on April 5, 1976, as being counterrevolutionary, was reversed and the incident was relabeled as a revolutionary event. In November 1980, the Gang of Four were indicted and tried on forty-eight counts of counterrevolutionary crimes.

The challenge facing Deng's group was how to repudiate all that had been done in the name of Mao during the Cultural Revolution while at the same time affiliating their own monopolistic power with the tradition of the very revolution Mao had stood for. The campaign for "the smashing of the Gang of Four" remained a struggle over Mao's legacy. Yet, as one participant suggested, the more detailed the charges against the Gang of Four, the more it seemed that Mao himself was the de facto target of the criticism:

> Nobody in China, even in the most backward commune, can fail to see that Mao Tse-tung stood for all that the Gang of Four stood for; the Gang was strong until he died and then it collapsed—Mao was the Gang of Four. People now say it was really a Gang of Five, but really it was only a Gang of One. After all the arguing after the smashing of the Gang of Four it is clear that all the excitement is about only one thing and that is that Mao was a fool. They attack the Gang of Four, but really they are only afraid to say what they believe and that is that it was Mao who did all the crimes. . . . They [Deng's group] still believe that it is important to have Mao on their side, but they are just pretending. (Pye 1981, 243)

The successor regime had recourse to a somewhat sophisticated discourse in resolving the confusion. Fei Hsiao-t'ung, China's leading sociologist who had served as a judge in the famous 1980 Trial of the Gang of Four, gave a typical argument:

> This analogy may be helpful. Imagine that China is a large ship advancing at high speed along a course of socialism but the navigator makes an error and the ship enters hazardous waters, where there are treacherous shoals. At this moment, some of the people in charge of the vessel clandestinely get together, form cliques, commit murder, resort to various foul means to seize the ship and turn the several hundred million on board into their slaves. Under the circumstances, the navigator must answer for his error, but his error is different in nature from those who try to exploit the navigator's error for their own despicable ends. (Fei 1981, 3)

As the verdict of this great trial indicates, the ten principal culprits in the Gang of Four were convicted of multiple counterrevolutionary crimes. At the sixth plenary session of the Eleventh Central Committee on June 27, 1981, the Chinese Communist Party officially declared that Mao, the Great Helmsman, was partially responsible for the error when he launched the "catastrophic" Cultural Revolution ("Resolution" 1981). Now the only thing intact is the revolutionary course of socialism. Having cleansed the unscrupulous elements on board, the new shipmaster, hoisting the Marxist-Leninist-Maoist ideology, is ready to resume the incomplete voyage with full force.

Portrait Four: The Democratic Conspirator

In the power struggle, people's voices are indispensable. During the Cultural Revolution, Mao had formulated the "four great freedoms" of "speaking out freely, airing views fully, holding great debates, and writing big-character posters." It was now clear that these freedoms had been exploited by hypocritical manipulations and twisted into the form of uncontrolled Red Terror. Yet among the Red Guards, there were many brilliant young activists who could penetrate the cloak of the power struggle, cast a critical eye on the socialist system, and press their own views through big-character posters.

In the seemingly chaotic atmosphere of the Cultural Revolution, the Maoist authorities had an extremely sharp sense for detecting any independent, and thus threatening, thoughts. These young writers were invariably met with swift and vicious attacks. For example, Yu Lo-k'o, a young Red Guard who in 1967 posted a brilliant article, "On Inherited Status" (*Ch'u-shen lun*), challenging as a feudal practice the communist system of prescribed "class status," was brutally persecuted to death.

In 1974, Li Yiche, a pseudonymous poster-writing team in Canton, hung a critical poster entitled "On Socialist Democracy and Legality." This article, which was openly dedicated to Mao and the Fourth National People's Congress, shocked the Maoist authorities and was officially declared as "absolutely reactionary, extremely poisonous." The three authors were ferreted out, imprisoned, and tortured on the charge of counterrevolutionary crimes. But the article spread throughout China by underground mimeographs (Nathan 1985, 91; Dittmer 1987, 175).

In February 1978, amid the campaign for the "Smashing of the Gang of Four," when the people's voice was again needed for the post-Mao power struggle, the revised state constitution guaranteed the "four great freedoms" in Article 45. Soon a "Democracy Forum," in the form of posters, speeches, and demonstrations, grew rapidly around the so-called "Democracy Wall"—at the Hsi-tan intersection of Ch'ang-an Avenue, near Tiananmen Square. Literary and political journals mushroomed; among the well-known were *April Fifth Forum, Peking Spring, Explorations, Enlightenment, China Human Rights Paper, Today,* and *People's Voice.* With or without express commitment to Marxism, these journals demanded a more comprehensive reform and democracy.[6]

Immediately after Deng's group emerged from the post-Mao power struggle, they began whipping up resentment over the democrats. In Deng's speeches on March 16 and 30, 1979, he accused the democrats of forming secret or semisecret groups and of making connections with Taiwanese agents and foreigners. He laid down "four basic principles" that no exercise of democracy could contradict: the socialist road, the proletarian dictatorship, Communist Party leadership, and Marxist-Leninist-Maoist thought.

On March 25, Wei Ching-sheng's article "Do We Want Democracy or New Dictatorship?" appeared, accusing Deng of "metamorphosing into a dictator." A few days later, police arrested a score of democrats and dissidents, including Wei, and confiscated their mimeograph materials, books, notes, and funds. In October, the regime brought Wei to trial on the charge of leaking secret information to foreign reporters and publishing counterrevolutionary statements. The prosecutor proclaimed: "Our constitution stipulates that you have freedom of belief, and that you may believe or disbelieve Marxism-Leninism-Mao Tse-tung Thought, but it also states that you are definitely forbidden to oppose it—for opposition is a violation of the constitution" (Nathan!·985, 34).

Wei was convicted and sentenced to fifteen years in prison. At the same time, the press reported that the National People's Congress Standing Committee declared that "people with ulterior motives" were using the Democracy Wall, in collusion with foreigners, to "disrupt social order and security." In December, the regime closed down the wall. Even the democrats who considered themselves Marxists failed to convince Deng with their socialist credentials. He denied their role as a loyal opposition and charged them as a potential "sabotage force" to be dealt with by the police (Nathan 1985). In April 1980, under Deng's demand, the National People's Congress eliminated the constitution's article concerning the four freedoms.

Although the democracy activists were being tried at about the same time as the Maoist gang, and both were convicted on the charge of counterrevolutionary crimes, the two groups have no resemblance to each other. The democracy activists were the real kin and forerunner of the ever stronger democracy movement that grew during the 1980s. This is true even though, in the early 1980s, the democracy movement was effectively crushed in China.

For example, Liu Ch'ing, an editor of *April Fifth Forum* who had been sent for three years of "reform through labor" for distributing the transcript of Wei's trial, was sentenced in 1982 to another seven years for smuggling out a camp diary to the West. Hsu Wen-li, another editor of the *April Fifth Forum,* was sentenced to fifteen years of imprisonment; Wang Hsi-che, an independent Marxist theorist who edited the *People's Voice* in Canton was given fourteen years; Ho Ch'iu, former editor of *People's Road,* received ten years. They were all charged with counterrevolutionary incitement.

In fall 1983, teams of police and militia appeared at night on the streets of many cities, carrying lists and knocking on doors. An estimated one hundred thousand suspected criminals were arrested nationwide; most were sentenced to reeducation in labor camps in border areas (Nathan

1985). Nevertheless, the cause of the democrats became the inextinguishable spark that would start a prairie fire. In December 1986, prodemocracy demonstrations burst out in twenty-two cities, lasting for a whole month and involving college students from over one hundred fifty campuses. The suppression of the 1986 democracy movement became the direct cause of the Tiananmen demonstrations of April-June 1989, in which several million students and civilians took part. It would not be surprising if the brutal suppression in 1989 will, in turn, become a direct cause of the next protest, perhaps even on a more formidable scale.

The Conclusion of Revolutionary Justice

The foregoing portrayal depicts the various generations of counterrevolutionaries in the six decades of the Chinese communist revolutionary process. None of the generations resemble the others. The local bullies and bad gentry, war prisoners and party heretics, the president of the People's Republic, the Maoist gang, and the democracy activists were neither kin nor kindred but rather whirled together by the revolutionary current to bear the unlikely family name of counterrevolutionaries.

Yet the rhetoric of revolutionary justice, in whose name the counterrevolutionaries were condemned, has been strikingly similar throughout the sixty years. In the early 1930s, when some Chinese communists opposed the policy of Red Terror and favored a stricter adherence to legal formality, Liang Po-t'ai charged that such comrades "did not understand that law develops in accord with the needs of the revolution, and whatever benefits the revolution is law. Legal procedures can be changed and must not become an obstacle to the interest of the revolution" (quoted in Griffin 1976, 139).

Half a century later, the policies of the still-revolutionary party continue to constitute the law. A 1981 college law text states: "Legislation must take party policy as its basis, and administration of the law must take party policy as its guide. When legal provisions are lacking, we should manage affairs in accordance with party policy. When legal provisions exist they should be accurately applied, also under the guidance of party policy. . . . Policy occupies the leading position, . . . law serves to bring policy to fruition" (quoted in Nathan 1985, 117).

Summarizing the most important speech-related provision of the 1979 criminal code, Article 102, which prohibits counterrevolutionary incitement, *Red Flag* points out: "A person is free to express any opinion and will be protected by law so long as he stands on the side of the people. . . . [But] no one is allowed to air antiparty and antisocialist views" (quoted in Nathan 1985, 119).

Developed as a result of the post-Mao emphasis on the supremacy of law, the code defines counterrevolutionary offenses as "acts undertaken with the purpose of overthrowing the political power of the dictatorship of the proletariat and the socialist system and which harm the Chinese People's Republic" (quoted in Nathan 1985, 118). Yet, as Andrew Nathan has observed, the principle that counterrevolutionary crimes require an intention, an act, and a harmful consequence has been disregarded in practice.

The democracy activists were punished as counterrevolutionaries for the mere posting or mimeographing of critical essays or distributing leaflets, even though there was no explicit call for the overthrow of the regime, no inciting act beyond dissemination of written material, and no measurable damage done to the state. In practice, conversation, academic discourse, and correspondence can all be punished if their content is suspicious to the authorities; even diary entries have been used as evidence of counterrevolutionary intent (Nathan 1985).

Central to the rhetoric of "revolutionary legality" is the distinction between the category of "people" and those on the other side, who are antiparty, antisocialist, and thus excluded from the protection of law. But as the foregoing analysis has shown, in the ever changing course of the revolution, the categories of "people" and "counterrevolutionary" are two sides of the same illusion. In fact, neither loyalty to party nor dedication to socialism could serve as an ultimate criterion. The loyalist and the dedicated could find themselves disgraced overnight, as the tragicomic theater of the Cultural Revolution has shown. Instead, these categories depend on which power appropriates the revolutionary tradition and mobilizes its rhetoric. The very process of the revolution itself has become the source of all "laws," a source that has relentlessly produced decrees and ordinances that are soon obsolete, swept away by the course of the revolution that has just given birth to them (Arendt 1963).

From the mass mobilization in the early communist movement to the consolidation of power after liberation, Chinese revolutionary elites have been keenly aware that their success and survival depend on the image-play of revolutionary justice. Yet the rhetoric lured not only the revolutionary masses in China. As late as the 1970s, many Western intellectuals were still celebrating the Maoist model of "popular justice." In 1971, a group of French Maoist intellectuals, together with Jean-Paul Sartre, began a project to set up a "people's court" to judge the police and to investigate management's responsibility for mining casualties. In a 1972 debate with Michel Foucault concerning the issue of popular justice, the French Maoists repeatedly urged Foucault to acknowledge the value of the people's court as formulated in the thought of Mao Tse-tung (Foucault 1981).[7]

Pierre Victor, who coauthored with Sartre the treatise *On a raison de se révolter* (1974), enthusiastically supports Maoist rhetoric. He suggests that there are two stages in the revolution from bourgeois legality to popular proletarian justice. The first stage is simply when the masses revolt against their enemies. In this stage, he parrots Mao's saying: "I'm in favor of looting, I'm in favor of 'excesses'; the stick must be bent in the other direction, and the world cannot be turned upside down without breaking eggs" (Foucault 1981, 32). "But then a new stage in the process develops, with the formation of the People's Red Army" (ibid., 2). For Victor, this military and judicial power is a new type of state apparatus, a neutral institution between the masses and their enemies; at this point, he argues, the process of a people's court would discipline and transform the diverse and egotistical acts of vengeance into a new system of popular justice (Foucault 1981, 2–3, 7–10).

Ironically, at the same time Western intellectuals such as Victor and Sartre were faithfully propagating the Maoist model, the Chinese people in the Cultural Revolution were gradually awakening from the protracted "looting" and "excesses," a "stage" that had lasted for over forty years since the Kiangsi Soviet of the late 1920s. And at the point when the People's Army and People's Court were called to serve as a judicial power between the people and its enemies, as in the latest example in the 1989 Tiananmen episode, the entire rhetoric of revolutionary justice imploded into absurdity.

During the Tiananmen demonstration, some democracy activists appeared on Ted Koppel's *Nightline.* When asked whether they were engaging in a "revolution," they hesitated. For as they understood it, revolution is the worshipped tradition they had been taught ever since their first day in school; revolution is the party in power. The young democracy activists knew that in China their actions would be viewed as counterrevolutionary crimes. But, as Arendt once remarked, in theory and in practice, only a counterrevolution could stop a revolutionary process that had become a law unto itself (Arendt 1963, 183).

Epilogue

The genealogical portrayals of counterrevolution-as-simulation involve two sociologically interesting phenomena: the rhetoric of denunciation and the rituals of popular mobilization. The rhetoric constructed within the legitimizing framework of the revolution defines the enemies of the people. This denunciation, as the social construction of evil, uses semantic ambiguity and a perpetually changing set of objective enemies. The process of purging deviants, the mass surveillance, and the persecution rituals deflect any reflection on the nature of the violence people are perpetrating or condoning, thus defusing any responsibility.

The violence perpetrated against the objects of the denunciation is simply taken for granted as a logical outcome of the process of purging "dangerous elements." The action takes on a defensive nature not only for the individuals involved but for the entire society and the "good of the people."

These rituals constitute a spectacle. They do not just assassinate people to get rid of them but rather to create a public drama for the purpose of involving people. In "revolutionary legality," the contradictions between legal rationality and revolutionary rationality are synthesized: it is both calculated and passionate. It is deliberately humiliating and ferocious—yet it is a sort of organized ferociousness that may be a synthesis encompassing both ends of what Randall Collins (1974) has called a spectrum of violence: a bureaucratized callousness and personalistic ferociousness.

Jean Baudrillard's notion of simulation is not a completely cynical view. What makes the counterrevolutionary, heretic, and every other form of deviant insider so potent is that they bear important social consequences—that is, they create intragroup solidarity for the purposes of maintaining boundaries and thus social control. Revolution is like a ritual, a threshhold between an overthrow and a restoration. Indeed, it was by the rhetorical creation of a counterrevolution for ritual suppression, and by the production of an opponent against whom to struggle, that a revolution made its tragicomic progress.

Notes

1. This is the point where Arendt distinguishes the Bolshevik practice (as putting the mask on an objective enemy) from that of Robespierre's "terror of virtue" (as stripping the mask off the "disguised traitor") (1963, 100). I am less certain that Robespierre's terror is indeed a practice of "stripping off" rather than "putting on."

2. According to an account by the Chinese Red Cross, the death toll was about 2,600. This does not include the many bodies that were immediately trucked away and cremated.

3. The Nazis, foreseeing the completion of the Jewish extermination, had al-

ready taken the necessary steps for the liquidation of the Polish people, while Hitler even planned the decimation of certain categories of Germans. The Bolsheviks, having started with descendants of the former ruling classes, directed their full terror against the kulaks (in the early 1930s), who in turn were followed by Russians of Polish origin (1936–38), the Tartars and the Volga Germans during World War II, former prisoners of war and units of the occupational forces of Red Army after the war, and Russian Jewry after the establishment of Israel.

4. For a notorious example of changes in the definition of crimes, see Deutscher's analysis of the Moscow trial (1949, 337).

5. These figures reflect only those who were persecuted whose death was relatively known and directly shouldered by the Gang of Four, not the total number of victims who died because of the movement. In addition, this does not include the many young Red Guards who died in the armed struggle for seizing power for Chairman Mao.

6. *April Fifth Forum* and *People's Voice* declared their loyalty to Marxism and challenged the legitimacy of the party dictatorship on Marxist grounds.

7. For a thoughtful background on Sartre and the French Maoists, see Kellner's interview with Jean-Paul Sartre, Philippe Gavi, and Pierre Victor and his review of Victor and Sartre's book (1974).

Works Cited

Arendt, Hannah. [1951] 1968. *Totalitarianism: Part Three of the Origins of Totalitarianism.* New York: Harcourt, Brace, Jovanovich.

———. 1963. *On Revolution.* New York: Penguin.

Barnett, A. Doak. 1964. *Communist China: The Early Years, 1949–55.* New York: Praeger.

———. 1967. "On Khrushchev's Phoney Communism and Its Historical Lessons for the World" (14 July 1964). In *China after Mao.* Ed. A. Doak Barnett. Princeton: Princeton University Press.

———, ed. 1969. *Chinese Communist Politics in Action.* Seattle: University of Washington Press.

Cohen, Jerome Alan. 1968. *The Criminal Process in the People's Republic of China, 1949–1963: An Introduction.* Cambridge, Mass.: Harvard University Press.

Collins, Randall. 1974. "Three Faces of Cruelty: Toward a Comparative Sociology of Violence." *Theory and Society* 1:415–40.

Condorcet, Marie Jean. 1849. "Sur le sens du mot revolutionnaire." *Oeuvres* 12:619.

"Deng's Big Lie." 1989. *Time,* 26 June, p. 32.

"Despair and Death in a Beijing Square." 1989. *Time,* 12 June, p. 26.

Deutscher, Isaac. 1949. *Stalin: A Political Biography.* New York: Oxford University Press.

Dittmer, Lowell. 1987. *China's Continuous Revolution.* Berkeley: University of California Press.

"The Face of Repression." 1989. *Time*, 3 July, p. 27.

Fei Hsiao-t'ung. 1981. "Reflections of a Judge." In *A Great Trial in Chinese History: A Trial of the Lin Piao, Chiang Chin Counterrevolutionary Cliques, Nov. 1980–Jan. 1981*. Ed. Editorial Board of *Li-shih te shen pan* [The Verdict of History]. Pp. 3–20. New York: Pergamon.

Foucault, Michel. 1981. "On Popular Justice: A Discussion with Maoists." In *Power/Knowledge*. Pp. 1–36. New York: Vintage.

Gardner, John. 1969. "The Wu-fan Campaign in Shanghai." Pp. 510–22 in *Chinese Communist Politics*, ed. Barnett.

Godechot, Jacques. 1972. *The Counter-Revolution: Doctrine and Action, 1789–1804*. Trans. Salvator Attanasio. London: Routledge and Kegan Paul.

Griffin, Patricia E., ed. 1976. *The Chinese Communist Treatment of Counterrevolutionaries, 1924–1949*. Princeton: Princeton University Press.

Kellner, Douglas. 1974. "Interview with Jean-Paul Sartre, Philippe Gavi, Pierre Victor, and Review of *On a raison de se révolter*." *Telos* 22:188–201.

Lefort, Claude. 1986. *The Political Forms of Modern Society*. Cambridge: Polity Press.

Li-shih te shen p'an [The Verdict of History]. 1981. Peking.

Mao Tse-tung. 1989. "On the Correct Handling of Contradictions among the People" (speaking notes, 27 February 1957). In *The Secret Speeches of Chairman Mao*. Ed. Roderick MacFarquhar, Timothy Cheek, and Eugene Wu. Pp. 131–90. Cambridge, Mass.: Harvard University Press.

Meisel, James H. 1966. *Counterrevolution: How Revolutions Die*. New York: Atherton Press.

Michnik, Adam. 1985. "The Prague Spring Ten Years Later." In *Letters from Prison*. Trans. Maya Latynski. Pp. 155–59. Berkeley: University of California Press.

Nathan, Andrew J. 1985. *Chinese Democracy*. Berkeley: University of California Press.

Pye, Lucian. 1981. *The Dynamics of Chinese Politics*. Cambridge, Mass.: Oelgeschlager, Gunn, and Hain.

"Resolution on Certain Questions in the History of Our Party since the Founding of the People's Republic of China." 1981. *Beijing Review* 24(27): 10–39.

Simmel, Georg. 1971. *On Individuality and Social Forms*. Chicago: University of Chicago Press.

Thurston, Anne F. 1987. *Enemies of the People: The Ordeal of the Intellectuals in China's Great Cultural Revolution*. New York: Alfred A. Knopf.

Townsend, James R. 1969. "Revolutionizing Chinese Youth." Pp. 451–72 in *Chinese Communist Politics*, ed. Barnett.

"The Verdict of History, the Victory of the People." 1980. *Hung Chi'i* [Red Flag] 23:n.p.

Yu Lo-k'o. 1967. "Ch'u-shen lun" [On Inherited Status]. *Chung-hsueh wen-ko pao* [High School Cultural Revolutionary Gazette]. February. (n.p.). East-Asian Library, Hoover Institute, Stanford University, Stanford, Calif.

Civil Society and Violence: Narrative Forms and the Regulation of Social Conflict

Philip Smith

[This chapter examines the role of civil society in controlling violence, particularly through the use of narratives. Smith argues that narratives link the macrolevel realm of social structure with the microlevel realm of cognition. Thus, narratives allow individuals, groups, and communities to judge, and to some extent regulate morally, distant acts of violence. The author uses two case studies to demonstrate how legitimacy or illegitimacy of violence is established through narratives: one interpersonal (the Bernhard Goetz case) and the other global (the Persian Gulf War).

Smith argues that people are not just passive receptors of state actions, but rather civil society determines which acts are acceptable. Members of civil society seek to maintain a coherent view; thus, the requirements of narratives are the same for legitimizing both interpersonal and global violence. The author emphasizes the role of the mass media and the framing process in making violence acceptable.]

During recent years, much effort has gone into explaining the complex relationship between the state and violence. One perspective has come to predominate: it sees the state as controlling the use of violence at all levels from global to interpersonal. Yet Eastern European resistance to Soviet rule, domestic U.S. protests against the Vietnam War, and the recent riots after the Rodney King verdict in Los Angeles demonstrate that the state does not always have free reign.

Whether involved in foreign wars or domestic repression, the state is sometimes supported, but often confronted, by what political theorists call "civil society." Civil society, it would seem, can independently evaluate and respond to acts of violence. Civil responses to violence can be substantially explained through social narratives. Members of civil society and civil institutions—in particular, the mass media—use narratives to interpret particular acts of violence, thus diffusing social norms about appropriate or inappropriate uses of violence.

In this way, narratives link the macrorealm of events, social structure, and legitimacy with the microrealm of interpretation, typification, and cognition. Narratives can be understood as enabling the individual conscience to judge distant acts of violence—via their cultural refraction in the myths and symbols of the collective conscience (Durkheim 1915). Because violent actions are held morally accountable in this way, changes in the structure of the narrative forms that legitimate violence can influence whether social actors are able to perpetrate acts of violence without being sanctioned.

I begin by examining the social control of violence and its one-sided treatment under a dominant state-centered paradigm. Then I outline the nature of civil society and the role of narratives in producing civil legitimacy. The work of the enlightenment philosopher Adam Ferguson suggests a historical transformation that has occurred in violence-legitimating civil narratives. The implications of this shift for the social control of violence are explored in two case studies: (1) Bernhard Goetz, who in 1984 shot four people on a New York subway train and (2) the effort within the United States to legitimate the 1991 Persian Gulf War, which produced thousands—perhaps hundreds of thousands—of deaths in the Middle East. Although one of these examples is "interpersonal" and the other is "global," in both cases legitimacy—or illegitimacy—was established through specific narrative forms.

The State, Civil Society, and Violence

Thomas Hobbes (1928) argued that anarchic violence is the antithesis of social order. Regulating the use of violence through mechanisms of social control is therefore a prerequisite for every social system. For this reason, the relationship between violence and social order is a key issue in both the classics of social theory (Durkheim [1893] 1964; Weber 1947; Simmel 1964; Parsons [1937] 1968) and in more contemporary social thought (Giddens 1985; Foucault 1979; Girard 1977).

Ever since Max Weber (1947) defined the state in terms of its monopoly on the legitimate use of force, a central theme within sociology has been the exploration of the complexities of the relationship between the state and violence. This work has been conducted in conjunction with research into war, revolution, militarism, the military, and international relations (e.g., Shaw 1984, 1991; Mann 1986; Morgenthau 1985; Skocpol 1979). The result has been a paradigm arguing that the state is the key influence in the production, control, and sanctioning of violence.

Yet several major issues are obscured by this state-centered paradigm. The work of Georg W. F. Hegel and Karl Marx suggests that the state does not exist in isolation but rather enjoys a symbiotic relationship with an autonomous "civil society" (Hegel [1821] 1967; Marx [1843] 1970; cf. Perez-Diaz 1978). If so, then we should expect civil society to have its own autonomous procedures for controlling violence not only among its members but also by the state itself. Yet the role of civil societies located within and between states and their relationship to war, conflict, and violence has been neglected by social theorists (Shaw 1991).

Understanding the autonomy of civil society casts light on the formalistic nature of the claims of Weber and his successors. Weber argued, "Today, the use of force is regarded as legitimate only so far as it is either permitted by the state or prescribed by it" (1947, 156). With current thinking about the nature of the state dominated by Marxian, Weberian, and rational choice traditions, the *étatiste*[1] focus has led to a narrow, instrumental perspective on the legitimation of violence—a viewpoint that ignores the role of culture. The legitimacy of violence is seen as a product of a rational bureaucratic process, dominated by strategic interests and by formal legal and institutional procedures. If the issue of "meaning" is addressed at all, it is usually limited to the propaganda and ideology through which the state supposedly renders the masses inert, passive, and acquiescent (Althusser 1971).

In turning from the state to civil society, we can add to this awkwardly two-dimensional picture of the legitimation process the deeper, "thicker" perspective that comes from studying the culture, beliefs, and identities of a wider social community. With this deepening comes the people, the active, concerned, intelligent citizens, and—most important—their dialectical relationship with the state apparatus. For although the state may initiate violent acts consistent with prevailing interests and procedures, civil society need not accept such acts as legitimate, nor believe in the acts' value, worth, or necessity.

Civil Society, Discourse, and Interpretation

A broader approach to legitimacy and violence is possible. At its heart would be the religious sociology of Émile Durkheim (1915) and Max Weber (1956), which examines the commitment of social actors to ultimate and meaningful goals (cf. Ellison and Bartkowski, in this volume). This broader approach would also include narrative theory, which has shown the importance of "stories" as frames within which collective representations of the world are shaped—frames that subsequently inform social action (Smith 1950; Ricoeur 1984–88). And we can borrow from the tradition of phenomenology and symbolic interactionism, which emphasizes the significance of action, interaction, and interpretation in the construction of a coherent *Lebenswelt* (Blumer 1986; Pollner 1987; Garfinkel 1967; cf. Heritage 1984). In sum, we can demonstrate the significance of narratives for civil society as a resource that members use to make violence, both within and between states, legitimate or illegitimate.

Civil society is a historically specific complex of institutions, customs, and discourses, akin to Talcott Parsons's "societal community" and Jürgen

Habermas's "public sphere," which are relatively autonomous from the state (Parsons 1966; Keane 1988a, 1988b; Calhoun 1992; Habermas 1989). As Edward Shils puts it: "Civil society lies beyond the boundaries of the family and the clan and beyond the locality; it lies short of the state" (1991, 3). Civil society includes institutions such as the mass media, the legal system, and voluntary associations (Alexander and Smith 1993). It contains social relationships driven by norms of civility such as politeness, courtesy, and trust (Shils 1991), and it contains a "public" (Baker 1987) of informed and critical citizens.

In functionalist terms, civil society and its institutions are a subsystem charged with the moral regulation of society (Alexander and Smith 1993). For this reason, civil society in general and the mass media in particular (Smith 1994) are permeated with a moralizing discourse that is used to evaluate how well social actors and actions fulfill the ideals of any autonomous cultural system (Alexander 1993a).

At the microlevel, the discourse in civil society makes the social world morally accountable to, for, and by its members (cf. Garfinkel 1967). It organizes fragmentary events into coherent patterns, providing a concerted "intersubjectivity" (Husserl 1967; Schutz 1962–66; Heritage 1984). This coherence is established along two dimensions: the cognitive and the moral.

In the cognitive dimension, the orderliness of events is established with respect to issues of temporality, causality, and ontology (Pollner 1987; Atkinson 1978; cf. Heritage 1984). In the moral dimension, events and actors are aligned according to concepts of purity and pollution, salvation and sacrality (cf. Durkheim 1915; Weber 1956; Douglas 1970; Katz 1988). These two axes are applied to events and integrated by social narratives that members of civil society use to interpret the social text in which they live (Ricoeur 1984–88; Entrikin 1991; Wagner-Pacifici 1986; Smith 1950; Pollner 1987; Atkinson 1978).[2]

Only through language and the narratives it produces can the morality and identity of actors and events be established. Narratives concretize abstract and ill-defined values for members of civil society, providing interpretations of conduct. Narratives make the cultural system usable—they enable members to mobilize culture, which in turn provides the moral frames through which people can interpret social life.

Using narratives, members of civil society plot key actors in social dramas as "characters," as symbols to which they attribute specific roles and motivations (White 1987; cf. Burke 1969). Their actions are seen as in some way an index of a deeper nature, as understandable responses to "objective" social conditions, as necessary and valid, spontaneous or constrained.

Events are arranged around these attributed characters to form a prevailing master narrative for specific historical sequences—designating them as tragic, heroic, comedic, or simply mundane (cf. Frye 1957). Narratives and character attributions shift over time, as new information becomes available to members of civil society. Tensions and ambiguities are resolved by the relentless work members put into maintaining a coherent world.

From Interpretation to Social Control

Enlightenment scholars were fond of pointing to the fluctuating nature of social customs. Adam Smith, for example, noted customary behaviors in antiquity that are shocking in light of more contemporary sensibilities about violence:

> Can there be greater barbarity, for example, than to hurt an infant? Its helplessness, its innocence, its amiableness, call forth the compassion, even of an enemy, and not to spare that tender age is regarded as the most furious effort of an enraged and cruel conqueror. What then should we imagine must be the heart of a parent who could injure that weakness which even a furious enemy is afraid to violate? Yet the exposition, that is, the murder of new-born infants, was a practice allowed of in almost all the states of Greece, even amongst the polite and civilized Athenians; and whenever the circumstances of the parent rendered it inconvenient to bring up the child, to abandon it to hunger, or to wild beasts, was regarded without blame or censure. (Smith [1759] 1801, 38)

Observers such as Norbert Elias (1978), Anthony Giddens (1985), and Randall Collins (1974) have reinforced this view, arguing that contemporary civil society has been largely pacified in terms of interpersonal violence. By historical standards, acts of face-to-face violence such as fistfights, duels, and infanticide persist only at low levels. Martin Shaw (1991) has argued recently that a similar historical trend can be detected at the macrolevel in the movement toward a "postmilitary society." He notes that compared to the nineteenth century the public is now far more skeptical of militarism and far less willing to accept the loss of life in war.

This tendency toward pacifying both interpersonal and global forms of violence is based on more than just the evolution of the state system (cf. Giddens 1985; Mann 1986) or on the historical transformations of the economic system (Smith [1776] 1880; Marx [1867–94] 1956; cf. Mann 1986). It is also linked to the reformulation of specific narratives that legitimate violence. This is more clearly visible in an examination of a neglected line of inquiry first suggested by Adam Smith's great contemporary, Adam Ferguson.

Ferguson is probably the only great scholar to have theorized explicitly, albeit in a few brief paragraphs, the link between narratives, violence, and civil society. In discussing the "manners of polished and commercial nations," Ferguson argued that the modern attitude to violence had changed:

> The hero of the Greek fable, embued with superior force, courage, and address, takes every advantage of an enemy, to kill with safety to himself; and actuated by a desire of spoil, or by a principle of revenge, is never stayed in his progress by interruptions of remorse or compassion. . . . Our modern fable, or romance, on the contrary, generally couples an object of admiration, brave, generous, and victorious; or sends the hero abroad in search of mere danger, and of occasions to prove his valor. . . . Indifferent to spoil, he contends only for renown, and employs his valor to rescue the distressed and to protect the innocent. . . . [He] professes a contempt of strategem and unites in the same person, characters and dispositions seemingly opposite: ferocity with gentleness, and the love of blood with sentiments of tenderness and pity. ([1767] 1966, 200–201)

Ferguson claimed that these narratives profoundly affected the behavior of members of civil society: "Whatever was the origin of notions, often so lofty and so ridiculous, we cannot doubt of their lasting effects on our manners. The point of honour, the prevalence of gallantry in our conversations, and on our theaters, many of the opinions which the vulgar apply even to the conduct of war," he claimed, had their origins in the chivalric ethic ([1767] 1966, 203).

Ferguson's point is at once simple and profound: attitudes toward violence in civil society are mediated through narrative structures, and these narratives in turn inform the actions of members. Ferguson is sketchy about how narratives affect social action. But the aforementioned "micro" processes, such as fitting events into moralizing narrative frames, help provide an answer. Ferguson also argued that there was a historical shift in the kinds of narrative frames that could be used to justify acts of violence.[3] Indeed, the very motives that made violence legitimate for the Greeks are now held to be profoundly tainted.

The narratives that allow disinterested, selfless, "legitimate" violence can be arrayed along a continuum. At one end, they depict violent actions undertaken in self-defense; at the other end, they describe heroic actions taken for the good of the other, the human species, or even the world. Yet in both cases, and in all points between, violence is deemed acceptable only when it can be narratively constructed as necessary, inevitable, or a last resort undertaken by people with pure or innocent motivations (cf. Emerson 1981; Katz 1988; Smith 1991). This is usually accomplished by contrasting the motivations and qualities of the perpetrator and recipient of violence and by placing them within a narrative frame that accounts for the inescapable need for confrontation. The presence of an "evil other," itself dedicated to unswerving violence, is therefore a precondition for the "hero's" use of violence.

The historical transformation of violence-legitimating narratives has significantly influenced the social control of violence. Because self-interest and the will to power and economic gain are no longer sufficient motives for violence—as they were for the Greeks—it is more difficult to legitimate, and therefore to perpetrate, violent acts.[4] Here we are less concerned with whether the perpetrators of violent acts are actually motivated by selfless sentiments and forced to act as a last resort. Instead, we are more interested in the public accountability (cf. Garfinkel 1967) of violent acts in civil discourse. Those who would use violence must make their actions accountable in the sense of developing an acceptable narrative form (cf. Mills 1967; Skinner and Tully 1988). As Marcel Proust wrote: "The motives actuating humanity are too sacred for him, before they are invoked, not to bow down to them, whether he believes them to be sincere or not" ([1921] 1949, 368).

The need for actions to be narratively accountable can operate both prospectively and retrospectively to regulate violent actions. Would-be violent actors are tempered by the need to produce forms of violent behavior that are appropriate to legitimating narratives. Obviously, this constraint does not always prevent violence. Retrospectively, members of civil society use narratives to judge violent acts that have already occurred and to sanction or reward violent actors according to the verdict the narratives provide. The question of retrospective accountability is nowhere more clear than in the courts, where prosecuting and defending counsel might offer conflicting narratives to account for the same murder.

Every society has taboo lines that differentiate acceptable and unacceptable uses of violence. At one level, we should understand narratives as a resource used by actors to enforce these lines: to judge whether specific acts of violence are inside or outside moral boundaries (Ellison and Bartkowski, in this volume). Yet Ferguson's work suggests that narratives do more than this. They also indicate where the lines should run. Historical shifts in violence-legitimating narratives have shrunk the boundaries. Confronted with a narrower zone of legitimacy, contemporary violent actors have a harder time justifying their actions than their erstwhile Greek counterparts. Simply using extreme force is no longer possible—violent actions must appear to be controlled if they are to remain legitimate.

As devices for interpreting the play of events and for establishing the ground rules of the game itself, narratives significantly influence the social control of violence. We can define this regulatory process in Durkheimian terms by understanding that narratives reflect the collective conscience. Narrative frames mobilize sentiments of outrage by defining normative transgressions that must be punished (Durkheim [1893] 1964) and by structuring the diffuse sentiments of the collectivity at each historical point.

The moralistic sentiments arising in the collective conscience of civil society can affect other parts of the social system in several ways. On the one hand, there are formal mediating mechanisms such as voting behavior, the judicial system, and public inquiries. On the other, there are informal mechanisms such as demonstrations (and occasionally riots), the withdrawal of "goodwill," mass media campaigns and investigations, and the diffuse pressure of public opinion. The ability of civil society to sanction or reward perpetrators of violence using these mechanisms gives narrative interpretations power as instruments of social control over the state and its citizenry.

The following case studies examine the role of narratives in legitimating and delegitimating contemporary violence. Although the first example looks at an act of violence committed by a member of civil society, while the second looks at one committed by the state, both show a remarkably similar pattern of discourse.

The Case of Bernhard Goetz, New York Vigilante

On December 22, 1984, Bernhard Goetz, by his own admission, shot four youths in a lower Manhattan subway car with a .38-caliber handgun. He fled immediately but eventually turned himself in to the police. Over the weeks and months that followed, civil society struggled to make sense of his action.

During the first few weeks, Goetz's violent action was viewed as highly legitimate. Across the nation, the vast majority of letters to the editor strongly favored Goetz. So did calls to talk-radio shows, by a ratio of fifty to one. New Yorkers sported "Thug-Buster" T-shirts and supportive baseball caps, knapsacks, and bumper stickers. Transit patrol officers were told by passengers how much they admired Goetz. Goetz turned down book and movie offers. The Guardian Angels collected money for his defense. A New York police hot line, set up to seek evidence, was flooded with calls supporting Goetz and demanding that he run for mayor. One telephone company worker even offered his life savings to pay Goetz's bail (*Time,* 21 Jan. 1985; *Newsweek,* 7 Jan. 1985, 25 Feb. 1985; *People,* 21 Jan. 1985).

This response was the product of a narrative that placed Goetz in a position between the romantic hero acting for the good of all and the person acting out of simple, mundane concern for his own safety. In general, conservatives and the political right tended to promote the heroic perspective (cf. the coverage in the *New York Post,* Jan.–Feb. 1985), while the center adopted the narrative of self-defense. In both narratives, Goetz was seen as a fragile and timid man, typical of the frightened subway rider. He was a geek, an electronics expert, who lived in a "$650-month three-room apartment." He shot the four youths because they were threatening him and he feared for his life.

He seemed to want to shun publicity, telling the media, "I am amazed at this celebrity status. . . . I want to remain anonymous [and] . . . avoid . . . any sense of triumph or self-justification" (*Time,* 21 Jan. 1985). According to *Time,* he had a "low profile for a legend" and spurned "aid and celebrity" (21 Jan. 1985). He even cooperated with the police, to the absurd point of "providing most of the evidence that may be used against him" (*Time,* 21 Jan. 1985).

In contrast, the youths who had attacked him were, according to the Guardian Angels' leader Curtis Silwa, "sleaze and slime" (*People,* 21 Jan. 1985). These "thugs and punks" were carrying "sharpened screwdrivers" and had a collective total of "nine convictions, twelve outstanding cases and ten bench warrants for non-appearances in court." The man Goetz's bullet had crippled and hospitalized was "awaiting trial on charges of robbing three men with a shotgun" (*Time,* 21 Jan. 1985).

To see the full narrative frame, however, we must look beyond Goetz and his "assailants." A third character was latent behind the frontstage drama, namely, the state. Federal statistics suggest that the actual rate of violent crime declined by almost 20 percent between 1980 and 1984 (*Time,* 8 Apr. 1985). The reasons for this decline were largely demographic, as the last wave of baby-boom juveniles moved into a later life-cycle stage. Still, public perceptions of the crime rate were to the contrary. Fueled by Ronald Reagan's anticrime rhetoric, which tried to convert minority groups into scapegoats, a strong "moral panic" arose over the issue of street crime (cf. Hall, Critcher, Jefferson, Clarke, and Roberts 1978).

Ironically, Reagan's rhetoric boomeranged when the state itself was labeled as deficient. The perception that Goetz's action was justified came from a viewpoint of the state as having somehow failed in what enlightenment theorists such as Hobbes called its social contract with civil society. According to contract theory, civil society hands over power to the state, such as the right to use force, in return for guarantees of liberty and security. In the Goetz case, the violence was condoned precisely because the state had failed to uphold its part of the bargain. As one informant told *People,* "When the police can't look after you, you have to do it yourself" (21 Jan. 1985).

In this sense, Goetz's use of violence was encoded not merely as an act of self-defense but also as a symbolic action that highlighted popular discontent with the state. "The criminal justice system is not working in America. It is absurdly slow, overburdened, understaffed, random in its selection of who is to be punished," wrote *Time* (8 Apr. 1985), echoing the sentiments of one expert who argued that "to live today in urban America means that you are severely at risk and essentially helpless to deal with the problem of crime" (*Time,* 21 Jan. 1985). In the specific context of New York, the subway system—the locus of Goetz's fateful deed—epitomizes the breakdown of social order and a return to the nightmarish world of the urban jungle. "Thundering trains, their walls inscribed with dizzying layers of graffiti, roar through blackened tunnels as expressionless straphangers brace against the lurch of the cars. The trains always seem either too crowded or too dangerously empty. And there lurks constantly a vision of young men—two, three, four—'asking for money' and backing their demand up with a fist or a knife or a gun" (*People,* 21 Jan. 1985).

Within the narrative of a social fabric torn by uncontrolled violence, Goetz's act of violence could take its necessary and heroic form. His violence struck a blow on behalf of the average American citizen—the ideological center of civil society. A Media General–Associated Press poll conducted soon after the event found that 47 percent of Americans approved of what Goetz did, while 17 percent disapproved, and 36 percent said they did not know enough of the details to decide. A *People* magazine poll also conducted in this early phase showed that 64 percent of men and 48 percent of women considered Goetz correct in shooting his assailants, while only 18 percent and 30 percent, respectively, said he should have pulled the gun but not shot. On January 25, 1985, a grand jury decided not to press charges against Goetz.

In the next few months, doubts that had earlier been expressed by only a few—usually liberals, radicals, and minority representatives—were more widely aired. These doubts emerged from the incompatibility between the heroic narrative and certain, deviant "facts": Goetz was carrying an unlicensed gun, he shot some of his assailants in the back, and he had not known whether his assailants were carrying screwdrivers or, indeed, any weapons at all. These details had been known in early January but the American mainstream considered them as minor inconsistencies that were ignorable, as Harold Garfinkel would say, "for all practical purposes." After the verdict, they became discursively central. With these doubts came a new narrative about Goetz and his "attackers" or, as they now became known, his "teenage victims." A law suit filed against Goetz by one of his victims was one of the first attempts to redefine events:

> The suit alleges that when Troy Canty, 19, one of Goetz's shooting victims, approached Goetz and asked him for $5, he immediately drew his illegal .38 caliber gun and shot the four youths. . . . [The gun] was loaded with . . . dumdum bullets—designed to cause a maximum of serious physical injury and pain to a victim. When [Cabey] attempted to flee . . . [Goetz] deliberately, wilfully, and with malice aforethought aimed at [Cabey's] back and fired his weapon severing his spinal cord. (*New York Amsterdam News*, 2 Feb. 1985)

This alternative narrative spread gradually from the African American community into other parts of civil society. Goetz underwent a symbolic transformation as members considered the competing narrative. While perhaps not completely discredited, he was redefined in a more ambiguous light. From being symbolic of a typical American citizen reacting on behalf of an enraged civil society, Goetz became abnormal, a "monster" somehow different and alien from the majority. From being a rational, autonomous hero who had unfortunately been embroiled in a nasty scene, Goetz became a sinister, dependent psychopath driven by mysterious, impulsive forces beyond his control.

The new Goetz emerged with vigor in *Time*'s issue of April 8, 1985. On the cover he appears as a thin, reedy figure, eyes piercing behind thick-rimmed glasses, emerging from a surreal and crepuscular subway station into the blackness of the New York night. In the text, Goetz is no longer a figure with whom we can identify. He is a weird, creepy, twilight figure—a "frightened, brooding, obsessive man" living in a "spartan meticulous apartment." The article suggests he has been mentally scarred by an earlier (1981) mugging and by his father's conviction for child molestation.

His separation from normal society is displayed in a psychiatrist's claim that Goetz had "acted out dreams of retaliation that most people resolve through fantasy." The new Goetz appears to take a malicious, sadistic pleasure in using violence, and he seems to enjoy public attention. No longer is his violence seen as simply disinterested and coerced. Now it seems that perhaps Goetz had sought out violence and was now receiving a social and psychological payoff for his violent actions: "Why did Goetz, by his own account, bend over one slumped youth and say, 'You seem to be doing all right. Here's another,' and then fire a shot that may have crippled the youth for life? And if Goetz was a shy, retiring person as he claimed, why was he parading around town with reporters, making pronouncements on the need for law and order?" (*Time*, 8 Apr. 1985). Just six weeks after the first grand jury's decision, a second one convened and indicted Goetz on several charges including attempted murder.[5]

The Case of the United States and the Persian Gulf War

The Prevailing Narrative

In August 1990, Iraqi troops invaded the neighboring state of Kuwait. The United States responded with a military blockade, and in January 1991 began a war against Iraq. The prevalent narratives in U.S. civil society viewed Iraq's initial act of violence as illegitimate.[6] In contrast, the U.S. military buildup and subsequent use of force were encoded as both necessary and altruistic. At the center of the master narrative was an apocalyptic vision of a titanic struggle between good and evil, with the Iraqi leader Saddam Hussein as the malefactor. Hussein was portrayed as having an affinity for violence. He was so intensely tainted in the U.S. consciousness that he was likened to Hitler—that is, characterized as insane, selfish, and obsessed with power. Only violence could stop him. A massive military showdown was thus the only option: "How many millions of people perished because we failed to stop Hitler on his first conquest? We are not in Saudi Arabia to protect our supply of oil. The real justification for being in Saudi Arabia is to stop World War III before it starts" (Letter to the editor, *Time*, 14 Jan. 1991).

Hussein's biography was constructed as evidence of his unshakable propensity for systematic violence: "He is a man who respects might more than diplomacy. Politicized in his teens, Saddam's first role was as a hit man for the political party he'd later take over. At the age of 22, he poured a hail of bullets into President Abdul-Karem Kassim's car. . . . When he took power for himself, in 1979, he arranged to have 22 of his top rivals executed. The taste for violence persists" (*Newsweek*, 13 Aug. 1990).

His own country showed the evils of his rule. It was characterized as secretive, repressive, and built on violence. As *Newsweek* put it, there was an "elaborate network of security agents, backed by a draconian set of laws. . . . Jails are full of the regime's enemies and international agencies claim that torture, even against infants, is commonplace" (13 Aug. 1990). Hussein's armed forces threatened to extend this dominion to other nations. He had a range of potent, infernal weapons including a chemical arsenal and other "doomsday machines" (*Newsweek*, 29 Oct. 1990). "Saddam already has missiles tipped with warheads full of poison gas. Most experts believe that within five to seven years Saddam could have the capacity to build nuclear weapons. Israel, the country Saddam has threatened to 'burn,' is already within range of his rockets. Eventually, Saddam may be able to build an intercontinental ballistic missile capable of reaching, say, New York" (*Newsweek*, 3 Sept. 1990).

In contrast to Hussein and Iraq was the victim, Kuwait. Kuwait was encoded initially as an innocent, nonbelligerent state with a "free press" and "noisy National Assembly," a country where "Kuwaitis thought they would live happily ever after—until Iraq came and took Never-Never land away" (*Newsweek*, 13 Aug. 1990). The United States was encoded in a narrative frame akin to a chivalric romance. As the dominant force in the rescue of Kuwait from its enslavement and "rape" by Hussein's forces, the United States was elevated to heroic status. America was the leader of a fraternal brotherhood embedded in the "new world order": "The burden of leadership has fallen upon the U.S. May we prove worthy," wrote one correspondent to *Time* (14 Jan. 1991).

While this perspective remained dominant and even strengthened between August 1990 and the war's effective end in April 1991, this hegemony was not attained effortlessly. In a closer look, we see various struggles and puzzles revolving around the master narrative. The narrative of apocalypse, which claimed a war was necessary to stop an otherwise irresistible force, was countered by another narrative couched in the genre of realism. According to this "realist" narrative, war itself would bring political, human, and economic disasters. The evil represented by Saddam Hussein was different only in degree, rather than in kind, from normal "badness."

The U.S. military-industrial complex and its leaders, such as George Bush, were seen in this second narrative as being almost as bad as Saddam Hussein. Peace activists argued that elites were taking America into a war for self-interested, economic, and political reasons (e.g., editorials in the *Nation*, 10 Sept. 1990, 24 Sept. 1990, 3 Dec. 1990, 10 Dec. 1990). This narrative denied the hegemony of a generalized (Parsons and Smelser [1956] 1984) cultural steering media and claimed the "exchangeability" of Hussein and his deeds with other social and moral evils (cf. Bohannan and Bohannan 1968).

Yet this competing narrative failed to influence the "silent majority," as had happened during the Vietnam War era. Indeed, the alternative narrative actually weakened as Desert Shield became Desert Storm. Opinion polls showed increasing support for both the war and Hussein's downfall and assassination (Gallup 1992). As the heroic master narrative strengthened, most members of U.S. civil society experienced these events as intensely important: in addition to identifying with the armed forces, an amazing 52 percent displayed a yellow ribbon and 49 percent flew a U.S. flag (Gallup 1992).

The success of the master narrative over its challenger can be explained by two factors. First, salient new material was successfully assimilated into the original narrative, enhancing its plausibility. Second, possibly contradictory material was dealt with in ways that made it "dismissible" for all practical purposes.

We can illustrate the first factor with Hussein's actions from the time of the invasion to the end of the war. He took hostages, thus bringing upon himself the level of symbolic pollution previously reserved for Iran, he continued issuing threats against Israel, and he continued his military build-up. Footage televised worldwide showed him fondling an innocent child who was squirming with anguish—a factor that was particularly important in getting women to support the war. He called for the use of hostages as "human shields." Worst of all, on television he displayed brutalized allied pilots, in a misguided attempt to weaken U.S. public opinion.

The second factor explaining the success of the master narrative was the ineffectiveness of contradictory information. Strangely, peace activists' strategic attacks against the war were less damaging than those that were more "innocent" or accidental. From August 1990 to April 1991, several incidents occurred that seemed inconsistent with the narrative of a heroic, chivalric America and that belied the promise of a new world order.

To understand how the master narrative withstood these challenges, we must draw upon the macrolevel realm of the sociology of knowledge and the more microlevel realms of ethnomethodology and conversation analysis, both of which show that, for innocent or self-interested reasons, members of the civil society will work to "repair" and maintain a coherent worldview (Evans-Pritchard 1976; Pollner 1987; Heritage 1984; Bloor 1978; Schegloff, Jefferson, and Sacks 1977). By stretching concepts, denying evidence, or placing events in distinct frames of reference, the coherence of narratives can be maintained over time.

Clearly, there are limits to this process. In the Goetz case, the inconsistencies became so great that a competing narrative seriously threatened the dominant version of events. Yet in the case of the Gulf War, the master narrative was preserved with greater integrity despite several threatening events. The lesser threats included the double standard toward Soviet repression in Lithuania and the U.S. invasion of Panama, U.S. censorship and manipulation of the mass media, the vested interests of the oil multinationals and the military-industrial complex, the overrepresentation of African Americans in the U.S. armed forces, and the redefinition of Kuwait as a patriarchal, dictatorial, and elitist nation. Important as these were, I shall discuss here the four most significant threats to the Manichean and heroic master narrative of the Gulf War.

Threats to the Narrative

The first threat was George Bush's own status. The heroic master narrative had invested Bush with remarkable, almost prophetic powers of leadership. Like Weber's Hebrew prophets, Bush had provided an all-embracing interpretation of "the world as a meaningful totality" (Weber 1978, 450–51) through his "vision of a new world order" (*Time,* 7 Jan. 1991). Yet a domestic crisis over taxes and the budget made him look weak and made his vision look fragmented and foolish. As *Time* put it, "His domestic policy, to the extent that he has one, has been to leave things alone until he could no longer avoid taking action" (*Time,* 7 Jan. 1991). This problem was solved by arguing that Bush had two distinct "characters," one oriented toward foreign policy and the other toward domestic policy: "He seemed almost to be two Presidents last year, turning to the world two faces that were not just different but also had few features in common. One was a foreign policy profile that was a study in resoluteness and mastery, the other a domestic visage just as strongly marked by wavering and confusion. . . . For better and for worse the two George Bushes are *Time*'s 1990 Men of the Year" (*Time,* 7 Jan. 1991).

This argument—that the same man could simultaneously embody sacred and profane characters, hermetically sealed in differing spheres—allowed Bush's foreign policy vision to stand reassuringly intact. As foreign events eclipsed domestic affairs in early 1991, Bush benefited from the unblemished hero side of his profile, receiving approval ratings consistently around 80 percent (Gallup 1992).

The second substantial threat to the master narrative was the U.S. relationship with Iraq prior to the Kuwait invasion. As we saw in the Goetz case, enduring narratives must strongly contrast the protagonists in order for violence to be legitimated. The master narrative of the Gulf War relied on a separation of America from Hussein's tainted actions, yet increasing information seemed to undermine this: "Surely, Saddam Hussein must have been out of his mind to invade Kuwait. . . . Or was he? As the Iraqi strongman contemplated the price of aggression last July, Kuwait must have looked like a free lunch. . . . George Bush may be full of resolution now, but before the invasion the signals sent to Saddam by his administration were, at best, mixed. At worst, it can be argued, Saddam was given a green light to gobble up his oil-rich neighbor" (*Newsweek,* 1 Oct. 1990).

Although potentially devastating to the heroic master narrative, U.S. complicity in Hussein's invasion was reframed as a mere glitch. Attention centered on an interview between the U.S. Ambassador to Iraq, April Glaspie, and Saddam Hussein, which occurred a few days before the invasion. Because of this tight focus, other possibly more damaging issues (such as U.S. arms sales to Iraq or the opposition by U.S. senators to agricultural sanctions against Iraq only six days before the invasion) were barely discussed. The interview tape made it impossible to claim that Hussein was lying about tacit U.S. approval. Initially, the hapless Glaspie became a scapegoat. The ambassador's message—that America had "no opinion on Arab-Arab conflicts"—was widely portrayed as a personal blunder, demonstrating her incompetence. In this way, the administration's integrity was repaired, and its separation from the tainted act was maintained.

Then it was learned that her message and tone toward Hussein had come from state department directives. In addition, Bush had issued no warning to Hussein even when he knew the invasion was imminent. Repair strategies then changed. Those raising objections to preinvasion U.S. policy were accused of opportunistic and hypocritical "finger-pointing" (*Time,* 1 Oct. 1990) and of exploiting their "20-20 hindsight" (James Baker, quoted in *Washington Post,* 24 Sept. 1990). Once tainted in this way, the arguments of administration critics were devalued.

It was also claimed that "Bush and Baker, neither of them expert in Middle East affairs, were advised to pursue that course by their moderate Arab friends" (*Time,* 1 Oct. 1990). Responsibility for the blunder, then, lay not so much with the state department but rather with America's foreign allies. A further defense—even though it contradicts the previous one—was that the upper echelons had little personal responsibility because of the state department's size and bureaucracy. For example, James Baker claimed that "there are probably 312,000 cables or so that go out under my name as Secretary of State from the Department of State" (quoted in *Washington Post,* 24 Sept. 1990).

Finally, and perhaps most important, the administration claimed that diplomacy is a complex business and that errors are at times inevitable. As *Time* noted: "There are only two basic ways to deal with a rogue nation—isolation (the stick) or involvement (the carrot)—and the argument over which path to pursue is unending" (1 Oct. 1990).

A third threat to the master narrative was the use of violence itself. Because Hussein was viewed as absolutely ruthless, it was assumed that his citizens were, at heart, both opposed to him and his ideological and political captives. As such, they were blameless and innocent—and in no way could they be a legitimate target of violence. In the war's early events, American claims of chivalry were strengthened by its allegedly careful use of force to minimize civilian casualties. This was reinforced by the promise of "smart" weapons technologies whose culturally "formatted contrasts" (cf. Atkinson 1983; Heritage and Greatbatch 1986; Roth 1992) distinguished them from Hussein's indiscriminate weaponry (cf. Alexander 1993b). Weapons experts quickly pointed out the deficiencies of the Scud missile. It is unwieldy and inaccurate, practically antique, a dinosaur compared with the sleek, precise Tomahawk cruise missile (*Time*, 23 Jan. 1991): "The Scud, with a targeting error radius measured in miles, is a mistake before it is launched. Do not compare the Scud, a haphazard weapon useful only in terrorizing civilian populations, to computer and laser-guided arms designed for precise delivery with a minimum of civilian casualties. The coalition cares; Saddam Hussein doesn't" (letter to the editor, *Time*, 25 Feb. 1991).

The U.S. government's skillful use of propaganda in the form of distorted video footage, combined with news footage of Scud damage in Israel, "visibly" verified the contrast in weaponry. But contradictory video evidence, of the U.S. bombing of an Iraqi bomb shelter in mid-February—which killed many civilians—almost destroyed the distinction between clean and dirty weapons. American leaders used several strategies to repair the damage. First, they reaffirmed that their policy was civilian friendly: "Noting that Iraqi civilians feel free to visit markets during air raids, and again charging that Iraq has moved headquarters, artillery positions and warplanes into schools, hostels and residential areas, General Schwartzkopf contended that 'the very actions of the Iraqis themselves demonstrate that they know damn well that we're not attacking civilian targets'" (*New York Times*, 15 Feb. 1991).

Second, U.S. leaders argued that Hussein had cynically placed civilians in the military command post, either to act as human shields or to manufacture a change in public opinion. In this way, the illegitimate violence could be attributed to the evil rather than the good character: "Although he and other American officials declined to say so publicly, the General [Neal] suggested that the command believed Mr. Hussein had purposely sacrificed Iraqi women and children for propaganda purposes by putting them in what he knew to be a military target likely to be hit" (*New York*

Times, 15 Feb. 1991). "Pentagon officials maintained that the Iraqi government was ultimately responsible for the deaths by having allowed civilians to take refuge at a military command post" (*New York Times,* 14 Feb. 1991).

This account was rendered implausible by reporters who visited the scene and reported that "they found no sign of a military command-and-control center, only piles of concrete and twisted steel and the charred and broken bodies of scores of civilians, including many women and children" (*New York Times,* 15 Feb. 1991). Having failed to control the damage, the administration finally admitted that a mistake had been made. "We were as careful as we possibly could be," General Kelly said. "We didn't know civilians were in there. We struck it. We suffer remorse as a result of that" (*New York Times,* 15 Feb. 1992).

Mistakes have the unusual language-game property of allowing responsibility for actions to be simultaneously affirmed and denied. By allocating an event to the category of a "mistake," causal responsibility can be admitted while intent about its consequences can be disavowed. There is also a confessional quality to such a public admission that, by demonstrating the pure quality of honesty, helped redeem the American military elite. Finally, the repair work was capped by having a plausible (to some) explanation for the intelligence failure to detect the presence of civilians: "Maybe they didn't go in and out until after dark last night and we didn't have a picture of it" (Kelly, quoted in *New York Times,* 14 Feb. 1992).

The last threat to the master narrative came after the war and centered on the Kurdish question. When their rebellion against Hussein was crushed, the plight of the Kurds was viewed with dismay in U.S. civil society. By following a policy of nonintervention, Bush had in effect become Hussein's ally: "The truth is that by betraying the rebels the U.S. is truly intervening—on the side of the killer Hussein," wrote one contributor to the *New York Times* (2 Apr. 1991). From being a prophetic leader, the foreign-policy Bush had become—like the domestic-policy Bush before him—a passive and acquiescent figure in the grip of a "paralyzing fear," no longer driven by high moral purpose in a quest to destroy evil.

> President Bush, in his zeal to avoid the prime sin of military intervention, is committing the second sin of almost total passivity. (Op-Ed, *New York Times,* 3 Apr. 1991)

> The reasons for the abandonment of Iraq's opposition are cynical, misguided and ill-informed—a fair match for the misjudgments and self-delusion that gave Mr. Hussein the capacity for aggression. (Op-Ed, *New York Times,* 3 Apr. 1991)

> If we refuse to take steps to protect them [the Kurds] from his vindictiveness, we will taint our troops' victory in Operation Desert Storm. (Sen. Orrin Hatch, quoted in *New York Times*, 13 Apr. 1991)

The Bush administration ignored these assaults as long as possible. In the end, however, it was driven to intervene to repair the damage to its reputation. The resulting political and military action—encoded as tardy, half-hearted, and coerced—was only moderately successful in this respect. The Kurdish issue scratched the teflon Bush had acquired during the Gulf War and initiated a long slide in his popularity ratings.

The Dialectics of State and Civil Society

Although the state has accumulated considerable power and destructiveness over the past several centuries, violence-legitimating narratives in civil society have helped limit this power. Just as technological advances and the increasingly centralized state have made it easier to destroy life in war, so have cultural shifts and an evolving civil society made it harder for the state to effect destruction. Meanwhile, citizens' use of violence has been regulated by both state and civil society. On the one hand, the state has outlawed forms of violence like assault, assassination, gunfights, spouse abuse, murder, rape, and infanticide, as well as "victimless crimes" like brawls and duels. On the other hand, civil society has regulated itself through narratives. These case studies illustrate three stringent narrative conditions that the state and the citizen must meet to legitimize their violent acts to contemporary civil society: (1) violence must be a last resort, restrained to minimum levels, and there should be no peaceful alternatives; (2) the violence must be undertaken by a quasi-heroic "pure" figure against an "evil other"; and (3) the violence must be undertaken for selfless and universalistic reasons.

In the cases of Goetz's vigilante shootings and the Gulf War, the narratives were constructed to combine these three features and to keep the violence within the taboo lines. First, Goetz's action was initially justified as a last resort because of his precarious situation in the subway car and because the state was viewed as having failed to control street crime. Similarly, the Gulf War was encoded as a last resort, the product of Iraq's objective danger and failed negotiations. Retreat was impossible because Iraq posed a long-term threat akin to Nazi Germany. Second, Goetz embodied the diffuse purity of the ordinary American while confronting tainted low-life characters who were apparently committed to crime. Likewise, in his prophet role, Bush confronted an intensely tainted Hussein who was apparently committed to limitless violence, torture, conquest, and repression. Third, Goetz did not seem (initially) interested in exploiting his violent action for money or publicity. Likewise, the United States was portrayed as entering war reluctantly with an eye not to national (or multinational) profit but to rescuing an innocent Kuwait and building a fraternal and democratic new world order.

In both cases, the "within bounds" characteristics of violence were threatened and almost discredited by competing narratives that probed three sensitive issues. First, both Goetz and Bush were viewed by their detractors as hungry for violence rather than reluctant. Goetz was carrying a gun loaded with dumdum bullets, and he shot his assailants in the back. Bush and the U.S. military bombed a civilian shelter and entered a war without serious negotiations. Second, Goetz's heroic image was tarnished by revelations about his character, actions, and words, while the tainted image of his assailants was modified by their more innocent "teenage" identity. Similarly, even though Hussein remained intensely tainted, the moral polarization between him and Bush was deflated by reports about Bush's domestic ineptitude, revelations of diplomatic complicity in the Iraqi invasion, and Bush's failure to support the Kurds. Third, Goetz came to be viewed as seeking publicity and profit from his celebrity status. Likewise, Bush was viewed eventually as opportunistic in his treatment of the Kurds, even though he withstood radical claims that he had gone to war for personal glory and for the benefit of the military-industrial complex.

Weber may have been correct when he argued that the state claims a monopoly on the legitimate use of violence. Yet whether or not civil society accepts the state's claim to a monopoly, or its particular uses of violence, is another matter altogether. These case studies suggest that the pattern of violence and its civil legitimacy is far more interactive than the state-centered paradigm suggests. Consent for violence can come and go with a speed that is at first disconcerting but that can be understood once we examine the shifting narrative frames of civil discourse.

The case of Bernhard Goetz reveals one side of this issue: the ability of civil society to revoke the state's monopoly on legitimate violence and to applaud the use of violence by citizens. The case of the Gulf War shows that civil consent to state violence is as provisional as the monopoly. The state risks losing public support when it cannot align its violent actions with legitimating narratives. For this reason, narrative frames deployed by civil society can exert a braking force on violent policies employed by the state.

The state will, as it were, think twice before committing violent acts that might be hard to legitimate.

We can better examine the social control exerted by the three narrative conditions by contrasting them with the heroic epics of the Greeks. It is considerably harder today to wage a war or shoot another citizen and legitimate it as a last resort undertaken for selfless motivations against an evil other than it was for a Greek to legitimate violence as a desirable action in itself, intended for shameless personal profit and economic or political booty. In a sense, the Greeks needed no legitimation at all other than success in using violence. Despite changes in the technology of death, in the cultural sphere Bush was at a disadvantage compared to Alexander the Great, and Bernhard Goetz was at a disadvantage compared to Achilles when it came to conducting and legitimating violent acts.

Yet, while more complex than the *étatiste* model, we should not overly simplify the dialectical state/civil society relationship. The presence of radically divergent narratives of violence in the two cases alerts us to the possibility of polarization, conflict, and struggle over legitimacy, not only between state and civil society but also within civil society itself. Factions and groupings, often divided along class, ethnic, or ideological grounds, will advance competing narrative interpretations of violent events. The result is a constant struggle in civil discourse over the narration of events—and hence legitimacy—such as that between the "moral majority" and African Americans in the Goetz case, or between leftist and conservative intellectuals in the Gulf War case. Although opponents of violence may not always win these struggles, shifts in legitimating narrative structures have provided them with a formidable cultural weapon that, by historical standards, makes it easier to discredit violent acts.

It is tempting to see the emergence of this narrative counterbalance to violence as a providential quirk of history. The truth may be more commonplace. Scholars as divergent as Adam Smith ([1776] 1880), Karl Marx ([1867–94] 1956) and Émile Durkheim ([1893] 1964) have argued that violence is antithetical to modernity. Just as the market and industrialization gave rise to the unparalleled power of the modern state, so did they precipitate a reformulation of social relationships and new forms of sociability both within and between states. We can account, then, for the simultaneous rise of state power, civil society, and narrative controls by recognizing an underlying process of social differentiation. In this context, the narrative regulation of violence within and by civil society should be understood as a distinctively cultural contribution to what Norbert Elias has so aptly named the "civilizing process."

Notes

I would like to thank Jeffrey Alexander, John Heritage, Andrew Roth, and Steven Jay Sherwood for their helpful and encouraging comments on an earlier draft of this essay.

1. The strict interpretation of *étatiste* implies an advocacy of state power. The theorists examined here are not necessarily *statisti* hoping for the triumph of the centralized totalitarian state. Yet analytically rather than normatively, there is a strong tendency toward *étatisme* in the dominant paradigm since it advocates, as an empirical truth, the extreme authority of the state over the control, legitimation, and regulation of violence. It is almost as if social scientists investigating the state and violence have had their theoretical horizons foreshortened by the ideologies promoted by the very object of their study.

2. Ethnomethodological studies do not address explicitly the issue of narrative. Still, ethnomethodological sociology can be reconceptualized, in part, as the study of the methods through which members produce the narratives that make their actions accountable. Pollner (1987) and Atkinson (1978) show how institutional procedures yield officially recognized and internally consistent accounts of "what happened." Garfinkel's (1967) study of "Agnes" illustrates how biographical details are used to construct a narrative of gender identity. From a more phenomenological interactionist perspective, Katz (1988) shows how the lived experience of "deviants" is embedded in the narrativity of the *Lebenswelt.* The focus of these studies on accountability and reflexivity is a useful corrective to the structural and social-structural focus taken by macrolevel theorists of narrative.

3. I am not interested in accounting for this narrative shift or its subsequent adoption by civil society. I see no causal priority in connecting the rise of civil society and the modern state to this narrative shift. My main purpose is to describe the narrative forms and their use by contemporary civil society. In the conclusion, however, I suggest an elective affinity between the emergence of complex social organizations and of new narrative forms that help control the use of violence.

4. I might add here that certain deviant traditions within civil society—most notably associated with Nietzsche—have bucked the historical trend and employed narratives closer to the Greek model to justify their violence.

5. Goetz was eventually acquitted of all charges except possession of an unregistered handgun. Without access to the jury deliberations, I cannot reconstruct the narratives used by the jury to produce this verdict. But from the public record we can see that the attorneys' courtroom strategies centered heavily on constructing and deconstructing the credibility of the two narratives I have identified.

6. The section that follows is heavily indebted to Alexander and Sherwood's (1991) unpublished essay, which replicates many of the findings of my own independent research (Smith 1994). For comparison, see Shaw, *Post-Military Society* (1991), which examines British public opinion and the Gulf War.

References

Alexander, Jeffrey C. 1993a. "Citizen and Enemy as Symbolic Classification: On the Polarizing Discourse of Civil Society." In *Where Culture Talks.* Ed. Marcel Fournier and Michèle Lamont. Pp. 289–308. Chicago: University of Chicago Press.

———. 1993b. "The Promise of a Cultural Sociology: Technological Discourse and the Sacred and Profane Information Machine." In *Culture and Sociological Theory.* Ed. Neil J. Smelser and R. Munch. Pp. 292–323. Berkeley: University of California Press.

Alexander, Jeffrey C., and Steven Jay Sherwood. 1991. "Bush, Hussein, and the Cultural Preparation for War." Manuscript. Department of Sociology, University of California, Los Angeles.

Alexander, Jeffrey C., and Philip Smith. 1993. "The Discourse of American Civil Society: A New Proposal for Cultural Studies." *Theory and Society* 22:151–207.

Althusser, Louis. 1971. *Lenin and Philosophy.* New York: Monthly Review Press.

Atkinson, J. Maxwell. 1978. *Discovering Suicide.* London: Macmillan.

———. 1983. "Two Devices for Generating Audience Approval." In *Connectedness in Sentence, Discourse, Text.* Ed. K. Ehlich and J. Riemdisk. Pp. 199–236. Tilburg: Tilburg Studies in Language and Literature.

Baker, Keith M. 1987. "Politics and Public Opinion under the Old Regime: Some Reflections." In *Press and Politics in Pre-Revolutionary France.* Ed. Jack R. Censer and J. D. Popkin. Pp. 204–46. Berkeley: University of California Press.

Bloor, David. 1978. "Polyhedra and the Abominations of Leviticus." *British Journal for the History of Science* 11:245–72.

Blumer, Herbert. 1986. *Symbolic Interactionism.* Berkeley: University of California Press.

Bohannan, Paul, and Laura Bohannan. 1968. *TV Economy.* Evanston, Ill.: Northwestern University Press.

Burke, Kenneth. 1969. *A Grammar of Motives.* Berkeley: University of California Press.

Calhoun, Craig. 1992. *Habermas and the Public Sphere.* Cambridge, Mass.: MIT Press.

Collins, Randall. 1974. "Three Faces of Cruelty: Towards a Comparative Sociology of Violence." *Theory and Society* 1:415–40.

Douglas, Mary. 1970. *Purity and Danger.* New York: Praeger.

Durkheim, Émile. [1893] 1964. *The Division of Labor in Society.* Glencoe, Ill.: Free Press.

———. 1915. *The Elementary Forms of Religious Life.* London: Allen and Unwin.

Elias, Norbert. 1978. *The Civilizing Process.* New York: Urizen Books.

Emerson, Robert. 1981. "On Last Resorts." *American Journal of Sociology* 87:1–22.

Entrikin, J. Nicholas. 1991. *The Betweeness of Place.* Baltimore: Johns Hopkins University Press.

Evans-Pritchard, Edward E. 1976. *Witchcraft, Oracles and Magic among the Azande.* Oxford: Oxford University Press.
Ferguson, Adam. [1767] 1966. *An Essay on the History of Civil Society.* Edinburgh: Edinburgh University Press.
Foucault, Michel. 1979. *Discipline and Punish.* New York: Vintage.
Frye, Northrop. 1957. *The Anatomy of Criticism.* Princeton: Princeton University Press.
Gallup, George. 1992. *The Gallup Poll: Public Opinion 1991.* Wilmington, Del.: Scholarly Resources.
Garfinkel, Harold. 1967. *Studies in Ethnomethodology.* Englewood Cliffs, N.J.: Prentice-Hall.
Giddens, Anthony. 1985. *The Nation State and Violence.* Berkeley: University of California Press.
Girard, Rene. 1977. *Violence and the Sacred.* Baltimore: Johns Hopkins University Press.
Habermas, Jürgen. 1989. *The Structural Transformation of the Public Sphere.* London: Polity Press.
Hall, Stuart, Chas Critcher, Tony Jefferson, John Clarke, and Brian Roberts. 1978. *Policing the Crisis.* London: Macmillan.
Hegel, Georg W. F. [1821] 1967. *The Philosophy of Right.* London: Oxford University Press.
Heritage, John. 1984. *Garfinkel and Ethnomethodology.* London: Polity Press.
Heritage, John, and David Greatbatch. 1986. "Generating Applause: Political Rhetoric and Response." *American Journal of Sociology* 92:110–57.
Hobbes, Thomas. 1928. *Leviathan.* London: Dent.
Husserl, Edmund. 1967. *Ideas: A General Introduction to Pure Phenomenology.* London: Allen and Unwin.
Katz, Jack. 1988. *The Seductions of Crime.* New York: Basic Books.
Keane, John, ed. 1988a. *Civil Society and the State.* New York: Verso.
———, ed. 1988b. *Democracy and Civil Society.* New York: Verso.
Mann, Michael. 1986. *The Sources of Social Power.* Cambridge: Cambridge University Press.
Marx, Karl. [1843] 1970. *A Critique of Hegel's Philosophy of Right.* Cambridge: Cambridge University Press.
———. [1867–94] 1956. *Das Kapital.* Moscow: Progress Publishers.
Mills, C. Wright. 1967. "Situated Actions and Vocabularies of Motive." In *Symbolic Interaction.* Ed. Jerome Manis and B. Meltzer. Pp. 393–404. Boston: Allyn and Bacon.
Morgenthau, Hans. 1985. *Politics among Nations: The Struggle for Power and for Peace.* New York: Alfred A. Knopf.
Parsons, Talcott. [1937] 1968. *The Structure of Social Action.* New York: Free Press.
———. 1966. *Societies: Comparative and Evolutionary Perspectives.* Englewood Cliffs, N.J.: Prentice-Hall.

Parsons, Talcott, and Neil J. Smelser. [1956] 1984. *Economy and Society.* London: Routledge and Kegan Paul.
Perez-Diaz, Victor. 1978. *State, Bureaucracy and Civil Society.* London: Macmillan.
Pollner, Melvin. 1987. *Mundane Reason.* Cambridge: Cambridge University Press.
Proust, Marcel. [1921] 1949. *The Guermantes Way.* London: Chatto and Windus.
Ricoeur, Paul. 1984–88. *Time and Narrative.* 3 vols. Chicago: University of Chicago Press.
Roth, Andrew. 1992. "Culture and the Collaborative Management of Disagreement in News Interviews." Master's thesis. University of California, Los Angeles.
Schegloff, Emmanuel, Gail Jefferson, and Harvey Sacks. 1977. "The Preference for Self-Correction in the Organization of Repair in Conversation." *Language* 53:361–82.
Schutz, Alfred. 1962–66. *Collected Papers.* 3 vols. The Hague: Martinus Nijhoff.
Shaw, Martin, ed. 1984. *War, the State and Society.* New York: St. Martin's Press.
———. 1991. *Post-Military Society: Militarism, Demilitarization, and War at the End of the Twentieth Century.* Oxford: Polity Press.
Shils, Edward. 1991. "The Virtue of Civil Society." *Government and Opposition* 26(1): 3–20.
Simmel, Georg. 1964. *Conflict: The Web of Group-Affiliation.* New York: Free Press.
Skinner, Quentin, and James Tully. 1988. *Meaning and Context.* London: Polity Press.
Skocpol, Theda. 1979. *States and Social Revolutions: A Comparative Analysis of France, Russia, and China.* Cambridge: Cambridge University Press.
Smith, Adam. [1759] 1801. *The Theory of Moral Sentiments.* Vol. 2. London: Strahan.
———. [1776] 1880. *The Wealth of Nations.* Oxford: Clarendon Press.
Smith, Henry N. 1950. *Virgin Land.* Cambridge, Mass.: Harvard University Press.
Smith, Philip. 1991. "Codes and Conflict: Towards a Theory of War as Ritual." *Theory and Society* 20:103–38.
———. 1994. "The Semiotic Foundations of Media Narratives." *Journal of Narrative and Life History* 4(1–2): 89–118.
Wagner-Pacifici, Robin E. 1986. *The Morality Play.* Chicago: University of Chicago Press.
Weber, Max. 1947. *The Theory of Social and Economic Organization.* New York: Free Press.
———. 1956. *The Sociology of Religion.* Boston: Beacon Press.
———. 1978. *Economy and Society.* Berkeley: University of California Press.
White, Hayden. 1987. *The Content of the Form: Narrative Discourse and Historical Representation.* Baltimore: Johns Hopkins University Press.

5

A Culture of Violent Solutions

Robert Elias

[In this chapter, Elias argues that the United States responds to social problems with violence, leading to a cycle of violence. He demonstrates that social issues that seem discreet—war, drugs, development and economic problems, childrearing practices, and treatment of women—are actually interrelated. In our politics both abroad and at home, Elias argues, we promote violence by responding with a "get tough mentality" to our social ills.

The author emphasizes the distinction between legitimate and illegitimate violence: that is, violence committed in the interests of those in power is usually considered legitimate, while violence committed by those on the margins is not. Elias raises the interesting question of the direction of cause and effect. Do the microprocesses cause the macro, or vice versa? This chapter emphasizes the impact of politics and economics on broader U.S. culture.]

I want to win the peace war. *George Bush*

I am violently opposed to the atrocities [in Bosnia].
General Norman Schwartzkopf

It is organized violence on top which creates individual violence on the bottom.
Emma Goldman

While Americans deplore violence, we nevertheless live in a very violent society. But our society is not merely plagued by "illegitimate" violence. Even more violence is generated by "legitimate" behavior, engaged in by individuals as well as institutions ranging from corporations to governments. On various levels, violence is standard behavior in U.S. society. It is justified by rationales as diverse as "buyer beware," "the need for domestic order," "protecting U.S. interests," and "promoting national security." Thus, much American violence is tolerated, perhaps even encouraged.

Even more important, violence is viewed as a legitimate means of solving problems, even if the problem is violence itself. To address a problem seriously, we must declare war. Arguably, we are a culture of violent solutions. Indeed, the use of violence to solve social and other problems comprises a large portion of the violence we commit in U.S. society.

But who are "we"? As we will see, "we" are sometimes all, or most, of us in this society. The public widely endorses legitimate violence and sometimes even illegitimate violence, although we should recognize the powerful forces of socialization and propaganda that often underlie that public support. At other times, "we" is the society characterized less by its members and more by its leaders—that is, those who wield power. Of course, in a purportedly democratic society, our leaders claim to exercise power in our name—but the reality is quite different (Parenti 1991).

Thus, while we should be concerned with the "we" of the general public, we should be even more interested in the "we" of the powerful few people and institutions who really run our society, undoubtedly more for their own interests than for ours. So let us consider the American people but also the American state—those elites both in and out of government who really rule our nation.

With this in mind, we can survey the way we as a society use wars and other violence to solve various American problems, ranging from problems such as Saddam Hussein to escalating crime. This will allow us to examine the role our own legitimate violence plays in creating new violence, which we then come to regard as a social problem. We will see how we routinely react to that violent social problem by committing more legitimate violence to try to solve the problem—thus producing a cycle of violence. What are the characteristics and results of using violence as a policy for solving problems? Who benefits and who loses? What are the alternatives?

Our Violent Society

We are an undeniably violent society, where violence has become not merely a characteristic but rather a way of life, proliferating throughout American culture. First, the United States has the highest crime rate in the world. Beyond the tremendous violence to property, from theft to wanton destruction, there is an even greater violence against people, including muggings, beatings, sexual assaults, and murders. Moreover, violence is becoming more organized and systematic, with an increase in serial or mass murders, gang violence, and hate crimes against women and other groups in society.

Second, for all the violence of crime, even more violence results from harmful behavior that we have thus far refused to define as crime. Even more than from crime, people suffer from the violence (measured in terms of losses, illnesses, disabilities, and deaths) of extensive but preventable workplace injuries and diseases, of environmental degradation, of unsafe food, pharmaceuticals, and other products, of unnecessary surgery and incompetent emergency care, and of corporate and government wrongdoing that devastates individuals, groups, and communities alike (Reiman 1988).

Third, violence permeates American culture. For example, it characterizes our sporting life. Some of our sports, like hockey and football, exist specifically to measure which team can administer the most effective violence against the other. Increasingly, the violence spills beyond the "game," such as in bench-clearing brawls. But our less violent sports have become more violent, too, and being a sports spectator is now more likely to involve us in violence, either as a victim or as a perpetrator. Consider the recent "kneecapping" of an Olympic-bound ice skater and the beer bottles thrown at professional baseball players. Likewise, we have an overwhelming amount of violence in our news, and we daily ingest hundreds of images of the violence of crimes or wars.

Our visual entertainment is also dominated by violence, from television programs to films. With the advent of videos, even more of that violence enters our homes. Violence has become an increasing part of our children's play: it is in the cartoons and other television programs they watch, in the movies they see, and in the computer games that now overwhelm so many of our households. But this violence is not play: it is neither appropriate as play in the first place, nor is it play when it makes us and our children more violent in our daily lives.

Fourth, however regrettable to admit, our system routinely represses various groups and communities in our society. The powers-that-be use social institutions to administer violence against politically unpopular groups such as the American Indian Movement, the Black Panthers, and Earth First! Social institutions use violence as social control (rather than as crime control) when they warehouse people of color into the nation's burgeoning prisons, when they promote forced sterilization campaigns against minority women, when they conduct drug and radiation experiments on unsuspecting subjects, when they discriminately administer the death penalty, when they conduct police raids to terrorize communities, and when they tolerate the institutionalization of police brutality.

Fifth, our society suffers from the violence of neglect and irresponsibility. Tens of millions of Americans are unnecessarily victimized, in the richest nation in the world, by the structural violence of hunger and malnutrition, homelessness, unemployment, illiteracy, untreated illness, and other symptoms of poverty, racism, and sexism.

This violence is escalating, both tangibly and symbolically. Indeed, there is more actual violence: the new scares about juvenile violence (Kantrowitz 1993) and workplace violence (Solomon and King 1993) are but two of the latest symptoms. And there is more symbolic violence, in our language (Elias 1993a) and in our various representations of violence, especially in the media (Gelman 1993).

While as a people we claim to deplore this violence, alarming numbers of us practice it in our daily lives. We also celebrate it in our heroes and, increasingly, in our heroines. As Jack Levin has suggested, "Violence is hip right now" (Gelman 1993, 48). Moreover, as David Gelman argues, it is "better than hip: it's commercial" (1993, 48).

In 1989, a young woman was brutally assaulted by six youths in New York's Central Park. The violence was bad enough but the attitude displayed by the perpetrators was even more shocking. They had committed a savage crime but showed neither remorse nor surprise that they had committed such an act. Raping and beating someone to near death seemed almost appropriate or at least acceptable—it happens all the time. From this apparent smugness and insensitivity was born the term "wilding."

Wilding became the new violence of American society: the indiscriminate violence of "mindless marauders seeking a thrill." It was violence committed by people who "seemed stripped of the emotional veneer of civilized humans, creatures of a wilderness where anything goes" (Derber 1992, 8). But as Charles Derber argues, wilding is hardly reserved for exceptional groups in our society; rather, wilding permeates our culture, from Main Street to Wall Street. The hyperindividualism and anything-goes environment of the "Age of Greed" in the 1980s has turned most of us into actual or potential wilders. No means to "get mine"—and everyone else be damned—is too extreme, not even murder (Derber 1992).

Just as alarming, we increasingly use violence to solve our problems—both legitimate and suspect. Upon examination, it is remarkable how many problems we now believe, or say we believe, can be solved by using violence.

Doing Violence to Our Problems

The problems to which we now routinely apply violence are both domestic and global, and sometimes both simultaneously. Indeed, we can see the interrelationship between our domestic problems (from the interpersonal to the national) and our global problems, and the interrelationship of the techniques of violence we use against them.

Yet what elites might view as "problems" might not be viewed as such by the masses. Violence, drugs, poverty, and even enemies (depending on who is targeted) might be legitimate problems to address. But what about when children, women, or minority races or religions are treated as problems, as we so often see in our society? What about when enhancing profits for the few or maintaining American-dominated international capitalism are treated as problems to solve? Whether legitimate or suspicious, the following problems (at home or abroad) have nevertheless been addressed most often by seeking solutions through violence.

Violence

As just illustrated, violence itself is a major social problem. At home, for example, there is a concern about controlling the high level of violent crime. Yet we routinely respond by escalating the violence. We declare "wars" on crime. Our police adopt more sophisticated weapons and military models. Our punishments increasingly promote deprivation, physical abuse, longer sentences, capital punishment, even sterilization. When physically abused children grow up and commit their own violence, we call for greater violence against them to "teach them a lesson."

We unleash the police and tolerate increased levels of brutality, making incidents like Rodney King's beating commonplace rather than exceptional (Davis 1992). When communities like South Central Los Angeles erupt in response to state violence and injustice, we send military troops to violently quell the riots. When state violence fails and citizens like Bernhard Goetz—the so-called subway vigilante—use their own violence against the threat of criminal violence, we applaud (Rubin 1986).

Abroad, we claim we are concerned about the problem posed by two other forms of violence: state repression and group terrorism. Yet most often, we respond with new violence. We send military aid to "professionalize" the Salvadoran army and its allied death squads. We bomb Libya to curb its terrorism campaign in Europe. We declare war on Iraq to reverse its invasion of Kuwait. When officials are too slow in responding with their own violence, they are chastised, such as Bill Clinton's initial reluctance to "get tough" in Bosnia (Whitaker 1993).

Drugs

Another major problem is the proliferation of drugs in our society. Yet predictably, we respond first and foremost by declaring a war on drugs. No need to spend much time on better health, education, or rehabilitation—only a violent response will seriously address drug users and dealers at home. So what if these wars have turned many parts of our cities into armed battlefields (Elias 1993b; Lusane 1991)?

Abroad, we follow the same policy. One response has been to sponsor police and militaries in drug-producing or drug-processing nations so they can conduct their own campaigns of violence. When that is not good enough, we send our own police (such as the Drug Enforcement Agency) and military abroad to raid suppliers, poison crops, kill druglords, and commit other violence to solve the problem (Elias 1991; Marshall 1991).

Poverty

The United States also has a growing problem of poverty. Even in the 1960s, when we were willing to consider "softer options" for dealing with poverty, our response was still a war: the War on Poverty. As we have moved from then to the 1980s and early 1990s, our solutions for poverty have grown ever more abusive and violent. Instead of confronting poverty, we have been fighting the poor: cutting assistance, pushing people off welfare, blaming them for their poverty, brutalizing and jailing the homeless, and swelling—rather than reducing—the ranks of the destitute (Piven and Cloward 1982).

Abroad, we purport to solve the problem of underdevelopment. Yet in practice, we intensify underdevelopment with policies that can only be viewed as escalating the structural violence that already plagues most people in the world. Our development model—based on austerity programs and "structural adjustment"—undermines local economies, ravages the environment, steals natural resources, exploits workers, represses communities, and generally enhances the misery of the world's poor (Hayter 1971; Lappe 1986). When confronted with millions of starving people, we ignore the institutional causes of hunger, such as the incentives we give other nations to squander their resources on militarism instead of nourishment. When we intervene, we commit our military troops to "take the problem seriously," even when—as in Somalia—the military solution only makes the problem worse (Marland 1993).

Enemies

Americans have been preoccupied, perhaps uniquely, with the problem of our "enemies." Yet we may not agree what constitutes the enemy. For example, at home we might be united in thinking that criminals are our enemies, but the more we examine the double standards used to define crime and criminals the more we might begin to disagree.

After criminals, our "real" enemies might be even more obscure. Are dissidents, for example, our enemies, or are they, as some would argue, those most responsible historically for promoting rights and social progress? In practice, we have treated most dissidents as enemies. And we have routinely used violence to fight those enemies, whether in the assassination of Black Panthers (Blackstock 1975), the "turkey shoot" attack on Attica prisoners (Bell 1985), the armed raids on American Indian Movement members at Wounded Knee (Matthiessen 1989), the crippling or killing of antiwar activists in Oakland, or the bombing of the MOVE group in Philadelphia and the Branch Davidians in Waco (Cleaver 1994; "War" 1993).

Dissidents are not alone among our domestic enemies. We often perceive other threats, especially to our economic well-being, such as from other races, ethnicities, religions, classes, or genders. The state might respond to these threats directly, such as by its racist immigration policies or its racist attacks on African Americans such as Rodney King, or indirectly, by abetting (through divisive policies that, for example, pit races against each other in a competition for artificially scarce public resources) individual (usually white male) responses to these threats. In either case, the response is violence more often than not, emerging as state repression or, increasingly, as hate crimes. Mexican "wetbacks" are terrorized by border patrols or attacked by citizens for stealing American jobs. Asian Americans are bashed for ruining the U.S. auto industry. Arab Americans are victimized for threatening "our" oil in the Middle East.

Abroad, we face the problem of enemies or aggressors who we believe want to attack us or otherwise undermine our way of life. Again, violence dominates our choice of responses. During its two hundred years, the United States has launched two hundred military interventions, varying in scale but all with the same statement: "We will beat you into submission." If Muammar al-Qaddafi insists on promoting international terrorism, then we can only stop him by bombing Libya and killing one hundred innocent civilians. If Manuel Noriega continues running drugs and refuses to toe the American line any longer, then we can only stop him by invading Panama, killing several thousand people, and leaving tens of thousands homeless.

For the decade of the 1980s, solving the problem of Central American unrest relied on promoting the unrelenting violence of U.S.-sponsored murder, assassination, torture, terrorism, repression, invasions, starvation, military coups, crop poisoning, economic destabilization, psychological warfare, environmental destruction, and low-intensity warfare (Barry and Preutsch 1988; Tifft and Markham 1991; Huggins 1987). As the former Assistant Secretary of State Elliot Abrams said, the purpose of the contras in Nicaragua was "to permit people on our side to use more violence" (Chomsky 1988, 48). The contras never had and never claimed they could gain the support of the Nicaraguan people: "Nothing counted except for the increase in violence" (Chomsky 1988, 49). U.S. policy makers had similar concerns about whether the violence was sufficient when we were in Vietnam.

The "new world order" promises no respite from this pattern, as the United States prepares itself for new interventions against other nations, revolutionaries, and terrorists (Watson 1993). The United States still promotes weapons sales to nations around the world, further buttressing the profitable war system. Yet we threaten violence against nations whose growing conventional and nuclear weapon capabilities begin to concern us, even if we were instrumental—as in the case of Iraq—in creating them. The United States delivers "spankings" to "teach lessons," such as George Bush's outgoing attacks on Iraq, and Clinton's bombing strikes on Baghdad—to prove he was not a foreign policy "wimp" (Ehrenreich 1993). When we attacked Iraq during the Gulf War and killed two hundred thousand people, we had not attacked Iraqis but rather their leader, Saddam Hussein, whom we demonized as Hitler and invested with mythical powers that had to be defeated.

Nonviolent alternatives to violence and to military intervention against our enemies are options undertaken only at the risk of "backing down" or "appearing weak." A question asked in one news poll of American popular support for the Gulf War best reflects the lack of alternatives to violence. When asking Americans what we should do in the Gulf, the poll offered only the following options: attack now, attack later, attack by air, attack by ground, and no opinion. So much for the possibility of not attacking at all.

Children

Yet another problem is how to successfully raise our children. Somehow, childrearing often gets reduced to the problem of disciplining children at home and in school. Curiously, we seem more preoccupied with the "negative" problem of keeping our children in line instead of the more "positive" problem of providing a stimulating and fulfilling environment for them. Youngsters seem more like an impediment than a national resource. In any case, again our solution seems to emphasize violence.

Certain ideologies, such as conservative Protestantism, encourage this violence in particular: "sacralizing" violence has been linked to the values of salvation, divine will, and obedience to authority. Accordingly, people are born with sin, and it is their human nature to rebel, to be selfish and evil. From this perspective, corporal punishment is not only acceptable, it is crucial to good child development (Ellison and Bartkowski, in this volume). These views, once treated as old-fashioned, have made a comeback not merely among fundamentalists but also throughout society, despite the overwhelming evidence that such violence is actually harmful and counterproductive.

Abroad, our problem is not our children but people we routinely treat as children. Foreigners are viewed as unruly, immature, disobedient, ignorant, incapable, and underdeveloped, precisely the traits we attribute to our children. Thus, they require the same kind of discipline, and violence seems to be the "only language they understand." As with our children, we are not beating them down for our own sake but rather so that we can, paternalistically, do what is in their best interest (Black 1992).

Women

As with children, women are often treated as problems. Rather than being valued for what they contribute to society, they are often viewed as threats to that society not only by the few in power but also by the masses. Gains in equality for women have been welcomed by some, especially those who have directly benefited. Yet for many more, gains against sexism and the movement—feminism—that has produced those gains are regarded as threats, even by many women.

Thus, another problem has been the challenge of maintaining a patriarchal society. Routinely, violence is the means used to help preserve male control in U.S. society (Tifft and Markham 1991). Men's power relies on the control of authority, resources, reproduction, and decision making (Dobash and Dobash 1988). Much of this is established in contemporary U.S. households, most of which are still organized on an authoritarian model. Family violence, which has grown to epidemic proportions, not only results from patriarchy (Hutchings 1992) but also provides a major means of enforcing patriarchy.

Likewise, women are often systematically victimized by other kinds of violence in U.S. society. They are sexually and physically assaulted. They are subjected to dangerous and unnecessary surgery. They are the major victims of the increasing serial and mass murders in the United States. Moreover, women are economically deprived, bearing—along with children—the growing "feminization of poverty." Increasingly, women are the victims of hate crimes: violence committed against women, implicitly or explicitly, because they are women and because they constitute some threat to men.

Abroad, we can see further, sometimes more severe, instances of global sexism. Despite human rights rhetoric to the contrary, preventing the victimization of women abroad has been a very low priority (Eisler, in this volume). In fact, we are more likely to promote this victimization through our policies. Equality for women abroad provides the same threat as it does at home. Thus, the real problem is maintaining, not eliminating, global patriarchy (Brock-Utne, in this volume). Again, the means are primarily violent. For example, our foreign and development policies help promote or condone prostitution, the sex trade and sex vacations, female labor exploitation, female circumcision, sexual assault, and life-threatening female poverty (Barry 1984; Enloe 1989).

Profits (for the Few)

In American society, we must also be concerned with business profits. Driven by capitalism, we worry about how to maximize profits, to produce the direct and indirect rewards they promise all Americans. Yet even (and some would say, especially) here, violence is routinely used to solve this problem.

Business-as-usual entails a stream of violence that, if effectively checked, would challenge the viability of the American economic system. Unchecked, it primarily victimizes workers and consumers—in other words, most of us. It is justified as the means of making profits, even if they are profits for the few rather than the many. Business success, usually measured by the bottom line, seems to hinge on violent policies.

The doctrine of "buyer beware," for example, generally means that to maximize profit, a seller can rip off the consumer, or even injure or kill the consumer with the product. To enhance profits, Ford can decide not to recall tens of thousands of Pintos that contain gas tanks that it knows will explode on impact, causing injuries and deaths. To increase the bottom line, U.S. companies can underpay their workers compared to the value and profit created by their labor. They can also lay off workers in profitable enterprises, such as General Motors in Flint and U.S. Steel in Youngstown, to relocate where profits (and usually labor exploitation) are even higher. In both cases, workers must endure the structural violence of low or nonexistent wages, and devastated communities—that helped build those companies—must endure their own deterioration.

Other kinds of violence are also used to maximize profits. Large U.S. companies can use predatory policies to fuel "hostile" takeovers or drive smaller competitors out of business. Savings and loan banks can squander the life savings of thousands of elderly people who will now spend their waning years in poverty. Business enterprises can maintain dangerous or lethal environments in their workplaces, thus sacrificing the lives of tens of thousands of Americans annually to workplace "accidents" and diseases. U.S. firms can, with minimal restrictions, pollute the natural environment, promoting illness and premature death. And as suggested, this kind of violence intensified in the "Age of Greed" of the 1980s, as wilding in U.S. society moved from the back alleys to Washington and Wall Street (Derber 1992).

Abroad, the problem is promoting capitalism and maximizing profits for U.S. multinational firms. Many of the same strategies used at home are used abroad. Thus, violence figures prominently in promoting business success; indeed, there are even fewer reservations on the use of violence. Violent business practices are perpetrated not merely by U.S. multinationals but also by governments. Local governments such as those in El Salvador or South Korea use state repression to promote foreign business on their soil. At the same time, the U.S. government promotes its multinationals through aggressive, often military, strategies that help develop a "favorable business climate" abroad.

Such a climate is produced by blocking, often violently, progressive change and by combatting challenges to the capitalist system, such as the "threat of a good example" provided by the economic reforms of the former Sandinista government in Nicaragua. Being a good example means accepting "austerity programs" that prime the economy by further impoverishing and violating local populations abroad. It means the violent repression of workers, especially if they try to organize for better conditions, wages, and benefits (Chomsky 1988).

An Anatomy of Our Violent Solutions

Defining Problems

How can we explain the violent solutions we so routinely apply to our problems? First, how we define our social and other problems determines whether there is a problem, which ones will be recognized, and perhaps even which solutions will be adopted. Who helps us define our problems? Which language helps identify problems and their solutions? What process do we use to work through problems? And how do we choose among possible solutions to those problems?

Intellectuals As suggested, violence is the solution of choice for many of our most critical social problems. We have an intellectual culture that is so committed to the rule of force that it never ceases to be baffled when that violence routinely fails (e.g., in winning over the Vietnamese, in stopping crime, and so forth). Domestic and foreign policy makers insist that violence is the answer (Chomsky 1988). Experts such as criminologists are largely responsive to officials and their warmongering (Klein, Luxemburg, and Gunther 1991; Elias 1986; Immarigeon 1991). Arguably, criminology perpetuates violence by accepting official (often violent) models and ideologies and by producing criminal justice technocrats who continue the violence process (Caulfield 1991).

Media After the policy makers and experts, the media then dutifully set the context and report the solution to our problems: The Committee in Solidarity with the People of El Salvador (CIESPES) is violent, former President Duarte is a democrat; antiwar activists are violent, military planners are peaceful (Caulfield 1991). Violence in response to these threats is a regrettable but necessary evil. The media routinely "forget" our violence's past failures (such as our failed crime and drug wars) and its disgraceful "successes" (such as the Gulf War and our nuclear buildup) (Elias 1993a). Or the media only selectively report violence, such as "their" human rights abuses but not "ours" (Herman 1982; Lee 1993).

Narratives Language can make all the difference in defining our problems and in making violence the inevitable solution. Officials have learned this lesson and have co-opted peaceful language to disguise violent activities: police officers are now peace officers, offensive weapons are peacekeepers, the war department is the Defense Department, and—according to military billboards—"peace is our [the military's] profession" (Elias 1991). Nevertheless, the media is filled with the language of war and violence when it describes our response to problems such as crime (Elias 1993a).

Beyond words, our view of the world, and of our problems and their solutions, is shaped substantially by public narratives. While there are competing, alternative narratives, the state has the resources to ensure that the dominant narratives describing our public problems are convenient for elite purposes, often demonizing the enemy to help justify a violent response (Smith, in this volume).

Accordingly, most official narratives insist on violence to solve (or allegedly solve) our problems. Those narratives describe our violence as necessary, heroic, or altruistic. We use violence only as a last resort (it is a shame how often it comes to that), pursuing innocent motives against satanic forces. Or we are only defending ourselves or rescuing others—and we have been asked to help. Or it is a struggle between good and evil, for our legitimate interests, and besides, violence is an inevitable part of human nature.

For example, in the international realm, the dominant narrative of the Gulf War demonized Saddam Hussein as the enemy, painted Kuwait as the innocent victim raped by Iraq, and portrayed the United States as the heroic avenger, coming to the rescue. Similar narratives have been played out in Panama, Libya, Vietnam, and so forth. In the domestic realm, we saw Bernhard Goetz—the so-called subway vigilante vindicated for his violence by narratives that justified his individual aggression because the state had failed (in using its own violence) to stop crime. Thus, Goetz was portrayed as acting in self-defense: he was the romantic hero while his victims were unfairly demonized. Even though this narrative eventually weakened, it kept Goetz from being dealt with seriously for his violence (Smith, in this volume).

As John Galliher (1991) has suggested, so strong are these narratives of violence that they can cause us to begin with the solution—violence—even before we have sufficiently understood or defined the problem. For example, we often seem to begin with a violent solution, such as capital punishment, and then look for theories or definitions of the problem that warrant such violence: such as the inevitability of "evil, black male savages." After this kind of analysis, resolving crime through social and economic change, such as through conciliation, mediation, education, and other more peaceful means, becomes impossible by definition, and the warmaking solution moves forward (Galliher 1991).

Narratives of violence make violence legitimate; that is, some violence is legitimized if put into acceptable narrative form. Almost all state violence is thus legitimized and excused. Legitimacy is determined not just by raw power or position but by public beliefs that are substantially shaped by successive state narratives about good and evil (Smith, in this volume). Thus, public opinion supports most state violence.

Assumptions There are several apparent assumptions behind America's use of violence to solve problems, both at home and abroad. First, violence is considered natural and inevitable, despite evidence to the contrary (Adams 1992; Goldstein 1992). Second, the United States and the men who run it are entitled to control. Third, violence is viewed as permissible because it helps achieve appropriate ends, such as instilling obedience, stimulating development, promoting democracy, protecting national security, and teaching lessons. Fourth, U.S. male aggressors are acting morally. Fifth, violence will be effective. Sixth, suffering is predestined, not created. Seventh, violence will not produce threats or harms for ruling U.S. males since there will be insufficient legal enforcement or counterforce against them (Tifft and Markham 1991).

Legitimizing Violence

Elites do not always need legitimacy to rule but having it makes their exercise of power far easier. They want to first portray themselves as addressing legitimate problems. Then, they want to legitimize their choice of violence as the solution. But official versions of legitimacy may differ dramatically from more objective assessments.

Which Problems? For example, what are the legitimate social problems that should be addressed? In line with some of the examples discussed here, we, the public, might say that safety is a problem. Yet while officials may pay lip service to that objective, they might privately be worried far more about the problem of their own power. We might want crime control, but officials might prefer the social control of disgruntled groups such as poor African Americans—and might be using the criminal law to pursue it, quite apart from any real questions of public safety (Szykowny 1994).

We might view all crimes and drugs as the problem while officials might care only about certain crimes and drugs. We might want to stop all repressors and aggressors while officials might want to stop them selectively, according to old cold war divisions, for example. We might view the problem as poverty while officials might view it as welfare. We might see productive international relations as a challenge while officials see other nations as the problem (i.e., as enemies). We might see the problem as one of eliminating weapons while officials might want to maintain them. We might want to prevent wars while officials might want to conduct and win them (table 5-1).

Admitting these motives would usually put officials in a bad light. These definitions of the problems are considered illegitimate. Instead, officials rhetorically commit themselves to a higher duty and more acceptable defi-

Table 5-1. Real Legitimacy?

Legitimate	Illegitimate
PROBLEMS	
Safety	Power
Crime control	Social control
For everyone	For the few
All crimes	Some crimes
All drugs	Some drugs
All repression	Some repression
All aggressors	Some aggressors
Poverty	Welfare
Underdevelopment	Foreign autonomy
Childraising	Controlling children
Authoritarianism	Too much democracy
Race relations	Other races
International relations	Other nations
Eliminating arms	Maintaining arms
Female/male relations	Controlling women
Decent work	Controlling workers
Wars	Conduct/win wars
SOLUTIONS	
Real attempts	Feeble attempts
Reasonable means	Unreasonable means
Good motives	Ulterior motives
Substance	Rhetoric
Solve	Manage
Attention	Neglect
For the many	For the few

nitions of public problems even if they abandon them in actual practice. Indeed, taking the "high road" of addressing "legitimate" problems gives them greater freedom to choose the solutions.

Which Solutions? To be legitimate, the state must approach the solutions to our public problems as follows: The solutions must be real, not feeble attempts, and must use reasonable not unreasonable means. Valid solutions require attention, not neglect, and must be substantive not merely rhetorical. They must proceed from good not ulterior motives, attempt to solve (not merely manage) the problem, and be designed to help the many not merely the few. When officials choose violence as a solution, it must generally be done and justified within this framework.

For example, it would be scandalous for the public to learn that our violent crime policy does more to maintain rather than reduce crime and that it serves both ideological and social control functions for the powerful (Reiman 1988). Nor would it be wise for the public to know that our violent drug policy has often done more to promote the drug trade than to stop it, especially when it helps promote other objectives such as our anticommunist crusades abroad (Marshall 1991) or our ghetto-control crusades at home (Lusane 1991).

Taking the correct rhetorical approach to addressing social problems provides the building blocks for creating narratives that justify the use of violence. Typically, such narratives will be filled with distortions to achieve the desired effect but will be convincing enough to bestow legitimacy on the violent policy.

Using Violence Despite all the efforts to justify their own violence, elites draw a sharp line between what they regard as legitimate state violence (or violence the state finds acceptable) and illegitimate violence directed at the state or that the state finds otherwise threatening or unacceptable (table 5-2). Certainly the state would not admit to most of the violence it views as legitimate; rather, it acknowledges only the violence it commits or endorses in response to the high-sounding, legitimate problems we have just enumerated.

For example, despite the democratic rhetoric, in practice officials accept violence committed against women but not by women, and against immigrants, workers, activists, prisoners, foreigners, the poor, and people of color but not the violence committed by them. Officials accept violence by the police but not against them, by the rich but not against them, and by the medical profession but not against it. The state accepts violence caused by

Table 5-2. Violence

Officially Legitimate (What the State[a] Does or Finds Acceptable)	Officially Illegitimate (What the State[a] Finds Unacceptable)
By government	Against government
By corporations	Against corporations
By the rich	Against the rich
Against women	By women
Against children	By children
Against foreigners	By foreigners
Against immigrants	By immigrants
Against people of color	By people of color
Against workers	By workers
Against homosexuals	By homosexuals
Against environmentalists	By environmentalists
Against the poor	By the poor
Against the powerless	By the powerless
Against activists	By activists
By the workplace	At or against the workplace
By the police	Against the police
Against prisoners	By prisoners
Murder by rich	Murder by poor
Capital punishment against poor people	Capital punishment against rich whites
Against terrorists	By terrorists
Against revolution	For revolution
By medical profession	Against medical profession
Against environment	By environment
By sports athletes	By sports spectators
In the media	Against the media

a. Ruling elites and institutions, both inside and outside government.

the workplace but not violence that invades the workplace and threatens the business. It accepts capital punishment against poor people but not against rich whites. Officials accept government and corporate violence but not violence committed against these institutions.

War Model

We use violence routinely to address our social problems. When that fails, we typically choose between two alternatives. On the one hand, we might give up, assuming the problem cannot be solved. As George Santayana once suggested: "Americans never solve any of their problems; they just amiably bid them good-bye" (1922, 52). On the other hand, we might just as easily conclude that we were not using enough violence to address the problem. Sally Gearhart explains how we trap ourselves into assuming that our only possible responses are either to be a victim or to strike back with more violence:

> Objectification is the necessary, if not sufficient component of any violent act. Thinking of myself as separate from another entity makes it possible for me to "do to" that entity things I would not "do to" myself. But if I see all things as myself, or empathize with all other things, then to hurt them is to do damage to me. . . . Our world belongs to those who can objectify . . . and if I want to protect myself from them I learn to objectify and fight back in self-defense. I seem bound to choose between being violent and being victimized. Or I live in a schizophrenic existence in which my values are at war with my actions because I must keep a constant shield of protectiveness (objectification) intact over my real self, over my empathy or my identification with others; the longer I keep up the shield the thicker it gets and the less empathetic I am with those around me. So every second of protecting myself from violence makes me objectify more and ensures that I am more and more capable of doing violence myself. I am caught always in the violence-victim trap. (1982, 268)

When we choose violence, as we usually do, we often declare war, both symbolically and tangibly. As the former prosecutor Alice Vachss argues: "A rapist is a single-minded, totally self-absorbed, sociopathic beast—a beast that cannot be tamed with 'understanding.' We need to stop shifting the responsibilities, to stop demanding that victims show 'earnest resistance,' to stop whining and start winning. And one of our strongest weapons must be fervent intoleration for collaboration in any form. We need to go to war" (1993, 36). Apparently, only going to war will show how serious we are about the problem.

The linkages between our crime wars and our international wars are also revealing. We are a nation at war with ourselves: a civil war, the war of law enforcement against the forces of crime. We imagine this, however cynically, as a conflict between good and evil where only superior firepower will ensure our security and win the day. We imagine the same things when we attack Panama, Grenada, or Iraq. Thus, as Kay Harris suggests:

> The civil war in which we are engaged—the war on crime—is the domestic equivalent of the international war system. One has only to attend any budget hearing at which increased appropriations are being sought for war efforts—whether labeled as in defense against criminals, communists or other

> enemies—to realize that the rationales and the rhetoric are the same. The ideologies of deterrence and retaliation; the hierarchical, militaristic structures and institutions; the incessant demand for more and greater weaponry, technology, and fighting forces; the sense of urgency and willingness to sacrifice other important interests to the cause; the tendency to dehumanize and objectify those defined as foes; and the belief in coercive force as the most effective means of obtaining security . . .
>
> People concerned with international peace need to recognize that supporting the "war on crime" is supporting the very establishment, ideology, structures, and morality against which they have been struggling. (1991, 91)

To perpetuate the war model of solving problems, officials co-opt the vehicles of peace for violent purposes. We noted earlier the co-optation of language, brought to its full absurdity and Orwellian dimensions in George Bush's claim, "I want to win the peace war," and Norman Schwartzkopf's comment, "I am violently opposed to the atrocities." But it is also a matter of co-opting institutions. During the 1980s, the United States used the Arms Control and Disarmament Agency as a forum for promoting weapons. In the early 1990s, the United States has co-opted the United Nations—purportedly created to promote world peace—to allow instead the United States to assume its unchallenged role as the world's policeman and to justify its continuing military conquests.

Guns and other weapons figure prominently in the war model. Just as we resist any real gun control at home, we also shun any real arms control abroad. Arms, we are told, are allowed, even encouraged, to protect us from our enemies. In fact, they expose us to more not less danger. Weapons escalate the violence we claim we are trying to protect ourselves from in the international realm. And in the United States, our guns are more likely to be used against us or result in violent accidents. Nevertheless, we persist, figuring we can use more violence than the enemy and thus triumph.

Even when we win (usually superficially) any particular war, we know little about how to win the peace. If we were ever to really win a war on crime, wouldn't the prisoners of that war soon be the enemies in future wars? Although we won the Gulf War, with an awesome display of violence, what have we really won in terms of peace?

The Impact of Violent Solutions

How well has violence worked to solve our problems? The answer is mixed. Violence has failed to solve our legitimate problems—those that affect the broader society. But violence has succeeded in solving some of our illegitimate problems, that is, violence has helped elites fend off challenges to their power and resources. That, rather than a serious concern about solving legitimate problems, is primarily why violence is used in the first place.

Failures

Violence has failed to solve our legitimate social problems for many reasons. As Emma Goldman's words (in the epigraph for this essay) suggest, organized violence on the "top" only escalates violence on the "bottom." Rather than inhibiting violence by others, official violence provides a model that legitimizes such behavior. Violence hardly seems appropriate to address the problem of the violence that results when we willingly provide the instruments for such behavior to others, such as when we arm foreign dictators like Hussein. Violence provides a poor solution to problems, such as terrorism, that were generated by violence in the first place.

Not only should we avoid violence for moral reasons, but violence is also inefficient, ineffective, even counterproductive. It not only fails to solve problems such as crime and foreign threats, it intensifies them. It promotes resentments if not hatreds, stimulates new problems, and invites retaliation in kind (Elias 1993b). Even though violence itself is becoming even more highly organized (Chomsky 1988), its use reflects a dysfunctional and disorganized society. Violence is a substitute for the kind of honest policy, resolve, organization, and social change required to solve most social problems.

Violence purposely avoids solving problems, perhaps because those practicing violence have other ulterior motives. Some may want to use violence to deal with crime even though they know it will not work, perhaps because they are more interested in punishing certain groups than in really reducing crime (Chomsky 1988; Elias 1993b). As Carol Nagy Jacklin puts it, "On the one hand, we seem to deplore [the problem of] violence but, on the other, we are not stopping it in the ways we know it needs to be stopped" (quoted in Macmillan and Klein 1974).

More specifically, violence has been counterproductive in solving the problem of crime. The violence of imprisonment has only increased the violence prisoners commit in our overcrowded prisons—whose population has quadrupled in the last dozen years—and then in society when they are released, sometimes prematurely, because of that very overcrowding (Zoroya 1993). Imprisonment helps officials, not victims, who may not be so intent (as we assume they are) on revenge anyway (Elias 1993b). The war model of crime control applies military concepts (such as viewing criminals as the enemy) and solutions (such as violent punishment) to social, political, and economic problems. It contradicts the offender's need not for violence but for restoration and resocialization (Knopp 1991).

Thus, our crime policy, like our foreign policy, was founded on violence. Coercive force has been legitimized to protect what we assume to be a just and humane system when actually it is violence being used to protect violence (Sullivan 1980). It is force being used against people, like Rodney King, who are demonized as being inhuman (Harris 1991). Conventional crime programs such as Crime Stoppers, Neighborhood Watch, McGruff, and even the Guardian Angels adopt a violent worldview based on paramilitarization and a fortress mentality. Crime-control policy adopts the language, ideology, and methods of war, and then co-opts the public as the foot soldiers in battle. Preventing crime becomes a holy crusade (Klein et al. 1991), like the Christian Crusades, and just as violent (Fahey 1992). The violence of crime control is a substitute for social progress that could more effectively solve crime and other social problems (Klein et al. 1991).

Even as a response to crimes against women, where some believe we impose our weakest punishments, greater violence is not the answer. The biggest detriment to enforcement against crimes such as sexual assault comes not from the weakness of our laws against rape or from judicial lenience but from the discouragement victims receive from police and prosecutors. In fact, the conviction and punishment rate is as high for sexual assaults as for other violent crimes (Caringella-McDonald and Humphries 1991). Most feminist criminologists agree that, even with more convictions, the violence of imprisonment would be ineffective (Schneider 1990; Daly and Chesney-Lind 1988; Box-Grainger 1986; Edwards 1989; Knopp 1991; Caringella-McDonald and Humphries 1991). As J. Macmillan and F. Klein argue:

> If all men who had ever raped were incarcerated tomorrow, rape would continue outside as well as inside prisons. Incarceration does not change the societal attitudes that promote rape. In a society that deals with symptoms rather than causes of problems, prisons make perfect sense. Confronting the causes of rape would threaten the basic structure of society. . . . Prison is vindictive—it is not concerned with change but with punishment. And its real social function is similar to that of rape—it acts as a buffer, as an oppressive institution where a few scapegoats pay for the ills of society. (1974, 5)

Just as we lose our repeated wars on crime, so too do our wars on drugs routinely fail (Elias 1993b). For all the violence such wars entail, the results have been feeble, if not counterproductive. Drugs continue to flow into the country, drug abuse remains extensive, and civil liberties have all but disappeared. Double standards of enforcement promote injustice and racism. Criminalizing drugs has manufactured criminals and promoted the social violence that is the price of taking risks in the high-stakes drug world. Unnecessary new crimes of violence are committed for resources to buy drugs at state-generated, artificially high prices. We are worse off each time we launch these wars.

Likewise, using violence against our enemies has been counterproductive. Many of our so-called enemies are not our enemies at all. Shouldn't African Americans and Native Americans be embraced rather than scorned, after the victimization they have endured through the centuries? Shouldn't peace activists, who oppose our society's illegitimate violence, be applauded rather than persecuted? Shouldn't we recognize that rather than our enemies, those who come from different races, ethnicities, and genders have far more in common with us than not? We would all benefit by ending our classist, racist, and sexist society.

Rather than blaming impoverished immigrants, why not examine the violent U.S. domestic and foreign policies that have forced their flood into the country? As for foreign enemies, isn't our national security threatened far more by not having enough educated people than by too few weapons, and far more by threats to our natural environment than to the international economic environment (Renner 1989)?

At any rate, violence against our real enemies has been ineffective and inappropriate. We pursue violent national security policies that make us less rather than more secure (Miedzian 1991). Violence used to suppress those who want to pursue their own political and economic systems returns against us, many times multiplied in the form of revolutionary insurrections. Pushing weapons to maintain the war system inevitably generates new enemies that must be violently crushed, giving the defeated even more reason to retaliate violently at some future date. Thus, our violence has generated widespread hatred of the United States in places such as Asia, Latin America, and the Middle East.

A cost-benefit analysis of our violence in Central America would illustrate our role in causing the blood and misery of hundreds of thousands of deaths, millions of refugees, and unknown numbers of people tortured, raped, and starved. In exchange, we have created resentment among millions of our southern neighbors and a mockery of real democracy among the Central American governments (Herman and Brodhead 1988). The United States is militarily strong but politically weak. We can kill but not persuade: our violence will never win the hearts and minds of others.

Consider the problem of domestic poverty. Our violent crackdown on the "irresponsibility" of the poor has not reduced poverty. Instead, it has helped increase and institutionalize poverty. Rather than social policy that addresses poverty's causes, punishment is our policy: a rejuvenated social Darwinism where pain and further sacrifice are the cures (Ehrenreich 1993). But the pain is administered unequally, with children, women, the powerless, and people of color as the disproportionate victims (Knopp 1991; Elias 1993b).

The workplace has become an ad hoc battlefield for a "war of haves and have-nots." Rather than promoting the social change and full employment that would prevent disgruntled workers from returning to their workplace to do violence, instead only better protective strategies are proposed (Solomon and King 1993)—no need to address the sources of this violence when we can line up new violence to try to repel it.

Similarly, we ignore the causes of poverty abroad. The violence of "austerity" or military intervention is easier than promoting real development. Yet with that violence, the rich get richer and the poor get poorer. The violence of structural adjustment produces a net drain of resources from the have-nots of the developing world to the haves of the developed world and from the destitute to the already rich in the poor nations.

We may be more successful using violence to solve some of our other problems, such as controlling women and children or maintaining high profits for the few. But here we are using violence to solve illegitimate problems whose solutions do not help the masses; indeed, they make most people's lives worse.

Successes

With these kinds of failures, why would we continue using violence to try to solve our problems? First, although the quick fix of violence will not solve legitimate social problems, people are reluctant to accept the real social change our problems require. Thus, instead of challenging the use of violence, they often support it. Second, the few in power have little incentive to solve our legitimate problems: not solving those problems allows them to justify the continued use of violence, although for quite different ends. Violence also lets the elite few solve illegitimate problems that threaten their position and control of resources. Most violence in the United States is used to keep power, not to solve problems, no matter how high-sounding the rhetoric.

For example, violence does nothing to reduce crime; in fact, it helps maintain crime, targeting "common" criminals, diverting people's attention from much greater social harms, and enforcing the laws against the have-nots who most threaten mainstream social relations. In other words, violence promotes the real goal of social control, not the secondary objective of crime control (Reiman 1988; Szykowny 1994). Likewise, violent drug policies do nothing to curb drug traffic; rather, they help promote it. But those same policies provide elites with a cover for worldwide anticommunist crusades, for raising illegal foreign aid, for justifying military interventions, and for rationalizing the domestic social control of the nation's ghettoes (Marshall 1991).

The violence of antipoverty programs does not reduce poverty. It helps control the unruly masses, fuels economic gains for the few, generates a "reserve army of unemployed" to help suppress wages and labor agitation, and promotes—abroad—a model of development that helps the United States more than poor nations. Violence does not eliminate our enemies; it creates more enemies. And it provides at least short-term benefits for the few. It checks dissidents, blocks real democracy, assassinates unruly domestic and foreign leaders, controls foreign enemies, and rationalizes the profits and armaments of the military-industrial complex. Violence generated between races, ethnicities, and genders over artificially scarce resources diverts people's attention toward scapegoats rather than toward their real enemies: those few who monopolize the nation's power and resources.

Besides these legitimate problems, which have been slighted in order to pursue other motives, violence is also used—often successfully—to solve several illegitimate problems. Violence keeps children in line, training many of them to be pliant cogs in the domestic and world economic system, even though that violence sometimes resurfaces when some of those children become adults and commit their own violence. Violence maintains patriarchy, controlling and degrading women, keeping them subordinate and subservient to preserve male power and resources (Gil 1977; Flitcraft and Stark 1978; Brock-Utne 1985; Tifft and Markham 1991). Moreover, violence maintains both a favorable business climate at home and abroad, ensuring maximum profits for the few at the expense of the many, and the war system, a substantial source of those profits.

Micro- and Macrolinkages

Whether a failure or a success, violence predominates. In an environment so saturated by violence, a relationship between the violence occurring in different realms no doubt exists. Among the linkages, it is difficult to distinguish cause and effect. Does our violence abroad, for example, help promote violence at home, or vice versa, or both? Despite that difficulty, increasingly we see that the linkages exist: violence on the micro- and macrolevels is connected.

We know that intrafamilial violence against women and children results, in part, from the broader society's laissez-faire attitude toward the household. We know that family violence is in part responsible for subsequent violence committed by children who were previously abused (Masumura 1979; Straus 1983). We know that the tolerated victimization of women in the home has undermined women's full protection under the norms of international human rights law and enforcement (Eisler, in this volume). We know that the violence of woman beating escalates simultaneously with the structural violence of increasing unemployment (Boulding 1978). We know there are linkages between the violence of poverty and teenage violence in the United States (Wright and Sheley 1991).

We know that we use the war model to address our problems at home and abroad. The connections between the battering of children (and others) in the United States and the battering of foreigners (such as Central Americans) abroad are increasingly clear. These two kinds of violence have similar natures, sources, processes, justifications, and vocabularies. When we typically treat foreigners as people who must be disciplined like our unruly children, we can understand the connection between militarism and corporal punishment (Tifft and Markham 1991).

Even governments acknowledge the micro- and macrolinkages. Some U.S. states, for example, now offer tickets to professional football games to people who will surrender their guns. One (admittedly more lethal) form of violence is exchanged for another: state governments obviously know there is a connection. Internationally, another government—the United Nations—has acknowledged the linkage between criminal violence and state violence in passing its Declaration on the Victims of Crime and Abuses of Power (Elias 1993b; Barak 1991). Not surprisingly, the United States opposed this declaration.

Social Disintegration

Surely other linkages will emerge. As they do, we will see them comprising a seamless web of violence. Aside from these concrete results, what does our use of violence say about our society? This violence questions our social values, suggests our growing powerlessness and lack of control, and forebodes decline, even disintegration (Pepinsky 1992).

The former U.S. Supreme Court Justice Felix Frankfurter once warned: "Loose talk about war against crime easily infuses the administration of justice with the psychology and morals of war. . . . The process of waging war, no matter how it is rationalized, is a process of moral disintegration" (1965, 92). Similarly, the philosopher Walter Schafer has argued: "The quality of a nation's civilization can be largely measured by the methods it uses in the enforcement of the criminal law" (1972, 50). If so, then ours is a civilization in steep decline.

Our repertory of options for addressing social problems has narrowed, leaving little more than a menu of violence. Accordingly, our violence has grown in the last two decades: as official violence has increased, so too has public violence. We have more prisons and more corporal and capital punishment. We hit and punish our children more. We have more gang violence and hate violence. Violence permeates our homes. Indeed, crime has invaded new communities, such as more and more rural areas.

Our violence is increasingly gross, insensitive, and desperate. In response, society encourages violence (even when it breaks the law) as a means of resolving conflict and fighting back (Johnson 1993; Ingrassia 1991; Dobash and Dobash 1979; Schecter 1982; Breines and Gordon 1983). Ironically, Bernhard Goetz's vigilante violence was applauded because the criminal process was viewed as too lenient. In fact, the process had failed because it was too harsh, too violent (Rubin 1986).

When societies are fragmented, alienated, and disintegrating, they use more violence—even if they have other means—to maintain order and solve problems. Societies impose social control by using either ideology, the law, or violence. Sophisticated or developed societies like the United States rely more on ideology and the law than on violence (Wolfe 1978). When a once sophisticated society begins to decline, however, violence increasingly supplants ideology and the law (Wolfe 1978). While two decades ago the United States had been moving away from the "iron fist" toward the "velvet glove" for controlling society (Platt 1982), that process has now reversed. Even worse, we seem increasingly addicted to violence, gripped in a downward spiral that is capped by a politics of denial about our desperate situation (Wien 1992).

Internationally, the United States has lost considerable moral power (given its support of repression), political power (given its unpopular views in the United Nations), and economic power (given the competition from Europe and Japan). But the United States maintains its dominance, and has regained its leadership of the United Nations, through its undisputed military power. Despite appearances, militarism is often the last gasp of power for dying empires. Our obsessive rallying around the flag belies fundamental weaknesses and insecurities ("Flag" 1990). Militarism blocks the search for ways to rejuvenate our society, such as the military-to-civilian conversion we need so desperately to rescue our economy.

Despite the warning signs, the U.S. system will no doubt continue its violence. Under the new world order, we will continue careening around the world like a rogue elephant in a china shop. Thanks to our military aggressiveness in the 1980s—epitomized in the Gulf War—the United States has now overcome the Vietnam syndrome of the 1970s and stands ready to unleash more lethal violence worldwide. The absence of the cold war has led only to a search for new military targets: druglords in Latin America, communist holdouts in Cuba and Korea, regional conflicts in the Middle East and Eastern Europe, and even hunger in Africa.

Our relentless use of violence betrays both our national purpose and our moral and intellectual culture. No crime, no matter how grotesque, is too great to fit into our system of intellectual self-defense that labels our violence as simply a reflection of our good intentions (Chomsky 1988).

More Peaceful Solutions

We are a culture of violent solutions, but violence will not solve our problems and is itself a problem and the root of most of our other social ills. There are alternatives to violence for addressing public problems. We should consider those alternatives not merely in principle (for moral reasons) but also for pragmatic reasons: unlike violent solutions, peaceful and nonviolent alternatives actually work (Elias 1993b; Quinney and Wildeman 1991; Pepinsky and Quinney 1991; Thurston 1993; Derber 1992; Morrison 1990).

We should have no illusions about adopting more peaceful solutions to social problems. Pursuing them requires significant social change and a forceful political challenge to those who now benefit from our culture of violence. We have acquiesced too long to our leaders' justification of violence. We must decide whether we want the new world order of escalating U.S. violence or an alternative world order of peace and progress (Krieger 1993; Elias and Turpin 1994; Brecher, Childs, and Cutler 1993).

Works Cited

Adams, David. 1992. "The Seville Statement on Violence." *Peace Review* 4(3): 20–22.

Barak, Gregg, ed. 1991. *Crimes by the Capitalist State.* Albany: State University of New York Press.

Barry, Kathleen. 1984. *Female Sexual Slavery.* New York: New York University Press.
Barry, Tom, and Deb Preutsch. 1988. *The Soft War: The Uses and Abuses of Economic Aid in Central America.* New York: Grove Press.
Bell, Malcolm. 1985. *The Turkey Shoot: Tracking the Attica Coverup.* New York: Grove Press.
Black, George. 1992. *The Good Neighbor: How the U.S. Wrote the History of Central America and the Caribbean.* New York: Pantheon.
Blackstock, Nelson. 1975. *Cointelpro: The FBI's Secret War on Political Freedom.* New York: Vintage.
Boulding, Elise. 1978. "Women and Social Violence." *International Social Science Review* 30(4): 37–50.
Box-Grainger, Jill. 1986. "Sentencing Rapists." In *Confronting Crime.* Ed. Roger Matthews and Jock Young. Pp. 102–9. Beverly Hills, Calif.: Sage.
Brecher, Jeremy, John Brown Childs, and Jill Cutler, eds. 1993. *Global Visions: Beyond the New World Order.* Boston: South End Press.
Breines, Wini, and Linda Gordon. 1983. "The New Scholarship on Family Violence." *Signs* 8:490–531.
Brock-Utne, Birgit. 1985. *Educating for Peace: A Feminist Perspective.* New York: Pergamon.
Caringella-MacDonald, Susan, and Drew Humphries. 1991. "Sexual Assault, Women, and the Community: Organizing to Prevent Sexual Violence." Pp. 98–113 in *Criminology as Peacemaking,* ed. Pepinsky and Quinney.
Caulfield, Susan L. 1991. "The Perpetuation of Violence through Criminological Theory." Pp. 228–38 in *Criminology as Peacemaking,* ed. Pepinsky and Quinney.
Chomsky, Noam. 1988. *The Culture of Terrorism.* Boston: South End Press.
Cleaver, Kathleen. 1994. "Philadelphia Fire." *Peace Review* 5(4): 467–74.
Daly, Kathleen, and Meda Chesney-Lind. 1988. "Feminism and Criminology." *Justice Quarterly* 6:5–26.
Davis, Mike. 1992. "The Los Angeles Inferno." *Socialist Review* 22(1): 57–80.
Derber, Charles. 1992. *Money, Murder and the American Dream: Wilding from Wall Street to Main Street.* Boston: Faber and Faber.
Dobash, R. Emerson, and Russell P. Dobash. 1979. *Violence against Wives: A Case against Patriarchy.* New York: Free Press.
———. 1988. "Research as Social Action: The Struggle for Battered Women." In *Feminist Perspectives on Wife Abuse.* Ed. K. Yllo and M. Bograd. Pp. 51–74. Newbury Park, Calif.: Sage.
Edwards, Susan. 1989. *Policing Domestic Violence.* London: Sage.
Ehrenreich, Barbara. 1993. "Punishment as Policy." *Z Magazine,* March, pp. 5–6.
Elias, Robert. 1986. *The Politics of Victimization: Victims, Victimology, and Human Rights.* New York: Oxford University Press.

———. 1991. "Crime Control as Human Rights Enforcement." Pp. 251–62 in *Criminology as Peacemaking,* ed. Pepinsky and Quinney.

———. 1993a. "Crime Wars Forgotten." *Peace Review* 5(1): 83–92.

———. 1993b. *Victims Still: The Political Manipulation of Crime Victims.* Newbury Park, Calif.: Sage.

Elias, Robert, and Jennifer Turpin, eds. 1994. *Rethinking Peace.* Boulder, Colo.: Lynne Rienner Publishers.

Enloe, Cynthia. 1989. *Bananas, Beaches and Bases: Making Feminist Sense of International Politics.* Berkeley: University of California Press.

Fahey, Joseph. 1992. "Columbus and the Catholic Crusades." *Peace Review* 4(3): 36–40.

"Flag Waving." 1990. *Economist,* 24 February, p. 21.

Flitcraft, Anne, and Evan Stark. 1978. "Notes on the Social Construction of Battering." *Antipode* 10:79–84.

Frankfurter, Felix. 1965. *Of Law and Life and Other Things That Matter.* Cambridge, Mass.: Harvard University Press.

Galliher, John F. 1991. "The Willie Horton Fact, Faith and Commonsense Theory of Crime." Pp. 245–50 in *Criminology as Peacemaking,* ed. Pepinsky and Quinney.

Gearhart, Sally Miller. 1982. "The Future—If There Is One—Is Female." In *Reweaving the Web of Life: Feminism and Nonviolence.* Ed. Pam McAllister. Pp. 266–84. Philadelphia: New Society Publishers.

Gelman, David. 1993. "The Violence in Our Heads." *Newsweek,* 2 August, p. 48.

Gil, David G. 1977. "Societal Violence and Violence in Families." In *Family Violence.* Ed. J. M. Eckelnar and S. M. Katz. Pp. 63–74. Toronto: Butterworths.

Goldstein, Arnold. 1992. "Aggression Reduction Strategies." *Peace Review* 4(3): 14–18.

Harris, M. Kay. 1991. "Moving into the New Millennium: Toward a Feminist Vision of Justice." Pp. 83–97 in *Criminology as Peacemaking,* ed. Pepinsky and Quinney.

Hayter, Teresa. 1971. *Aid as Imperialism.* London: Penguin.

Herman, Edward. 1982. *The Real Terror Network: Terrorism in Fact and Propaganda.* Boston: South End Press.

Herman, Edward, and Frank Brodhead. 1988. *Demonstration Elections: U.S.-Staged Elections in the Dominican Republic, Vietnam, and El Salvador.* Boston: South End Press.

Huggins, Martha D. 1987. "U.S.-Supported State Terror." *Crime and Social Justice* 27/28:149–71.

Hutchings, Nancy. 1992. "Family Violence." *Peace Review* 4(3): 24–27.

Immarigeon, Russ. 1991. "Beyond the Fear of Crime." Pp. 69–82 in *Criminology as Peacemaking,* ed. Pepinsky and Quinney.

Ingrassia, Michele. 1991. "'Life Means Nothing.'" *Newsweek,* 19 July, pp. 16–17.

Johnson, Kevin. 1993. "Summit Called over Rise in Gang Crime." *Los Angeles Times,* 24 July, pp. B1, B6.

Kantrowitz, Barbara. 1993. "Wild in the Streets." *Newsweek,* 2 August, pp. 40–46.

Klein, Lloyd, Joan Luxemburg, and John Gunther. 1991. "Taking a Bite Out of Social Injustice." Pp. 280–98 in *Criminology as Peacemaking,* ed. Pepinsky and Quinney.

Knopp, Fay Honey. 1991. "Community Solutions to Sexual Violence." Pp. 181–93 in *Criminology as Peacemaking,* ed. Pepinsky and Quinney.

Krieger, David. 1993. "Ending the Scourge of War." *Peace Review* 5(3): 353–60.

Lappe, Frances Moore. 1986. *Aid as Obstacle: Twenty Questions about Our Foreign Aid and the Hungry.* San Francisco: Institute for Food and Development Policy.

Lee, Martin A. 1993. "Mainstreaming Human Rights." *Peace Review* 5(1): 71–82.

Levin, Jack. 1985. *Mass Murder: America's Growing Menace.* New York: Plenum.

Lusane, Clarence. 1991. *Pipe Dream Blues: Racism and the War on Drugs.* Boston: South End Press.

Macmillan, J., and F. Klein. 1974. *Feminist Alliance against Rape Newsletter,* September–October, pp. 1–10.

Marland, Tom. 1993. "'This Is Going to Go On'—Despite the Upbeat Talk, We're Stuck in Somalia." *Newsweek,* 12 July, p. 34.

Marshall, Jonathan. 1991. *Drug Wars.* Forestville, Calif.: Cohan and Cohen.

Masumura, Wilfred T. 1979. "Wife Abuse and Other Forms of Aggression." *Victimology* 4:46–59.

Matthiessen, Peter. 1989. *In the Spirit of Crazy Horse.* New York: Simon and Schuster.

Miedzian, Myriam. 1991. *Boys Will Be Boys: Breaking the Link between Masculinity and Violence.* New York: Doubleday.

Morrison, Roy. 1990. *We Build the Road as We Travel.* Philadelphia: New Society Publishers.

Parenti, Michael. 1991. *Democracy for the Few.* New York: St. Martin's Press.

Pepinsky, Hal. 1992. "Violence as Unresponsiveness." *Peace Review* 4(4): 93–98.

Pepinsky, Harold, and Richard Quinney, eds. 1991. *Criminology as Peacemaking.* Bloomington: Indiana University Press.

Piven, Frances Fox, and Richard Cloward. 1982. *The New Class War.* New York: Pantheon.

Platt, Anthony. 1982. *The Iron Fist and the Velvet Glove.* San Francisco: Crime and Justice Associates.

Quinney, Richard, and John Wildeman. 1991. *The Problem of Crime: A Peace and Social Justice Perspective.* Mountain View, Calif.: Mayfield.

Reiman, Jeffrey. 1988. *The Rich Get Richer and the Poor Get Prison: Ideology, Class, and Criminal Justice.* New York: John Wiley.

Renner, Michael. 1989. "Who Are the Enemies?" *Peace Review* 1(2): 22–26.
Rubin, Lillian. 1986. *Quiet Rage: Bernie Goetz in a Time of Madness.* New York: Farrar, Straus, Giroux.
Santayana, George. 1992. *The Life of Reason.* New York: Charles Scribner's Sons.
Schafer, Walter. 1972. *Schools and Delinquency.* Englewood Cliffs, N.J.: Prentice-Hall.
Schecter, Susan. 1982. *Women and Male Violence: The Visions and Struggles of the Battered Women's Movement.* Boston: South End Press.
Schneider, Anne L. 1990. *Deterrence and Juvenile Crime.* New York: Springer-Verlag.
Solomon, Julie, and Patricia King. 1993. "Waging War in the Workplace." *Newsweek,* 19 July, pp. 30–34.
Straus, Murray A. 1983. "Societal Morphogenesis and Intrafamilial Violence in Cross-Cultural Perspective." In *International Perspectives on Family Violence.* Ed. R. J. Gelles and C. P. Cornell. Pp. 137–52. Lexington, Mass.: Lexington Books.
Sullivan, Dennis. 1980. *The Mask of Love: Corrections in America.* Port Washington, N.Y.: Kennikat Press.
Szykowny, Rick. 1994. "No Justice, No Peace: An Interview with Jerome Miller." *Humanist* 54(1): 9–18.
Thurston, Linda M. 1993. *A Call to Action: An Analysis and Overview of the U.S. Criminal Justice System.* Chicago: Third World Press.
Tifft, Larry L., and Lyn Markham. 1991. "Battering Women and Battering Central Americans." Pp. 114–53 in *Criminology as Peacemaking,* ed. Pepinsky and Quinney.
Vachss, Alice. 1993. *Sex Crimes.* New York: Random House.
"The War in Waco." 1993. *The Nation,* 10 May, pp. 615–16.
Watson, Russell. 1993. "A New Kind of Containment." *Newsweek,* 12 July, pp. 30–31.
Whitaker, Mark. 1993. "Getting Tough at Last." *Newsweek,* 10 May, p. 22.
Wien, Barbara J. 1992. "A U.S. Domestic Agenda for Peace Studies." *Peace Studies Bulletin* 2(1): 20–23.
Wolfe, Alan. 1978. *The Seamy Side of Democracy: Repression in America.* New York: Longman.
Wright, James, and Joseph Sheley. 1991. "Teenage Violence and the Urban Underclass." *Peace Review* 4(3): 32–35.
Zoroya, Gregg. 1993. "Violence Grows at County Jails." *Orange County Register,* 15 July (Metro sec.), pp. 1–2.

6

Linking the Micro and Macro in Peace and Development Studies

Birgit Brock-Utne

[In this chapter, Brock-Utne demonstrates that feminist scholarship links the micro and macro in relation to both peace and development studies. While feminists have analyzed the links between both direct and structural violence, Brock-Utne also argues for the distinction between organized and unorganized violence. She maintains that unorganized direct microlevel violence (e.g., woman battering) is linked to organized indirect macrolevel violence (e.g., economic inequality).

Basic to feminist thought is the idea that "the personal is political," that is, what goes on in the household is political. Brock-Utne emphasizes the paucity of analysis of the household in both peace and development research, which seeks to understand macrolevel violence and inequality. The author argues that we must pay closer attention to the microlevel if we are to understand macrolevel violence.]

A Feminist Critique of the Concept of Peace

Linking the micro with the macro in analyzing direct as well as indirect violence is essential to both peace research and development studies. Although a few male researchers have made this connection, the micro- and macrolinkages in peace and development research have come primarily from women's feminist scholarship.

The concept of peace is different and more complete when seen from a feminist perspective (Brock-Utne 1985, 1988a, 1989). We can show this by using the well-known dichotomy of "negative" and "positive" peace. This dichotomy has characterized peace research since its inception. It appears, for example, in the editorial written by Johan Galtung for the first issue of the *Journal of Peace Research* in 1964.

Negative Peace

In the newest revision of his textbook on peace and conflict studies, Håkan Wiberg (1987) defines peace as being both negative and positive: negative peace is "the absence of organized, personal violence, that is, approximately the same as non-war," and positive peace is "the absence of structural violence" (1987, 4–8, my translation). He seems to find working with positive peace more unwieldy than negative peace. But even negative peace can get unwieldy if one examines it from a radical feminist perspective where an analysis of patriarchy and the personal-as-political is essential (Brock-Utne 1989).

Such an understanding was already included in Galtung's (1969) early discussion of the negative peace concept, but since then it seems to have been forgotten by most peace researchers. Galtung said: "When one husband beats his wife, there is a clear case of personal violence, but when one million husbands keep one million wives in ignorance, there is structural violence" (Galtung 1969, 171).

What if one million husbands beat their wives? That must also be a clear case of personal violence, even of a collective kind. In a society where this happens, there is an absence of negative peace. Barbara Roberts calls such violence "the war against women" (1983), and some radical feminists—criticizing women's "peace" work at Greenham Common—claim that women are constantly "at war" with male society (OWP 1983). Even in so-called peacetime, women live in fear of being burned (in India), raped, mutilated, and killed by their so-called protectors. On women and peace, one radical feminist writes:

> Because the violence of the war against women is so widespread, it is not seen as such by many of its victims and certainly not defined as such by those who do the naming—the war makers. It is the very personalized nature of the war against women that allows it to be so normal as to render it invisible. As far as I am concerned, the ultimate act of male violence happens everyday. And when I am walking around thinking of this and I hear phrases like "Women for Life on Earth" and "Women for Peace," I feel completely bemused. What on earth do they mean? (Green 1983, 9)

The concept of negative peace should include the absence of collective personal violence against women, the absence of what these feminists have called "war." But I share Wiberg's desire to have as clear a concept of war as possible.

In response, I have developed a four-part scheme that divides negative and positive peace into two: the micro and the macro (Brock-Utne 1989, 47). The term "war" is reserved for the absence of personal, direct, and collective violence at the macrolevel. The war against women can be placed at the microlevel, thereby categorizing it as a matter of negative peace but not labeling it as war per se. Admittedly, this distinction may be open for criticism. Does not the collective violence against women occur at the macrolevel? Does it not occur more so than internal wars? Wiberg provides a possible response to this conceptual problem in his concepts of organized versus unorganized violence.

By insisting that "negative peace is the same as the absence of *organized* personal violence," Wiberg (1987) excludes Galtung's example of personal violence, where a husband beats his wife. That beating has not been organized. Even when one million men beat one million women, that brutality is not organized in the same way as when soldiers are trained to kill, called to defend themselves and their nation, or when police are trained to combat riots, although some organized gang rapes may be on the definitional borderline.

We can extend Wiberg's negative peace definition: "Negative peace means the absence of both organized (usually 'war') and unorganized personal violence" (Brock-Utne 1989, 43). War is then defined as organized, collective, personal violence, usually between states but possibly within one nation-state (so-called domestic wars).

There are advantages to excluding violence against women in the concept of war. First, it is easier to analyze the work women do to uphold as well as to uproot the institution of war. There is also an advantage in having a concept that is precise.

On the other hand, the advantage of including violence against women in the concept of war may be that peace researchers would have to address it as much as they do war in the more conventional sense. Yet some of the same advantage can be gained by including in the concept of negative peace the absence of unorganized violence against women (and also against children and men).

Positive Peace

Wiberg (1987) admits that it is not enough to say that positive peace requires the absence of structural violence. What about cultural freedom and identity? What about Galtung's million husbands keeping a million wives in ignorance as an example of structural violence? To keep someone ignorant can be achieved by both denying them access to information and by denying them an environment conducive to consciousness-raising. It is a different kind of violence from that committed by the industrialized countries or the multinational companies toward the Third World, or that committed internally in a country through structures where the few may prosper while the many die from starvation.

A distinction between organized and unorganized violence could clarify our thinking here as well. The multinationals, commerce ministries, and other elites in each country are certainly organized. The million husbands are not organized even though they may behave as if they are, perhaps because patriarchal thinking is so much a part of their value structure (or even their laws and educational system).

Galtung uses the example of one million husbands and one million wives, but what about one husband keeping his wife in ignorance? Take, for instance, Friedrich Engels, whose "wife" (they never actually married, which was why Karl Marx would never invite them to his home) was ignorant of the alphabet when he first met her and remained so after living with him for more than twenty years (Janssen-Jurreit 1976). This example creates some problems.

More than in the case of the one million husbands, there is an actor or rather a nonactor here as well as a victim. The personalized nature of this repression should categorize it under the absence of negative peace, where the actors and victims are easily identified. Yet I have reserved that category for a more direct, physical violence (beating, torture, rape, physical and sexual assault, murder). So this leaves us with the prospect of including the million wives (or the one) within the category of structural violence.

This category would include all types of repression and exploitation, whether organized or unorganized, that lead to a premature death because of a lack of food or due to contaminated air and water, or that just lead to a more miserable life where human potential is crippled, not used to its fullest extent.

Keeping a wife ignorant will normally not kill her, but providing her with an inadequate diet will, in the long run. We can introduce, therefore, a distinction in the concept of positive peace (or the absence of indirect violence) between indirect violence that shortens the life span and indirect violence that reduces the quality of life (Brock-Utne 1989). Table 6-1 summarizes my discussion on negative and positive peace.

The table's six cells are logically independent of one another. For example, it is possible that a man may keep his wife ignorant, lock her up in the house, and not allow her to read or watch television in a country where the right to free communication is widely enjoyed. Likewise, there may be war in a certain country and no wife battering, or wife battering and no war. This logical independence of categories is often forgotten, however, in standard U.N. texts on peace. The United Nations often defines peace as "the absence of war" in one paragraph while the next paragraph argues that peace cannot exist without the full participation by everyone in decision making, the enjoyment of human rights, equality, and so on.

The logical independence of the cells does not mean there are no connections between them; indeed, there may be many. Whether such linkages exist is an empirical question. Feminist scholarship has shown that women receive more beatings in periods of high unemployment (e.g., Boulding 1978). Thus, unorganized direct violence on the microlevel is linked to organized structural violence on the macrolevel. Elise Boulding has found

Table 6-1. A Summary of the Concepts of Negative and Positive Peace

	Negative Peace	Positive Peace	
	Absence of personal physical and direct violence	Absence of indirect violence shortening life span	Absence of indirect violence reducing quality of life
Unorganized	1. Absence of, e.g., wife battering, rape, child abuse, dowry deaths, street killings	3. Absence of inequalities in microstructures leading to unequal life chances	5. Absence of repression in microstructures leading to less freedom of choice and fulfillment
Organized	2. Absence of, e.g., war	4. Absence of economic structures in a country or between countries so that the life chances of some are reduced or effects of damage on nature by pollution, radiation, etc.	6. Absence of repression in a country of free speech, the right to organize, etc.

that women feel themselves especially menaced when the level of general violence increases since there is a strong psychological nexus between violence and rape.

In periods of war, women are not only tortured and slaughtered, just as men are, but they are also commonly raped. There are, for example, reports of gang rapes of Vietnamese women by American soldiers during the Vietnam War. The last soldier "making love to her" would shoot her when he was done (Brownmiller 1975, 110). But usually rape is reported only when committed by "the other side."

Such selective reporting stimulates and justifies retaliation in kind by "our side." News of sexual abuse and rape caused by "our side" is not generally included in "All the News That's Fit to Print." Susan Brownmiller has shown that selective reporting of rape has provided an ideological excuse for men to rape women who "belong" to other men.

For each of the six cells in the table, we may ask research questions that are particularly relevant for women. Such questions may be asked from one or more of the six feminist perspectives I have outlined elsewhere (Brock-Utne 1989, 14–39), thus producing as many as thirty-six combinations. Only when we have gathered a vast array of studies from various feminist perspectives on each of the six cells shall we have a complete feminist analysis of peace. Such an analysis will widen the field and help it illuminate many more aspects of the problem of violence.

The Concept of Peace and the U.N. Decade for Women

In a study of the final documents from the first three U.N. Decade for Women conferences (Mexico 1975, Copenhagen 1980, and Nairobi 1985), we can see how the concept of peace has changed to gradually add the absence of violence against women (Brock-Utne 1988a). Only the final document from Nairobi includes the feminist insight of linking the micro and the macro, arguing that there is no peace as long as women are being beaten and mutilated (Brock-Utne 1986; 1989, 70–73). In paragraph 258, it states: "Violence against women exists in various forms in everyday life in all societies. Women are being beaten, mutilated, burned, sexually abused and raped. Such violence is a major obstacle to the achievement of peace." Paragraph 257 argues that "the question of women and peace and the meaning of peace for women cannot be separated from the broader question of relationships between women and men in all spheres in life and in the family. Discriminatory practices and negative attitudes towards women should be eliminated and traditional gender norms changed to enhance women's participation in peace."

The change in the concept of peace from the 1980 to the 1985 conference reflects some of the thinking within the network of feminist peace researchers in the International Peace Research Association (IPRA). This network, founded in Orilla, Canada, in 1981, has exerted a great influence, both as a direct consultant and as an indirect lobbyist, on redefining peace to include the absence of violence at the microlevel, especially in relation to women.

Toward a Feminist Theory of Development

Thus far, development theories—both the neoclassical modernization approach and more radical alternatives that embrace Marxist, dependency, world system theories—have paid little attention to women. Indeed, women are mentioned only as research variables. These theories view the household as a "black box" and not as a part of existing political arrangements, that is, as "the private, personal sphere."

Feminist thinkers reject this split between the personal and the political (French 1986, 477). Researchers trying to uncover the level of wife beatings in families have been told: "No one should inquire into the privacy of the home" (Brock-Utne 1989, 49). Yet Roberts (1983), who has written extensively on violence against women, claims that no place is less safe for a woman than her own home. Feminist peace researchers have long recognized the need to conduct research on what goes on within households.

Currently, development researchers with a feminist perspective have begun to react against the conventional conceptualization of the household in development research. Conventionally, no analysis is made of who does the work in the family, who makes the more influential decisions, who gets the rewards. A study reported in the Indian feminist magazine *Manushi* shows that the traditional male-constructed economic indicators, such as average household income, per capita income, and per capita food consumption, fail to show who actually gets how much of what (Horowitz and Kishwar 1982).

When Indian researchers examined the internal distribution of money, food, and decision-making power within landholding as well as landless Indian families, they found a steady pattern of discrimination against women that varied little from one class to another. B. Horowitz and Madhu Kishwar (1982) found that it was the men (mostly the husband, sometimes sons or fathers-in-law) who decided whether the women in the household would be available for paid work outside the family. Even when the women worked for wages, very few of them had much say in how the family's income would be spent or in other important areas of family decision making. The lives of the women were hampered by crippling restrictions. Women from landholding families were even more restricted and powerless than women in landless families.

This research shows us how gender-neutral economic indicators do a great injustice to women and provide an incomplete picture of reality. It is no wonder that the U.N. High Commissioner for Refugees found that even after adequate supplies of basic and supplementary food (earmarked for vulnerable groups) were available in refugee camps, women and children continued to suffer from malnutrition (UNHCR 1980). In such situations, the patterns of distribution, both within the refugee camps and within the refugee family, reflected the discriminatory socioeconomic relations prevailing in the refugee groups.

The development researcher Rae Lesser Blumberg (1989) takes her analysis a step further than most studies by looking at the discriminatory practices that occur within the black box of the household. She shows that without properly examining household practices in Africa, the African food crises cannot be understood. Gender is not just a research variable—it is a central theoretical concept. She shows, for instance, that the greater a woman's relative economic power within the household, the more likely her fertility pattern will reflect her own preferences rather than those of her mate, family, state, and so on (Blumberg 1989). Generally, women use their greater economic leverage to achieve lower fertility.

Microlevel fertility aggregates, of course, to a country's fertility rate. Referring to recent empirical studies supporting the hypothesis that reducing fertility contributes to ecomomic growth in Third World nations, Blumberg concludes: "In other words, the economic empowerment of women at the micro level—that is, their increased share of the 'internal economy of the household'—can generally be expected to help their country's economic growth indirectly by reducing its fertility levels" (1989, 165).

Blumberg also highlights the gender blindness of development planners. They fail to see that development projects that increase women's workload while giving the income to their husbands may easily undermine the nutritional levels of children and women in those families. Development experts seem oblivious to the well-documented role of women as producers: women produce, for example, about 80 percent of the locally consumed and marketed food in Africa (Sivard 1985, 5, 17). The Economic Commission for Africa estimates that females account for 60–80 percent of all labor hours in agriculture (U.N. 1987, 5).

Despite this, males are an estimated 97 percent of all agricultural extension agents, who provide adult education to farmers in Africa (Swanson and Rassi 1981). One often hears expressions such as "the farmer and his wife" or abstract talk about "farmers" without mentioning the fact that the food-growing farmers of Africa are mostly women. Male extension agents transmit agricultural information to the husbands when the wives are in fact the full-time farmers. When the men pass on information to the women, it is often incorrect (Carloni 1987, 16).

Most agrarian households in Africa also promote the practice of "separate purses." Women control what they locally produce. Thus, as Blumberg (1989, 176–177) suggests, the incentives for "the household" (meaning "the male") do not elicit as much of a response from women farmers as do incentives that they, as women, can control. For example, the Cameroon

SEMRY Irrigated Rice Project requires conjugal activity to cultivate the irrigated fields yet the husband gets all the income. Researchers found that wives were very reluctant to work in the rice fields because that work competed with the women's sorghum production and their other income-generating activities. Women preferred to spend their time growing sorghum, even though rice brought a better price. Sorghum is cultivated on an individual basis. Although a married woman uses her sorghum primarily to feed her family, it is her own sorghum. Blumberg shows that the few independent women (mostly widows) in the project who grew rice on their own account would spend much more time in the rice fields than the married women and less time with sorghum since they would get all the proceeds from the higher-paid rice cultivation.

One of the major aims of current development practices in Africa, especially the World Bank's structural adjustment programs, is "getting the prices right" (World Bank 1981). Feminist development researchers show that even the "most right" prices will not matter if the women producers of most of the continent's food crops receive too little of the income to provide any real incentive. Thus, inadequate attention to women producers seems to be a crucial but little recognized factor in African food crises. Blumberg claims: "And yet, ironically, if given appropriate technical/credit aid and incentives, African women farmers may be the single most cost-effective available resource to alleviate the food crisis" (1989, 182).

Lacking a feminist analysis that uses gender as a central theoretical concept and without looking at the internal economy of the household, development planners are puzzled about some basic facts of particular nations. For instance, since Tanzania introduced its International Monetary Fund (IMF) and World Bank–sponsored Economic Recovery Programme (ERP) in 1986, the country has shifted from being a net importer to a surplus producer of food. Agriculture in Tanzania has grown at a rate of 5–6 percent per annum during the ERP, compared to 3 percent in 1981–85. Without considering other statistics, this may look like a substantial achievement. But health statistics show that half the children in Tanzania are malnourished and 5–7 percent are severely malnourished.

Valerie Leach, the former head of the Analysis and Evaluation section of UNICEF in Dar-es-Salaam, claimed that the "successful" ERP has *increased* malnourishment for rural Tanzanian mothers and their children (Morna 1990, 4). A study of 1,350 households in Dar-es-Salaam's poorer neighborhoods showed malnutrition at 20–30 percent—slightly lower than the national average. She explains that the lower rate of malnutrition in the towns has occurred because women are at home more often in urban areas, and they frequently give the children some of the snacks they make and sell outside the house. Since 80 percent of the agricultural work in Tanzania is done by women and since more land has been cultivated under the ERP, Leach claims that the deteriorating health of rural women and children comes from the fact that rural women work harder on the land and have less time to feed their children. The incentives gained from the extra food production may have been a factor as well. Are the incentives given only to the men while the women get less time to grow food directly under their own control?

Conclusion

Linking the micro and the macro when analyzing direct as well as indirect (or structural) violence is essential to both peace research and development studies. Feminist scholarship has led the way in illuminating these connections. Without greater attention to the mechanisms responsible for direct and structural violence at the microlevel—such as within the household—we shall be unable to understand the direct and structural violence taking place at the macrolevel.

Works Cited

Blumberg, Rae Lesser. 1989. "Toward a Feminist Theory of Development." In *Feminism and Sociological Theory.* Ed. Ruth A. Wallace. Pp. 161–200. Newbury Park, Calif.: Sage.

Boulding, Elise. 1978. "Las Mujeres y la Violencia Social." *Revista Internacional de Ciencias Sociales* 30(4).

Brock-Utne, Birgit. 1985. *Educating for Peace: A Feminist Perspective.* New York: Pergamon.

———. 1986. "Feminist Perspectives on Peace and Peace Research." *PRIO-Report,* no. 17.

———. 1988a. "The Development of Peace and Peace Education Concepts through Three U.N. Women's Decade Conferences." In *A Just Peace through Transformation.* Ed. Chadwick Alger and Michael Stohl. Pp. 170–90. Boulder, Colo.: Westview.

———. 1988b. "Formal Education as a Force in Shaping Cultural Norms in Relation to War and the Environment." In *Cultural Norms in Relation to War and the Environment.* Ed. Arthur Westing. Pp. 83–101. Oxford: Oxford University Press.

———. 1989. *Feminist Perspectives on Peace and Peace Education.* New York: Pergamon.

Brownmiller, Susan. 1975. *Against Our Will: Men, Women and Rape.* New York: Simon and Schuster.

Carloni, Alice Stewart. 1987. *Women in Development: A.I.D.'s Experience, 1973–85.* Vol. 1. Washington, D.C.: Agency for International Development.

French, Marilyn. 1986. *Beyond Power: On Women, Men and Morals.* London: Abacus.

Galtung, Johan. 1964. Editorial. *Journal of Peace Research* 1(1).

———. 1969. "Violence, Peace and Peace Research." *Journal of Peace Research* 6(3).

Green, Frankie. 1983. "Not Weaving but Frowning." In *Breaching the Peace: A Collection of Radical Feminist Papers.* London: Only Women Press.

Horowitz, B., and Madhu Kishwar. 1982. "Family Life—The Unequal Deal." *Manushi* 11.

Janssen-Jurreit, Marie Louise. 1976. *Sexismus: Über die Abtreibung der Frauenfrage.* München/Wien: Carl Hanser Verlag.

Morna, Colleen Lowe. 1990. "1990 Tanzania: Overworked Mothers, Underfed Babies." *Women's Feature Service,* July–October, pp. 4–7.

Only Women Press (OWP). 1983. *Breaching the Peace: A Collection of Radical Feminist Papers.* London: Only Women Press.

Roberts, Barbara. 1983. "No Safe Place: The War against Women." *Our Generation* 15(4): 7–26.

Sivard, Ruth. 1985. *Women: A World Survey.* Washington D.C.: World Priorities.

Swanson, Burton, and Jaffe Rassi. 1981. *International Directory of National Extension Systems.* Champaign: University of Illinois, Bureau of Educational Research.

U.N. High Commissioner for Refugees (UNHCR). 1980. "The Situation of Women Refugees the World Over." Document No.A/CONF.94/24. New York.

United Nations. 1987. "Effective Mobilisation of Women in Development." Report of the Secretary General. UN/A/33/238. New York.

Wiberg, Håkan. 1987. *Konfliktteori och Fredsforskning* [Theory of Conflict and Peace Research]. Stockholm: Esselte Studium.

World Bank. 1981. *Accelerated Development in Sub-Saharan Africa: An Agenda for Action.* Washington, D.C.: World Bank.

7

Human Rights and Violence: Integrating the Private and Public Spheres

Riane Eisler

[In this chapter, Eisler calls on us to examine the relationship between violence and abuse in intimate relations and human rights violations in all spheres of life. She argues that this is a missing link in human rights theory as well as in most analyses of social violence.

Eisler introduces an integrated approach to human rights that looks at interrelationships between private and public spheres. She documents how in its parent-child and gender relations the family has often socialized people to accept human rights violations as normal. Instead of classifying gender relations as peripheral "women's issues," Eisler views these relations as a fundamental building block for all human relations. We can see this connection by looking at regimes known for their human rights violations: they also try to force women into subservience. Even in more democratic nations, the failure to adequately address domination and violence in gender and parent-child relations impedes the construction of what Eisler calls a partnership rather than dominator society.

Force-backed domination in the home is thus linked to force-backed domination by the state, and the domination of half of humanity by the other is a political rather than only personal issue. Recognizing the link between physical and structural violence at the micro- and macrolevels can help us develop adequate analyses and solutions.]

Everyone who watches television or reads the newspaper at some point has had to ask themselves why armed aggression, military coups, torture, and terrorism have been so impervious to appeals of either reason or emotion. Why, despite the great human yearning for peace, has warfare—be it in the name of God, nationalism, or tribalism—been so recurrent? Why have reforms and revolutions carried out all over the world in the name of liberty and justice at best been only partly successful? Why, instead of steadily moving forward against injustice and repression, are we chronically forced to defend gains already made? In short, why, despite the mounting struggle over the last three centuries against institutionalized violence and oppression, have we been unable to build the foundations for a world in which human rights are protected and respected in practice and not just in theory?

Probing for answers to these questions has led me to two other questions that, once articulated, make it possible to see these issues in a different and much larger context. How can people brought up in families where violence and abuse are commonplace be expected to respect the human rights of people outside their families? Can people brought up to accept brutal practices—such as child and woman beating and/or genital mutilation and the selective malnutrition of female children—in their private lives realistically be expected to create a society free of torture, repression, warfare, and terrorism?

The simple answer is they cannot. On the contrary, people who grow up in such families, or who are taught to acquiesce to such practices in other people's families for the sake of social convention, are in fact effectively conditioned to accept human rights violations, not only in the private sphere of the home but also in the public sphere of our nations and our world. In other words, human rights violations in the private and public spheres are interrelated, and only a new integrated approach to both violence and human rights can lead to realistic solutions to problems that otherwise seem insolvable.

This chapter outlines a new conceptual framework for human rights in which the public and private spheres are fully integrated.[1] It begins with a reexamination of the historical development of human rights theory and action that shifts the dialogue about institutionalized violence from issues of national and international relations to underlying questions about human relations (Eisler 1987b, 1993). It argues that an effective approach to the problem of violence requires a new analysis of human society, one that reassesses many conventional beliefs, both religious and secular, and goes to the foundations of what I have called a partnership rather than dominator model of social organization (e.g., Eisler 1987a, 1987c, 1991, 1994, 1995; Eisler and Loye 1990). Specifically, it shows that unless we address the institutionalization of violence, abuse, and domination in our most intimate relations, we will continue to have chronic human rights violations in all our relations—in *both* private and public spheres. And it concludes with proposals for specific actions designed to help us move toward the next phase in the worldwide struggle against institutionalized violence and domination by focusing on the foundations for a world in which human rights can be recognized and honored in reality, and not just rhetoric.

The Public and Private Spheres

Logically speaking, in a world where human rights are truly valued, the distinction between private and public violence, cruelty, oppression, and discrimination would be seen as absurd. Yet many people continue to see private or family relations as separate and distinct, or at best as far less important than, political and economic relations in the public sphere. And, though once it is analyzed, this view makes no sense, it is the view that has shaped—and by so doing, distorted and stunted—the historical development of both human rights theory and action.

A basic problem is that from its beginning the modern movement for human rights—for a world where violence, cruelty, and oppression are not considered "just the way things are"—was literally what it is still often called: the movement to protect the "rights of man." Philosophers such as John Locke in the seventeenth century and Jean-Jacques Rousseau in the eighteenth century, who proposed the then novel idea that men have "inalienable rights," never spoke of the same rights for women or children.

Indeed, since their concern with despotism was limited to relations among men and men (or more specifically, among free property-owning white men) in the public or political arena, they did not even address the question of despotism in the private or family sphere. On the contrary, while they frontally challenged the then widely accepted notion that kings had a "divine right" to rule over their "subjects" in the state, the supposedly also divinely ordained right of men to be "kings" in the "castles" of their homes was for these men sacrosanct. Rather than being individuals innately possessed of "natural rights," women and children were merely members of men's households, "naturally" to be controlled by them.[2]

There were women, such as Mary Wollstonecraft and Abigail Adams in the eighteenth century and Elizabeth Cady Stanton and Sojourner Truth in the nineteenth century, who argued that women too have human rights.[3] There were also a number of men who made this point. For example, in his essay "The Subjection of Women," published about 130 years ago, the English philosopher John Stuart Mill noted that only "when the most fundamental of the social relations is placed under the rule of equal justice" can a just society be realized ([1869] 1973, 238). Similarly, in *The Origin of the Family, Private Property, and the State* (1884), published shortly after Marx's death, Friedrich Engels recognized the family relations between women and men as the model for class oppression. But by and large, as they still generally are today, such writings were banished to the intellectual ghetto of feminism.

Thus, the splitting off of "human rights" from "women's rights" and later also "children's rights" was established. This in turn led to the accompanying distinction in human rights theory and practice between the "public" (or men's) world and the "private" world to which women and children were still generally confined by custom and sometimes also by law.

Yet human society is based, first and foremost, on the relations between the female and male halves of humanity and on their relations with their sons and daughters. Our very first lessons about human relations (and thus also about human rights) are learned not in the public but in the private sphere. This is where people learn to respect the rights of others to freedom from violence, cruelty, oppression, and discrimination—or where they learn violence, cruelty, oppression, and discrimination. Once we examine human rights from this unified perspective, many things that otherwise seem random and unconnected begin to fall into place. Specifically, the link between force-backed domination in the state and force-backed domination in gender and parent-child relations becomes visible.

We can then see why throughout history regimes noted for their human rights violations, such as Hitler's Germany, Khomeini's Iran, Stalin's Soviet Union, and Zia's Pakistan, have made the return of women to their traditional (or subservient) place in a male-headed family a priority. We can also see why today in the United States those who would push us back to the "good old days," when most men and all women still "knew their place" and "holy wars" were the order of the day, have likewise opposed equal rights for women. For example, it helps explain why rightist fundamentalists pushed for a "family protection" act that would have cut funding for battered women's shelters—thus protecting a family structure where male heads of household can violently exercise despotic control.

This connection between rigid male domination in the family and despotism in the state also helps explain the Muslim fundamentalist custom found in chronically violent areas—where terrorism continues to be seen as legitimate and honorable—of not bringing men to trial for the "honor" killings of their wives, sisters, and daughters for any suspected sexual independence. For it is through the rule of terror in the family that both women and men learn to accept rule by terror as normal, be it in their own societies or against other tribes or nations.

As Engels noted, in the despotic Roman Empire the male head of household had life and death powers, not only over his slaves but also over the women and children in his household. Similarly, under the English common law, which developed during a time when monarchs maintained their rule through fear and force, husbands were legally permitted to beat their wives if they disobeyed them—the well-known phrase "rule of thumb" going back to a legal reform decreeing that the stick a man used could be no thicker than his thumb (Eisler 1977; Blackstone [1765–69] 1908). Here too we clearly see the systems relation between force-backed domination in the home and force-backed domination in the state.

Moreover, as the psychotherapist Alice Miller (1983) points out, if we examine the childhoods of brutal despots like Adolf Hitler, we see yet another link between the institutionalization of domination based on cruelty and terror in childrearing and the institutionalization of domination backed by cruelty and terror in the state. The biographies of such demagogic archcriminals reveal that their cruelty and violence—and particularly their violent persecution of "inferior" or "dangerous" people, be they Jews in Germany, blacks in the American South, or "disobedient" women in the fundamentalist Muslim world—is in large part rooted in the violence and cruelty they experienced as children.

To be sure, not all people raised in violent households become violent and brutal. But studies such as the classic *The Authoritarian Personality* have documented how individuals who participate in and/or acquiesce to authoritarianism, violence, and scapegoating in the state tend to be individuals from families where authoritarianism, violence, and scapegoating were also the norm (Adorno, Frenkel-Brunswick, Levinson, and Sanford 1950). In other words, such studies verify what common sense tells us: that the link between cruelty and violence in the private sphere of the family and the public sphere of the state is all too real.

Personal and Family Rights

But, we might ask, should a government or international agency have the power to interfere in people's private affairs? Even granting that what we experience and learn in our families affects our attitudes and behaviors in all spheres of life, shouldn't what happens inside a family be free from outside interference? What about the right to privacy?

Certainly the right to privacy, or more precisely the right to protection from governmental interference with the right to privacy, is an important civil right. But the right to protection from governmental interference in certain areas of personal choice and action—such as with whom to speak and associate, with whom to have intimate (including sexual) relations, whether or not to conceive, and whether or not to carry a pregnancy to term—is a *personal* right. In other words, these are *not* family rights. Rather, they are individual rights—even though they may involve personal choices and actions that characteristically take place within the family.

Moreover, personal relations in families have always been socially regulated. For example, the killing of one brother by another in the privacy of their home is generally regarded as a crime in both tribal and modern codes of law. But while every society in fact interferes with internal family affairs through both custom and law, subjecting them to both legal regulation and outside scrutiny, all too often these customs and laws have been applied very selectively. Indeed, all too often they have served to permit rather than prevent violence, cruelty, oppression, and discrimination.

For example, Islamic laws still permit a husband to have more than one wife and to divorce wives (who are often completely dependent on their husbands for economic survival) by simply repeating "I divorce you" three times—while women do not have the same right. As late as the nineteenth century (long after the Declaration of Independence proclaimed that all men have inalienable rights to life, liberty, and property), women in most American states had few if any political or economic rights and upon marriage were legally divested of any right to control property, including property they brought into the marriage. Only a few years ago, the Kenyan legislature refused to enact a law that would forbid husbands to beat their wives—because, as some members of the Kenyan Parliament argued, this would interfere with men's traditional right to "teach their wives good manners."[4]

Even when there are laws on the books that ostensibly protect women or children, these laws are often selectively enforced—or not enforced—in ways that actually protect their violators from scrutiny and punishment. An example is the still widespread failure in much of the world to prosecute husbands who beat their wives (sometimes even despite laws prohibiting such battering) on the ground that this is a "domestic" or internal family affair. Still another example is how, despite laws and international conventions outlawing slavery, the practice of families selling girl children into prostitution (or sexual slavery) continues unabated in parts of the world (particularly Asia), in large part because it is generally not prosecuted.[5]

While there has been, and continues to be, much talk about protecting the family, the principle of noninterference in the private or family sphere has often in fact been used to maintain a particular kind of family—one in which women and children have few if any individual rights. Under cover of this mantle of "family protection," men can with impunity still dominate and hurt women, parents can do the same to children, and women and children have no recourse in either custom or law.

This is why the distinction between personal and family rights is so critical. Clearly, a person's right to make certain private decisions should be free from governmental interference. But that is not the same as immunizing family decisions—or more specifically, the decisions of those who wield power in a family—from public scrutiny and regulation. In short, *the protection of personal rights is not synonymous with noninterference in actions within the family—and in fact there often is a direct conflict between the two.*

Traditions of Domination

Another familiar argument against "outside interference" in family affairs is that the family is the repository of traditional religious and/or cultural values with which neither laws nor governments, much less international agencies, should be permitted to interfere. Once again, if we go beneath the rhetoric to the realities and reexamine what is at stake, we see that the issue is not so much one of preserving religious or cultural traditions but of preserving those traditions that maintain a particular form of familial and social organization. We also see that from the very beginning it has been precisely the reexamination—and rejection—of cultural and/or religious traditions that has fueled the modern movement for human rights.

In fact, the whole basis of the modern human rights movement is the rejection of autocratic cultural traditions backed up by fear and force. For instance, the autocratic rule of kings was once justified, and staunchly defended, by religious authorities who claimed that kings and other "noblemen" had a divinely ordained right to rule. Their right to rule was also vigorously defended by secular philosophers such as Edmund Burke, who argued that the doctrine of "the rights of man" would lead "to the utter subversion, not only of all government, in all modes, but all stable securities to rational freedom, and all the rules and principles of morality itself" (Burke, quoted in Castel 1946, 425).

This kind of rhetoric is all too familiar, as it is still used to oppose "women's rights" and "children's rights" by both religious authorities and secular writers who would have us see women's and children's rights as subversive of the moral order and a threat to family and social stability. Not only that, but violations of women's and children's rights—including brutal violence against them—are still often justified in the name of tradition.

Thus, the cry against interference with ethnic traditions is still raised to defend the genital mutilations that kill, maim, and blight the physical and psychological health of millions of women and little girls in parts of Africa and Asia every year. Unlike male circumcision, with which these practices are sometimes erroneously equated, these are not ceremonial cuttings of skin. They often consist of cutting off the clitoris (designed to deprive women of sexual pleasure and thus presumably the desire to "stray") or cutting off the labia and tightly sewing up the vaginal opening (making sexual intercourse impossible until a larger opening is again cut before marriage).[6]

Due to the challenge by women's rights advocates around the world, some national leaders have condemned such practices.[7] But to date, international human rights organizations have not taken a strong stand—even though genital mutilation is estimated to affect over 100 million women in Africa and Asia and is being brought by immigrants into Europe, Canada, and the United States.

This failure by international human rights organizations to speak out against an institutionalized, governmentally protected form of torture is all the more incomprehensible since the elimination of torture is universally accepted as a top human rights priority. One reason given by international human rights organizations, when they give a reason at all, is that genital mutilation is not torture in the conventional legal-political sense: an instrument of political oppression to exact conformity and suppress dissent. But while the practice of genital mutilation is embedded in religious rites and/or ethnic customs, its essential purpose is in fact extremely political. It is an effective means of perpetuating male power over—indeed, male ownership of—women. Moreover, like the torture of political prisoners, genital mutilation is an effective means of breaking a person's spirit, since it not only causes traumatic pain, even death, but also afflicts its survivors with major physical and psychological problems for the rest of their lives. Like the painful and deforming foot binding of girls in prerevolutionary China, genital mutilation thus exacts conformity and suppresses dissent precisely because even the victim is socialized—from childhood—into accepting it.

The idea that human rights organizations must not speak out against this form of torture out of respect for cultural traditions is not only illogical, it is ludicrous. Every institutionalized behavior, including cannibalism and slavery, is a cultural tradition. Surely no human rights advocate, or for that matter anyone else, would today dare to justify cannibalism or slavery (which were once also traditional practices in certain cultures) on cultural or traditional grounds.

Neither would any human rights advocate have justified apartheid or segregation based on race in South Africa as a cultural tradition—which it certainly was during the years of white rule. Yet segregation based on gender, which is still the norm in much of the Muslim world (including nations such as Iran, Saudi Arabia, Bangladesh, and Pakistan), is still defended by some Muslims and non-Muslims on the grounds that it is a cultural tradition. This is the case, even though it too effectively bars one group (women) from equal access to educational and employment opportunities, even freedom of movement, and even though this group is in fact half of the population!

Similarly, no human rights advocate would think of justifying house arrest. Yet, is this not what the cultural tradition of secluding women accomplishes when it confines women to special quarters that they may not leave without male permission? And while it is tempting to frame this issue in regional terms, because the examples from the Middle East, Africa, and Southeast Asia are so striking, it is important to remember that gender segregation, or what Dessima Williams calls gender apartheid, is to varying degrees a universal problem.[8]

For example, the custom of segregating jobs into women's and men's work, with work assigned to women given lower status and pay, regardless of requirements of technical skill, intellectual ability, or moral sensitivity, has been a major factor in maintaining women's subordination to men worldwide. Thus, in the former Soviet Union, where employment outside the home was encouraged for women, the occupations and professions where women were concentrated—from street cleaning to medicine (which in the United States has been dominated by men and extremely lucrative)—were poorly paid. In the United States, despite legislation mandating equal opportunities for women, the same pattern prevails. It is not inaccurate to say that for many American women the opportunity to enter the paid labor market has in practice meant the opportunity to work in jobs where they earn lower wages than white males.

This leads to another critical point. To note that the evils of gender-based segregation are not yet as fully recognized by human rights advocates as the evils of race-based segregation is not in any way meant to make invidious comparisons between traditions of racial discrimination and violence and traditions of gender discrimination and violence. Obviously, discrimination and violence based on race is a major problem worldwide all too graphically evidenced by the magnitude and injustice of the economic disparities between North and South.

But to recognize this should not blind us to the magnitude and injustice of the economic disparities between men and women—and to how truly shocking their omission from conventional discussions of either economic or political rights really is. This comes into even clearer focus when we consider that in most parts of the world women and children are the majority of the poor and the poorest of the poor (Eisler 1987a, 172–84). It becomes even more shocking in light of the fact that globally women as a group work much longer hours than men as a group; that, according to the U.N.'s *State of the World's Women Report* (1985), women perform two-thirds of the world's work, for which they earn only one-tenth of its income and own less than one-hundredth of its property.

In the United States, the fact that women who work for wages still do most of the child care and housework is commonly called the "double burden." In the former Soviet Union—because of the long hours women had to spend (after their jobs and in addition to taking care of children and home) standing in lines for food and other necessities—it could properly have been called the "triple burden."

Again, this is not meant to single out particular countries, such as the United States or the former Soviet Union. The sad fact is that economic discrimination (or to borrow Johan Galtung's term, "structural violence" [1980]) against women is ubiquitous, varying only in degree.

The Double Standard for Violence

Physical violence against women, which has only in recent years been systematically studied and reported, is also ubiquitous. Thus, domestic violence against women is a major problem in most parts of the world, including the United States, where, according to the U.S. Department of Justice (1986), a woman is beaten every fifteen seconds. It too is deeply ingrained in many cultural traditions, with study after study showing that it cuts across all national, racial, and socioeconomic lines. Study after study also shows that this tradition of domestic violence, which blights the lives of countless millions of women worldwide, has been passed on from generation to generation precisely because men have *not* generally been held accountable, much less prosecuted for this violence.[9]

Even the killing of female children and women is not prosecuted in some cultures if it is by a male family member.[10] Where statistics are kept by sex, they show that victims of family murders are overwhelmingly women and children, as, for example in Austria, where in 1985, 54 percent of all murders were committed within families and 90 percent of the victims were women and children (Bernard and Schlaffer 1986).

As Lori Heise (1989) writes, few phenomena are as pervasive, yet so ignored, as violence against women. She also notes that most of this violence is rooted in long-standing customs, like the habit of men around the world of using alcohol as an excuse for beating their wives and girlfriends. And these patterns of violence against women—from the selective starving of girl children and bride burnings in India[11] to the rape of a woman every six minutes in the United States (FBI 1988)—have continued precisely because they have for so long been generally perceived as "normal," even by the victims themselves, who have been socialized by their families to accept such brutality. Thus, in the United States, rapes have been widely reported only in recent years, since in the past—as is still the case in many cultures today—the rape victim and not the rapist would be punished, under traditions that blamed women for "tempting men to sin" or for "not being at home where they belong."

While government restrictions on foreign travel (as in the case of Soviet Jews) have been soundly condemned by international human rights organizations, the inability of millions of women (not only in Islamic nations but in many other parts of the world) to travel without male permission is still rarely noted in the general discourse about human rights violations.

Similarly, this discourse still generally fails to recognize how deeply ingrained the traditions of cruelty to children have been in all parts of the world. This includes traditions of physical abuse, such as beatings (which in most parts of the world are the norm rather than exception and sometimes are even condoned by law) and sexual molestations (which, according to some estimates, affect 25 percent of U.S. girls [Blume 1990, xiv]). It also includes more subtle traditions of psychological abuse that are now understood by a growing number of scientists as psychosocial, rather than purely individual, pathologies (Eisler 1995, esp. 182–87).

This double standard for human rights (that is, men's rights) and women's and children's rights obviously has extremely adverse consequences for the quality of women's and children's lives—often even resulting in their deaths. But it also has extremely adverse consequences for boys and men. This is documented by a recent study based on data from eighty-nine nations, which shows how gender discrimination and violence undermine the overall quality of life for everyone (Eisler, Loye, and Norgaard 1995).

It is ironic—and politically dangerous—that the systems connection between what happens in the private and public spheres is more often recognized by those working against, rather than for, human rights. For example, U.S. right-wing fundamentalists accurately see male authority in the family as the cornerstone of the kind of society they would impose. But it is also understandable because right-wing fundamentalists draw upon integrated traditions of domination that span the entire spectrum of human relations—from the family to the tribe or state.

All of this takes us back to the urgent need for a new integrated approach to human rights. For, like the submerged mass of an iceberg with only its tip in view, traditions of domination and violence in the private sphere provide the foundations for domination and violence in the more visible political or public sphere (Eisler 1995).

Indeed, it is only when we begin to apply a single standard to human rights violations, whether they occur in our intimate or international relations, that we see how the distinction between the public and private spheres has prevented the application of human rights standards to the most formative and fundamental human relations. For the basic fact is that people learn in their families what behaviors will be punished, or will not be punished and thus effectively condoned. As long as cruelty and violence in families are condoned rather than condemned and prosecuted, not only will these continue from generation to generation but so also will acts of cruelty and violence outside of the family (Eisler 1995).

From Domination to Partnership

Today the world stands at a crossroads. On one side is the well-trodden path of violence and domination—of man over woman, parent over child, race over race, nation over nation, and man over nature. This is the road leading to a world of totalitarian controls and ecological or nuclear disaster. On the other side lies a very different path: the road to a world where our basic civil, political, and economic rights—including protection from domination and violence and, just as urgently, protection of our natural environment from man's fabled "conquest of nature"—will at long last be respected. This road could take us to a new era when partnership and peace, rather than domination and violence, are the accepted norms.

I use the terms domination and partnership in a specific way. They describe two contrasting configurations or models of social organization that make it possible to see patterns that are not visible using conventional categories such as capitalism versus communism, religious versus secular, or right versus left (Eisler 1987a, 1995; see also table 7-1).

In the *dominator model,* human differences—beginning with the differences between male and female—are automatically equated with inferiority or superiority, with those deemed superior (such as men) dominating and those deemed inferior (such as women) being dominated (see figure 7-1). In this model, human rights are, by definition, severely limited, as the whole system is ultimately held together by fear and force.

By contrast, in the *partnership model*—again beginning with the difference between women and men—difference is *not* automatically equated with inferiority or superiority. Boys and girls do not learn early on to divide humanity into in-groups and out-groups. Instead, both halves of humanity are equally valued, and "softer," more stereotypically "feminine" values such as caring, nonviolence, and empathy can in fact (not just rhetoric) be given social and economic precedence, since men do not have to be socialized for domination and conquest—be it of women, other men, other nations, or nature. In short, in this model human rights can in fact and not merely theory be protected in both the so-called private and public spheres.

Models are abstractions. But the degree to which a society orients to one or the other profoundly affects all areas of our lives (see table 7-1 and figure 7-1 for some salient features of both models).

It is noteworthy that new evidence from archaeology indicates that, contrary to what we have been taught, many societies were oriented primarily to the partnership rather than dominator model for thousands of years in

Table 7-1. The Dominator and Partnership Models

	Basic Configurations	
Component	Dominator Model	Partnership Model
1. Gender relations	The ranking of the male over the female as well as the higher valuing of the traits and social values stereotypically associated with "masculinity" rather than "femininity."[a]	Equal valuing of the sexes as well as of "femininity" and "masculinity," or a sexually egalitarian social and ideological structure, where "feminine" values can gain operational primacy.
2. Violence	A high degree of institutionalized social violence and abuse, ranging from wife—and child—beating, rape, and warfare to psychological abuse by "superiors" in the family, the workplace, and society at large.	A low degree of social violence, with violence and abuse not structural components of the system.
3. Social structure	A predominantly hierarchic[b] and authoritarian social organization, with the degree of authoritarianism and hierarchism roughly corresponding to the degree of male dominance.	A more generally equalitarian social structure, with difference (be it based on sex, race, religion, or belief system) not automatically associated with superior or inferior social and/or economic status.

a. The terms "femininity" and "masculinity" as used here correspond to the gender stereotypes appropriate for a dominator society (where "masculinity" is equated with dominance and conquest) and *not* with any inherent female or male traits.

b. As used here, the term "hierarchic" refers to what we may call a domination hierarchy, or the type of hierarchy inherent in a dominator model of social organization, based on fear and the threat of force. Such hierarchies should be distinguished from a second type of hierarchy, which may be called an actualization hierarchy (e.g., of molecules, cells, and organs in the body: a progression toward a higher and more complex level of function).

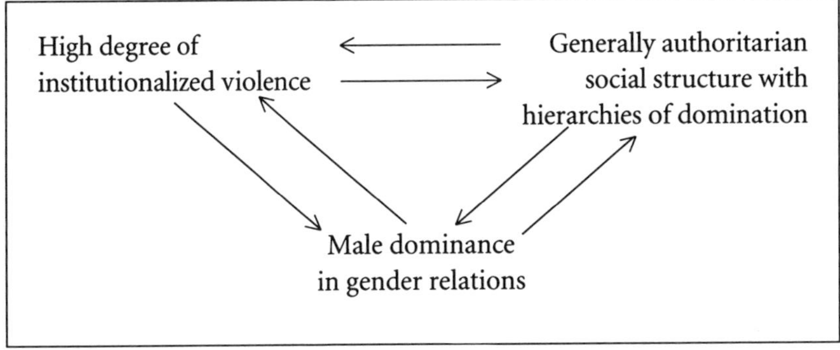

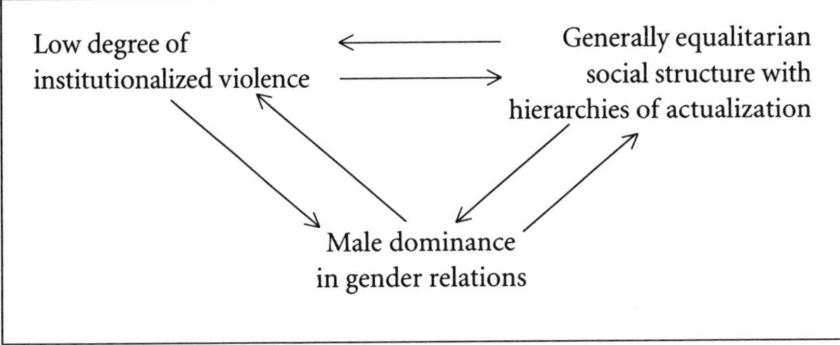

Figure 7-1.

our prehistory. That is, strongman rule, in the family or the state, has not always been the human norm (Eisler 1987a, 1995; Eisler and Loye 1990).

A detailed discussion of these models is beyond the scope of this chapter. The main point I want to emphasize is that if we look at the modern human rights movement as a key element in the struggle to free ourselves from a dominator model of human relations, we can see that the first phase of this movement challenged what we might term the top of the dominator pyramid: domination—and with it, institutionalized violence—in the public or political sphere. We can also see that *the next essential step is the challenge to the base upon which that pyramid rests and continues to rebuild itself: domination and institutionalized violence in the private sphere of family relations, and even more specifically, in the day-to-day relations between women and men and parents and children.*

Indeed, the "culture wars" launched in the United States by the heads of the right-wing fundamentalist movement call for strengthening a male-headed family where women must render unpaid services (with no independent access to income) and children of both genders must learn that orders from above have to be strictly obeyed on pain of severe physical punishment. Viewed from the dynamic perspective of the "cultural transformation theory" I have proposed (e.g., Eisler 1987a, 1987c, 1991, 1995), this reinforcement of traditions of domination in gender and parent-child relations by those who consider rigid rankings of domination divinely ordained makes sense. It is a reaction to the growing challenge to traditions of force-backed domination in the so-called private sphere of our foundational day-to-day interpersonal relations.

For example, not so long ago, the common wisdom was "spare the rod and spoil the child." Now we are beginning to recognize child beating as child abuse. People used to joke that "if rape is inevitable" a woman should "relax and enjoy it." Now rape is increasingly recognized as an act not of sexual passion but of aggression and violence. Gradually, the ethnic tradition of genital mutilation is being recognized as a brutal means of maintaining male sexual control over women. Increasingly, customs like the payment of "bride price"—where women (often mere children) are purchased from their own families for arranged marriages where they must not only bear a man children but often work from dawn to dusk—are recognized for what they are: a form of slave trade.

These are major changes in consciousness that could presage a new integrated stage in the modern political movements to shift from a dominator to a partnership model—and with this, to real respect for human rights. But changes in consciousness must be accompanied by social and political action if they are to result in changed institutional infrastructures.

A Call to Action

Recent meetings, such as the U.N. Human Rights Conference in Vienna in 1993, have brought increased attention to violence against women and other human rights violations in the private sphere.[12] The next step is a reformulation of human rights theory and action to integrate fully the private and public spheres. More specifically, what needs to be formulated are new human rights guidelines for use by governmental and nongovernmental agencies for altering their charters, policies, and most important, action agendas.

This is not as difficult as it may seem, since many of the building blocks for an integrated approach to human rights are already in place. Most notably, during the past two decades there have been two U.N. conventions that dealt specifically with the human rights of the hitherto generally excluded majority—women and children. The first was the 1979 U.N. Convention on the Elimination of All Forms of Discrimination against Women, which for the first time moved beyond the spurious distinction between the public and private spheres, specifically addressing the need to integrate "women's rights" into the purview of both human rights theory and action. The second was the 1989 U.N. Convention on the Rights of the Child, which likewise focused heavily on the private or familial sphere.

Other conventions have also provided materials for constructing a new integrated framework for human rights. For instance, U.N. conventions condemning slavery (or the ownership of one human being by another) and UNESCO reports such as the 1975 analysis of prostitution "hotels" in Europe (which document women's torture and imprisonment) could be extremely useful. So also could the Forward Looking Strategies from the U.N. Decade for Women (1975–85), the 1990–95 System Wide Medium Term Plan for Women and Development, the Fourth U.N. World Conference on Women Platform for Action (1995), and the research of INSTRAW (the U.N.'s International Research and Training Institute for Women).

There are also the resources of numerous nongovernmental organizations. Examples in relation to the problems and rights of women include the International Women's Rights Action Watch (organized by Arvonne Frazer at the Humphrey Institute of Public Affairs of the University of Minnesota to monitor, analyze, and encourage law and policy reform in accordance with the principles of the U.N. Convention on the Elimination of All Forms of Discrimination against Women), the Sisterhood Is Global Institute (currently headquartered in New Zealand), and groups such as Women Living under Muslim Laws International Solidarity Network (in Grabels, Montpellier, France) and Terre des Femmes (founded in 1981 in Lausanne, Switzerland, to include gender-specific persecution as political persecution under the provisions of the Geneva Refugee Convention of 1948).[13] Organizations that monitor the needs and problems of children include UNICEF, the Children's Defense Fund in Washington, D.C., the Inter-American Children's Institute in Montevideo, Uruguay, and Defense for Children International–USA in New York, to name but a few.

Moreover, the theme for the 1994 U.N. International Year of the Family was "building the smallest democracy at the heart of society." This too points to a growing consciousness of the need to move beyond the double standard for violations of the human rights of women and children in the family and violations of men's political and economic rights in the state.

Governmental reporting of human rights violations in the "private sphere" has also begun. Started during Jimmy Carter's administration but discontinued during Ronald Reagan's, the U.S. State Department—in response to years of tireless lobbying by human rights activists such as Fran

Hosken—in 1989 again instructed its embassies to report the extent to which foreign governments tolerate or condone violence against women, including domestic or "private" violence. Although they have been inadequately enforced, the two Percy Amendments (1973 and 1974) mandate U.S. and international agencies to study the impact of development programs on women. By 1987, the Netherlands, Norway, Canada, Sweden, and Denmark had also adopted policy guidelines to try to ensure that development funds are used to protect and strengthen women's rights, by requiring appraisal reports of their foreign development aid to include information about women (Hosken, personal communication, 1993).

These are important policy breakthroughs that have been sparked by social activists who want human rights applied equally to all. Further advances would be made if, for example, foreign aid policies imposed trade sanctions—such as those proposed by former Congresswoman Patricia Schroeder (*USA Today*, 27 Mar. 1990)—against countries that violate women's human rights, just as there have been trade sanctions against South Africa's racist treatment of blacks. Conversely, inducements, such as being placed in favored nation trade categories, could be provided for nations that enact and enforce legislation protecting women and children from domestic violence. Nations that provide evidence that such legislation is being enforced could also receive specific aid to support the enforcement of such laws, not only for humanitarian reasons but because family violence is a major impediment to successful economic development and a model for violence in all relations—including international relations (Eisler et al. 1995).

As a major contributor to the United Nations, the United States could pressure U.N. agencies, such as the World Bank, to adopt equal employment policies and increase their hiring of women, especially for decision-making positions. If we are committed to supporting democracy in the world, redressing the undemocratic underrepresentation of women in policy-making positions in all nations (including the United States) and at the United Nations should be a top policy priority.[14]

Such proposals have a much better chance of being implemented if they are backed by nongovernmental organizations, particularly human rights groups, which could forcefully lobby for them. These organizations could also launch an international human rights education campaign focusing on stopping violence and abuse in the family as the basis for a less violent, more peaceful, more democratic world.

As I write this, there rage in our world scores of armed conflicts, most of them civil wars where men, women, and children are being maimed, tortured, and killed (e.g., the carnage in Rwanda and the former Yugoslavia). Violence against traditionally disempowered groups is growing, be it against foreigners in Germany, immigrants in the United States, or women in places where Muslim fundamentalists are trying to seize power. For example, two young female students were gunned down in Algeria for the "crime" of standing at a bus stop without covering their heads, as is traditionally prescribed for Muslim women.[15] Terrorism is becoming commonplace, even in the United States, as tragically illustrated by the 1995 Oklahoma City bombing and the earlier bombing of the New York Trade Center.

Yet "heroic" male violence—in service to what its perpetrators consider a just cause—continues to be idealized, and we are daily bombarded with ever more brutal images of "entertaining" brutality. In the United States, movies are X-rated if they contain nudity or sex. Yet movies, comics, rock videos, and television programs that are watched by millions of young people constantly show men engaged in beatings, rapes, murders, and even dismemberment and torture—with women frequently portrayed only in the role of victims.[16] This effectively accustoms people to view domination and violence as normal, even "fun"—thus further teaching us to be insensitive to people's human rights (Eisler 1995).

In terms of the conceptual framework proposed by cultural transformation theory—of modern history as the tension between a powerful movement toward partnership and the strong, often violent, dominator systems' resistance—it is predictable that a social organization based on rankings backed by force and fear will promote violence to maintain its hold (Eisler 1995). While the contemporary escalation of violence in both reality and the mass media is not a conscious conspiracy, it serves a dominator systems' maintenance function. As we are learning from scientists such as Ilya Prigogine and Isabelle Stengers (1984), it is a matter of systems dynamics, of how living systems seek to maintain themselves. In other words, it is a function of systems self-organization (Csanyi 1989; Jantsch 1980; Loye and Eisler 1987). Just as the system of organs that constitutes the human body functions to maintain itself, so do the various institutions of a particular type of social system.

However—and this is of critical importance—despite these systems-maintenance mechanisms, living systems can and do fundamentally change. This happens, as Prigogine and Stengers (1984) describe, during times of extreme disequilibrium in the system. While they describe living systems on the chemical level, similar dynamics are observable on the level of human societies (Eisler 1987a, 1995). In human society, however, there is the added element of conscious choice, of making the commitment to alter not only belief systems but behaviors and social institutions.

People can—and do—decide to change both attitudes and behaviors. We see evidence of this around us every day—from changes in millions of people's smoking behaviors to changes in attitudes and policies about child abuse, rape, and sexual harassment. As noted earlier, during the past three hundred years there have been important changes in our family, political, and economic institutions.

A creative campaign to use the mass media to model nonviolent and humane interpersonal and international relations could help accelerate these changes (Eisler, forthcoming). Such a campaign can raise consciousness to something we see by simple observation: that human relations based on fear of force and pain (the dominator model) are not the only alternative. It would teach us to recognize human rights violations in our intimate relations: the day-to-day relations between men and women and parents and children. And it would help people make sense of all the contemporary talk of "supporting and strengthening the family," for it would open the way to raising a fundamental, though still rarely articulated, issue: what kind of family do we want to support and strengthen? If it is a dominator family where women and children have few if any rights, the prospects for human rights are grim indeed, as are the prospects for a less violent and more democratic world. If it is a partnership family where the rights of all members are fully recognized and implemented, there is reason for long-range hope.

It is on this note of hope for the future that I want to close. Completing the shift from a dominator to a partnership society is a long-range goal. But if we begin now to do the foundational work, we can begin to build a better future.

Ultimately, the only realistic way to break cycles of violence—whether interpersonal or international—is to help women and men and parents and children stop accepting the kinds of violent relations that in the international arena, through ever more deadly weapons, threaten our very survival. We can create a less violent and more humane world—but only if we first lay the necessary foundations by taking into account the link between the private and public spheres and addressing not only the rights of "man" but the human rights of the neglected majority: women and children.

Notes

1. For a more conventional review of human rights theory, from the natural law tradition derived from Aquinas to Marxist-constructionist approaches, see

Donnelly, *Concept of Human Rights* (1985). There is an extensive literature on human rights, including publications such as the *Human Rights Quarterly, Human Rights Watch, ICJ (International Community of Jurists) Review,* and *Encyclopedia of Human Rights.* Unfortunately, most of these publications have tended to address the human rights of women and children only in passing because they focus almost exclusively on the so-called public sphere, generally ignoring what happens in people's day-to-day relations in the so-called private sphere.

2. Eisler (1987b) provides a more in-depth discussion of the historical antecedents to the split between the private and public spheres and between women's rights and human rights. Bunch (1990) also addresses this split.

3. For example, in the first U.S. Women's Rights Convention in 1848 (the same year Marx and Engels issued the much more publicized *Communist Manifesto*), Stanton adapted the U.S. Declaration of Independence as a Women's Rights Manifesto by adding two critical words: "We hold these truths to be self-evident: that all men *and women* are created equal" (Stanton [1848] 1972, 72 [emphasis added]).

4. This comes from a *Time* magazine report quoted in *Women's International Network (WIN) News* (Autumn 1979, 42). Another legislator, Kimunai Arap Soi, even charged that the bill was "very un-African" (ibid.). But as the Kenyan women's magazine *VIVA* observed: "There is nothing 'African' about injustice or violence, whether it takes the form of mistreating wives and mothers, or slums, or circumcision. Often the very men who . . . excuse injustice to women with the phrase 'it is African,' are wearing three-piece, pin-striped suits and shiny shoes" (quoted in Heise 1989, 8).

5. A pioneering work on this subject is Barry, *Female Sexual Slavery* (1979). Barry is director of the Coalition against Trafficking in Women (P.O. Box 10077, State College, PA 16805), an organization trying to bring the worldwide traffic in women to the attention of the worldwide community. This campaign is particularly urgent because, due to the rapid spread of AIDS, the sexual enslavement of women not only condemns millions of girls and women to a miserable existence of sexually servicing men but in many cases to death. For example, in the all too accurately named "cages" of Bombay's red-light district, the World Health Organization estimated that 35 percent of the girls and women were already infected with the AIDS virus in 1992, up from 3 percent in 1988 (Drogin 1992). The situation may be even worse in other sex tourist centers, such as Bangkok, where girls from the poor northern parts of Thailand and other regions of Asia are regularly sold to sex entrepreneurs.

6. A groundbreaking work on this subject is Hosken's report (1984). Hosken's quarterly *Women's International Network (WIN) News* has a regular feature on genital and sexual mutilations. At a World Health Organization–sponsored conference in Dakar, Senegal, in 1984, the Inter-African Committee (IAC) was established as an umbrella organization dedicated to abolishing female circumcision and to dispelling the ignorance and myths that perpetuate this prac-

tice, such as the false belief that the Koran demands circumcision (an updated copy of the *Hosken Report,* is available from Fran Hosken, Women's International Network News, 187 Grant Street, Lexington, MA 02173). Hosken also distributes *The Childbirth Picture Book,* a valuable tool for women in developing countries that includes information on excision and infibulation. To date, *The Childbirth Picture Book* has been translated into French, Arabic, and Spanish. Hosken is currently working on a Somalian translation, as genital mutilation is almost universally practiced in that nation.

7. African nations that have begun to take measures against the continuation of genital mutilation include Egypt, Kenya, and Sudan, where at the Khartoum Seminar in 1979 the World Health Organization (WHO) recommended the eradication of these practices.

8. Williams introduced the term "global gender apartheid" at the First Minoan Celebration of Partnership, held in Crete in October 1992 and cosponsored by the Center for Partnership Studies.

9. Recent studies from the United States and Canada verify this, showing that when men are prosecuted and jailed for domestic violence (as people routinely are for violence against friends or strangers) this acts as a deterrent (e.g., Berk and Newton 1985). The experience in Minneapolis, where husbands are prosecuted and jailed, also shows the importance of holding men legally accountable for violence against their wives or lovers.

10. For example, so-called honor killings of women suspected of sexual independence are still not prosecuted in many parts of the Middle East, and the killing of baby girls, which reappeared in China after the government instituted its one-child policy, is likewise still condoned by custom, not only in parts of rural China but in other regions of the world as well.

11. "The Lesser Child: The Girl in India," a report prepared by the government of India to mark South Asia's Year of the Girl Child, 1990, has verified the heartbreaking situation of women in India. For example, it reports UNICEF findings that 25 percent of Indian girls die before the age of fifteen because of systematic patterns of neglect, discrimination, and sometimes infanticide, based on their gender (Crossette 1990).

12. I was particularly active in one of these conferences: "Empowering Women: Achieving Human Rights in the 21st Century," an international conference held October 29–31, 1992, at Coeur d'Alene, Idaho, which focused on some of the building blocks needed for a new integrated model of human rights as a vehicle for reducing violence worldwide.

13. For instance, Women Living under Muslim Laws International Solidarity Network and Terre des Femmes assiduously worked to obtain political asylum for Maryan Zerazi in Germany, on the grounds that women fleeing from honor killings, widow burning, genital mutilation, and other gender-specific human rights violations should be recognized as political refugees. Zerazi is a Syrian woman who has fled halfway around the world to protect herself from a

violent husband who threatened to kill her if she left him (letter from Women Living under Muslim Laws, 11 Nov. 1992).

14. To his credit, President Bill Clinton's appointments mark a major breakthrough in this respect. His own partnership with Hillary Rodham Clinton, two of whose major interests have long been advancing women's status and protecting children's rights, undoubtedly contributed to Clinton's commitment to policies to improve conditions for children and to advance the rights of women.

15. *Women Envision* (June 1994) reported these murders (published by Isis International, P.O. Box 1837, Quezon City Main, Quezon City 1100, Philippines). *Alert for Action* (27 July 1994), published by Women Living under Muslim Laws, reports that more than 550 women have been murdered in Kurdistan, with the government remaining silent or even encouraging this through various laws directed against women (Women Living under Muslim Laws, Boîte Postale 23–34790, Grabels, Montpellier, France). *Women's International Network (WIN) News* also has regular news on the global problem of violence against women, as well as on organizations all over the world working against it.

16. The Television Program Improvement Act of 1990 introduced by Senator Paul Simon has paved the way for change. It allows heads of television networks to meet to establish rules governing the use of violence in programs without fear of antitrust legislation for combining their efforts. It seems far-fetched that they would ever have been prosecuted under antitrust laws for this reason, but it was through Simon's efforts that ABC, CBS, and NBC officials met to discuss violence on television.

Works Cited

Adorno, Theodor W., E. Frenkel-Brunswick, D. Levinson, and R. N. Sanford. 1950. *The Authoritarian Personality.* New York: Harper and Row.

Barry, K. 1979. *Female Sexual Slavery.* New York: Avon.

Berk, R. A., and P. J. Newton. 1985. "Does Arrest Really Deter Wife Battery?" *American Sociological Review* 50:253.

Bernard, C., and E. Schlaffer. 1986. "A Case Study of Austria." In *Proceedings of the Expert Group Meeting on Violence in the Family with a Special Emphasis on Its Effects on Women.* UND BAW-EGN-86-CS.15. Vienna: United Nations.

Blackstone, William B. [1765–69] 1908. *Commentaries on the Laws of England.* 19th London ed. Philadelphia: Lippincott.

Blume, E. S. 1990. *Secret Survivors: Uncovering Incest and Its After Effects in Women.* New York: John Wiley.

Bunch, Charlotte. 1990. "Women's Rights Are Human Rights: Toward a Re-Vision of Human Rights." *Human Rights Quarterly* 12:35–52.

Castel, A. 1946. *An Introduction to Modern Philosophy.* New York: Macmillan.

Crossette, B. 1990. "Twenty-Five Percent of Girls in India Die by Age 15, UNICEF Says." *New York Times,* 5 October, p. A10.

Csanyi, Vilmos. 1989. *Evolutionary Systems and Society: A General Theory of Life, Mind, and Culture.* Durham, N.C.: Duke University Press.

Donnelly, J. 1985. *The Concept of Human Rights.* New York: St. Martin's Press.

Drogin, Bob. 1992. "HIV Spreading 'Out of Control' in India's Red-Light Districts." *San Francisco Chronicle,* 27 November, p. A4.

Eisler, Riane. 1977. *Dissolution: No Fault Divorce, Marriage, and the Future of Women.* New York: McGraw Hill.

———. 1987a. *The Chalice and the Blade: Our History, Our Future.* San Francisco: Harper and Row.

———. 1987b. "Human Rights: Toward an Integrated Theory for Action." *Human Rights Quarterly* 9:287–308.

———. 1987c. "Woman, Man, and the Evolution of Social Structure." *World Futures: The Journal of General Evolution* 23(1/2): 79–92.

———. 1991. "Cultural Evolution: Social Shifts and Phase Changes." In *The New Evolutionary Paradigm.* Ed. Ervin Laszlo. Pp. 179–200. New York: Gordon and Breach.

———. 1993. "The Challenge of Human Rights for All: What We Can Do." In *Creating the 21st Century: Rights, Responsibilities, and Remedies.* Ed. H. F. Didsbury. Pp. 99–117. Washington, D.C.: World Futures Society.

———. 1994. "From Domination to Partnership: The Hidden Subtext for Sustainable Change." *Journal of Organizational Change Management* 7(4): 35–49.

———. 1995. *Sacred Pleasure: Sex, Myth, and the Politics of the Body.* San Francisco: Harper San Francisco.

———. Forthcoming. "Communication, Socialization and Domination: The Idealization of Violence and the Hidden Subtext of Gender." In *Women Transforming Communications.* Ed. D. Allen, R. Bush, and S. J. Kaufman. Thousand Oaks, Calif.: Sage.

Eisler, Riane, and David Loye. 1990. *The Partnership Way: New Tools for Living and Learning.* San Francisco: HarperCollins.

Eisler, Riane, David Loye, and Kari Norgaard. 1995. *Gender Equity and the Quality of Life: A Global Survey and Analysis.* Pacific Grove, Calif.: Center for Partnership Studies.

Federal Bureau of Investigation (FBI). 1988. *Uniform Crime Report.* Washington, D.C.: Government Printing Office.

Galtung, Johan. 1980. *The True Worlds: A Transnational Perspective.* New York: Free Press.

Heise, Lori. 1989. "International Dimensions of Violence against Women." *Response* 12:8.

Hosken, Fran P. 1984. *The Hosken Report: Genital and Sexual Mutilation of Females.* Lexington, Mass.: WIN News.

Jantsch, Eric. 1980. *The Self-Organizing Universe.* New York: Pergamon.

Loye, David, and Riane Eisler. 1987. "Chaos and Transformation: Implications of a Non-Equilibrium Theory for Social Science and Society." *Behavioral Science* 32:53–65.

Mill, John Stuart. [1869] 1973. "The Subjection of Women." In *The Feminist Papers*. Ed. A. S. Rossi. Pp. 196–238. New York: Bantam.

Miller, Alice. 1983. *For Your Own Good: Hidden Cruelty in Child-Rearing and the Roots of Violence*. New York: Farrar, Straus, and Giroux.

Prigogine, Ilya, and Isabelle Stengers. 1984. *Order out of Chaos*. New York: Bantam.

Stanton, Elizabeth Cady. [1848] 1972. "Seneca Falls Declaration of Sentiments." In *Feminism: The Essential Historical Writings*. Ed. M. Schneir. Pp. 77–82. New York: Random House.

United Nations. 1985. *State of the World's Women Report*. Vienna: United Nations.

U.S. Dept. of Justice, Bureau of Justice Statistics. 1986. *Preventing Domestic Violence against Women*. Washington, D.C.: Department of Justice.

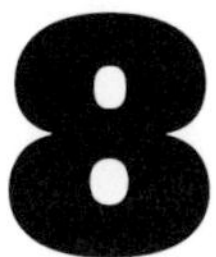

Is There a Therapy for Pathological Cosmologies?

Johan Galtung

[We began this volume with the psychologist Lifton moving from the level of individual psychology to its social context. We complete these selections with the broadest perspective, with the global conflictologist Galtung's speculations on how to treat pathological cosmologies. Painting a geopolitical picture of the late twentieth century with broad strokes, he identifies the cultural programs or codes of the major civilizations of the seven poles replacing the bipolar cold war world. He also identifies the traumas of each civilization that he claims can lead to a "collective megalo-paranoia syndrome" with a potential for catastrophic violent behavior. Galtung then ponders the possibility that an entire civilization might be treated for this pathology in a manner analogous to therapies for individuals.]

The Geopolitical Setting

A world of international feudalism is a good image for describing the successor system to the cold war, referred to by George Bush as the "new world order" (Galtung 1992). As suggested by table 8-1, we can divide our present world into seven spheres or regions, six of them headed by well-known hegemonic powers. One "hegemon" is primus inter pares, the hegemons' hegemon: the United States of America. The Arab/Islamic world does not have a hegemon on top but, arguably, Saddam Hussein tried to place Iraq in that position.[1]

Table 8-1 describes the motivations of these superpowers, three of them with global reach (the United States, European Union, and Japan), three have only regional influence (Moscow, Beijing, and India); three are Christian, one Shinto, one Confucian, one Hindu, and one Muslim. Generally, certain motivational syndromes that are embedded in their collective subconscious (in contrast to their consciously present ideology), here referred to as "cosmology," will carry in their wake the usual economic and military capabilities.[2] By stressing cosmology, we mean to assert the primacy of "culture" or civilization, as compared to the Marxist assumption of economic primacy, the "realist" assumption of military primacy, or the liberal assumption of the primacy of political institutions (e.g., as conceptualized in the democracy-dictatorship dichotomy).[3] We can characterize these civilizations in terms of their *chosenness,* their *myths,* and their *traumas,* in order to be closer to contemporary geopolitics.

Cosmology is the code, or program, of a civilization, usually better seen from the outside than by insiders who will typically find it too normal and natural, like the air around them, to be able to verbalize it. A civilization is a macroculture that spans considerable regions in space and time, such as the occidental civilizations with their basis in the religions of the *kitab:* Judaism, Christianity, and Islam. The distinction between expanding occidental civilization, or Occident I (the Greco-Roman period and the modern period), and contracting occidental civilization, or Occident II (the medieval period), may be more interesting, however, since these distinctions are meaningful for all three abrahamitic religions with their hard and soft, or gentle, aspects. There are also the Indic (Hindu), Buddhic (Buddhist), Sinic (Chinese), and Nipponic (Japanese) civilizations.

We want to know how civilizations program nations in general and national leaders in particular for patterns of international behavior. For this purpose, three dimensions of all cultures have been selected: (1) chosen-

Table 8-1. Geopolitics: Cultural Factors in a Seven-Polar World

Poles	Chosenness	Myths	Traumas
1. United States	By God, as New Cana'an	Post–WWII unipolarity	Vietnam syndrome Tehran hostages
2. European Union	Cradle of civilization	Europe as world center	World War II Nazism Fascism, communism Loss of empires U.S. junior partner
3. Japan	By *Amaterasu-O-mikami*	*Dai-tō-ā*	Pacific war defeat Nuclear holocaust
4. Moscow	By History (betrayed)	Bipolarity Russia	World War II Stalinism
5. Beijing	Simply *is*	Perfect autonomy	Humiliation of 1840s–1940s
6. India	Cradle of civilization	Hindu *raj* British *raj*	Colonialism Underdevelopment
7. Islam	By Allah	Islamic past Arab nation Ottoman Empire	Crusades, zionism Communism, consumerism *Divide et impera* Inner divisions

ness, the idea of being a people chosen above all others by transcendental forces, endowed, even anointed, as a light unto others, even with the right and duty of governing others, (2) myths, of a glorious past, near or distant, to be recreated, and (3) traumas, the phenomenon of being a people hit and hurt by others, possibly due to envy, by enemies lurking anywhere, prepared to hit again. Rooted in religion and history, these three dimensions are bound to be crucial, in addition to the more basic dimensions of space, time, and knowledge.[4]

Together, they form what might be viewed as a syndrome: the "chosenness-myth-trauma" (CMT) complex or, more provocatively, the collective megalo-paranoia syndrome. Chosenness induces collective sentiments of grandeur relative to all others. This is then built into the myths of a glorious past to be recreated, the present being suspended between the glorious past and the more glorious future. The myth is the bridge between the transcendentalism of being chosen—that moment when the deity pronounces, "Thou art mine," and concrete utopia—on this earth.[5]

History can be used as its own validation: "Because we had that past we must have been chosen" and "because we were chosen we had that past." But the traumas can also be used to validate the idea of chosenness: "We have suffered so much, there must be a deeper meaning to that suffering that will be revealed in a positive, even glorious future." Thus, new traumas are expected for the future, with a mixture of fear and the lustful anticipation of self-fulfilling prophecies.[6]

The three parts of the syndrome reinforce each other both socially and as ideas. People chosen to be a light unto others (e.g., Israel, America [the "castle upon a hill"], and Nazi Germany), even to rule others, will experience an endless chain of traumas. After an initial period of success that provides raw material for myths, resistance will set in, leading to traumas. Others in the world might not be interested in that light or in being conditioned by outsiders, preferring to be their own light and their own cause. They do not accept the notion that transcendental forces should rule through some other chosen people because they have not been a party to that covenant, have not been chosen themselves, or see the whole chosenness idea as morbid at best and a power strategy at worst.[7]

The chosen people will sulk ("My lord, why hast thou betrayed me") and find reasons for the traumas inflicted upon them anywhere and everywhere except in their own idea of chosenness in the first place, any notion of which they will brush aside as "blaming the victim" (a frequently used term in American Jewish political discourse). How could they bear traumas without the consolation of chosenness? In a Manichaean framework, the negation of being chosen in a drama with a transcendental author is to be the unchosen, even rejected, people. An unchosen people will not survive long, having ready-made explanations for their traumas, and self-fulfilling myths of predestined decline and fall.[8]

People suffering from the CMT complex will have two standard, non-contradictory explanations for why transcendental will is not fulfilled and why glory has not been ushered in: "Equal but opposed forces are at work,"[9] and "the Chosen People have strayed away from the transcendental will," thus no longer having its backing.[10] If the transcendental will is to rule others, then getting back to the path of righteousness will lead to even more trauma, such as the vicious circle that the hegemonic powers (and Israel) have built for themselves.

The focus here is on chosen people with positive myths and negative traumas, which together give them a sense of rights and duties. A diagnosis of collective megalo-paranoia is based on chosenness and myths that feed the megalomania and on traumas that feed the paranoia. The two sides are inseparable. The megalomaniac is always on the alert for signs of disrespect, avoiding situations that might falsify its illusions of grandeur.[11] The paranoid has to justify being the focus of so much hostility and so little appreciation of its extraordinary talent. Such people may become very dangerous when they demand an instant confirmation that their talents are recognized.[12]

Individual-Centered Therapy

Individuals socially defined as suffering from mental disorders have one thing in common: social incompetence, as defined by mainstream culture in that society. Incompetence is a socially unacceptable form of deviance seen as unwilled, that is, the individual cannot by an act of will become competent. If the incompetence is willed, then the individual is seen as wicked, a criminal entitled to punishment; if seen as unwilled, the individual is a patient in need of therapy.[13] But willed/unwilled is a matter of judgment, a decision sometimes made by juries. There is no sharp distinction, nor are the reactions very different.

Let us divide the standard repertory of reactions to mental disorder into "sociotherapy" (changing the social status of the deviant), "somatherapy" (changing the body of the deviant), and "psychotherapy" (changing the mind of the deviant). Clearly, the three categories do not exclude each other—reactions by any of the three affect the other two arenas.

First, applying standard sociotherapy would include killing, banishing, or institutionalizing the deviant: in other words, either physical or social elimination.[14] This therapy might try to restructure the deviant's relationship to the community. The deviant might be put with other deviants into a sociotherapeutic community, such as a halfway house. Many primitive or traditional societies already constitute, in themselves, a tolerant therapeutic community for deviants. Or a deviant might be "kicked upstairs," based on the decision that the individual's deviance constitutes competence on a higher level, such as when a shaman is identified (Yablonsky 1990). At the top of hierarchies, there is no need for people, only words.[15]

Imagine a megalo-paranoid person in a megalo-paranoid civilization. The person suffers from delusions of grandeur and persecution, as does the civilization. This does not immediately qualify a person for high positions; there are some additional conditions. The person has to talk the idiom of the nation's cosmology, that is, to give voice to the chosenness, myths, and traumas of the society in terms that are understood by the people and accepted by the elites. And the person must never express any doubt about those beliefs.[16] Self-centered talk of one's own chosenness will not qualify. There must be an acceptable link between individual and collective megalo-paranoia.

The individual must be seen as a chosen representative whose personal myths and traumas came about on behalf of the society, as individual manifestations or projections of collective destiny. Ideally, the individual should be a microrepresentation of the macrolevel collectivity—past, present, and future.[17] Jesus Christ and Mohammed are examples, as are Adolf Hitler, Joseph Stalin, and Ronald Reagan (Galtung 1984).

With this self-presentation, a psychopath equipped with megalo-paranoid syndromes may be seen as a strong leader, not suited for daily interaction with equals but ideal for the higher rungs of an impersonal, paper-oriented bureaucracy of the ministerial, corporate, or military varieties. Empathy with others would be a very low trait, another way of saying "socially incompetent." Indeed, the leader's adequacy for vertical advancement may be high because of a lack of consideration for others, found more often in males than in females (Gilligan 1986). The steeper the bureaucracy and the higher the production of mental disorder, the worse the situation.

Something in this may shed some light on how to explain Nazi Germany. Hitler and his possible "madness" fail to explain why he got so many followers. Attributing fascism to the German people alone, however, disregards the need for a competent executive, since the people alone cannot manage megalo-paranoia over the long term. Mass phenomena like the hysterical crowd or mob are short-term activities.[18] Far from socially incompetent, Hitler was rather pleasant in private company despite his ruthlessness in politics. His basic traits were really believing what he said and pushing a sickening ideology with relentless energy.[19]

In the end, Hitler developed psychosomatic symptoms, as would anyone under such stress. He saw himself as chosen, his own past richly endowed with both trauma and myths of glory. In other words, his psychocharacter identified intensely with the sociocharacter of the German people. It was not merely that the Germans were authoritarians in search of a leader or that Hitler was an authority in search of a people to rule. Rather, they recognized themselves in each other, "You and I, we are of the same kind," specificae of the same genus. Perfect fit.

In the periphery of that system, the Germanic *Neuordnung* (new order), a mini-Hitler took shape: the Norwegian Vidkun Quisling. He had the personal CMT complex well installed in his personality and tried to become *fórer*—Norwegian for Führer. Unlike Hitler, Quisling would never have won free elections, since his CMT complex was not mirrored in Norwegian cosmology.[20] A large-scale Norway, ten or a hundred times bigger, might have developed that cosmology and applauded. Quisling was a dictator and a clown on the wrong stage with the wrong script—no perfect fit.

Second, we can examine somatherapies. Here, there is an implicit idea of reversibility. Therapy is possible, as opposed to the sociotherapeutic idea of healing not the deviant but rather the society—by ridding itself of the deviant or by using the deviant's extraordinary talents. Individualism is also implicit in this approach. The context is not changed, only the individual body. Any intervention is in principle conceivable; physical-mechanical (lobotomy), physical-electrical (electroshock), biochemical (ataraxia), and so forth. These therapies can be divided into two groups: those that are openly painful and hence carry elements of punishment, and others.

If the therapists are instruments of social control on behalf of the social order, they will, like other authorities, tend to prefer apathy to revolt and thus organize their therapies accordingly. An apathetic patient, like a noncrying baby, is "kind." Lobotomy and ataraxia induce that state; as with killing, banishment, and institutionalization, patients are rendered powerless and punished. Apathy-inducing approaches are also seen as more humane.[21]

Third, we can contrast this with "psychotherapeutic" approaches. Unlike the other two therapies, this approach is in its infancy, notwithstanding the century since Freud opened the individual subconscious. The schools are proliferating, a good sign of pluralism. Psychotherapists see mental disorder as more or less reversible. Some approaches are individual-centered and some more sociotherapeutic, shading into the therapeutic approaches reviewed above. Somatherapy must be individualistic, given the lack of interbody connections; psychotherapy is not forced into that assumption.[22]

Here, we want to emphasize individual-centered psychotherapy. Within this, we can formulate a general Paradigm I with which to examine the problem of how civilizations program nations and their leaders. Paradigm I consists of seven phases, partly inspired by Talcott Parsons's (1951) work on medical sociology:

Phase 1: Individual recognizes and accepts being in a crisis.
Phase 2: Individual accepts crisis as preprogrammed in self.
Phase 3: Individual accepts need for help by competent other.
Phase 4: Individual accepts entering a patient-healer relationship.
Phase 5: Patient and healer cooperate in identifying hidden program.
Phase 6: Patient and healer cooperate in changing program of self.
Phase 7: Patient is born again with new self: catharsis.

The linkage between this paradigm and Judeo-Christian spirituality is obvious. The crisis is the sin. Preprogramming means at some stage having strayed away from God, even having given one's self to Satan, or still more basic: original sin. The competent other is Jesus Christ, and the acceptance of a relationship with Him is a necessary condition for union with God (i.e., the achievement of salvation/purification).[23]

Catholicism would add the church as a necessary condition for entering the relationship with the Supreme Healer: *extra ecclesiam, nulla salus.* The forces behind the acts of sin must be seen and then exorcised through repentance, expiation, and submission, asking for forgiveness, accepting new guidance, being reborn in Christ: catharsis. If not, the apocalypse of eternal damnation will result.

With these parallels to religion, it is no wonder that psychoanalysis was resisted. The Christian paradigm was secularized, with the individual psychoanalyst in the role of the priest, Freud in the role of the Christ, even endowed with God-like features—promising rebirth, on earth!

But let us contrast the Judeo-Christian-inspired Paradigm I with a more Buddhist-oriented Paradigm II. First, Paradigm II includes an element of consciousness-formation, or conscientization, as Paolo Freire (1981) calls it. The subconsciously known but consciously unknown become consciously known, available and explicit, to be countenanced and confronted. The general formula is self-knowledge through meditation.

Second, it includes an element of mobilization, with the individual self becoming increasingly aware. There is faith in the capacity of the self to provide its own others for inner dialogue (e.g., with one internal other being some superego and another the id), a view that would also be compatible with some types of medieval and Protestant Christianity. With an external other there would be a difference between the other above and the other at the same level. Christianity in Occident I sees God as transcendent, above, rather than as immanent, within. The need for human beings to be guided from above is reflected in the classical psychoanalytical insistence on an other-directing psychoanalyst as indispensable, as opposed to client-centered, self-directed therapy and humanistic psychology (as associated with Carl Rogers and Abraham Maslow). Paradigm II is neither, but it welcomes outer dialogues with others in the same situation.

Third, there is the element of confrontation, of challenging those subconscious forces that have been driving the self, picking one particular crisis as an example. Fourth, there is a struggle, the dialectic of liberating one's self from the old self while at the same time creating the new self. And this ends, fifth, with *moksha,* satori, self-reliance, born again, a new beginning, capable of conscious self-causation, not driven by hidden codes.

Paradigm II is similar to a paradigm for revolutionary struggle, also from below, to overcome structural violence (Galtung, n.d.a). In that case, the conscientization is aimed at understanding not the inner forces hidden in the deeper layers of the personality but rather the forces hidden in the deeper layers of society. In both cases, the word structure is useful; the personality has a structure, and so does society. A structure can do violence not only in society, to human beings—body, mind, and spirit—but also in personality. This opens the question of whether there could be some structural violence present in any personality merely by virtue of being a personality and in any society by virtue of being a society. The answer would indicate limits to inner and outer peace.

The relationship of all this to the problem of pathological cosmologies can now be elaborated. In this case, the pathology is rooted neither in the structure of the personality nor in the structure of the society but in both. There are similar elements in the subconsciousness of elite members of the society ("the ruling cosmology being the cosmology of the ruling class," to paraphrase Marx), and others, and in the deep culture of that society, such as the CMT complex.

The concept of cosmology links the structure of that culture to the structure of its personalities, the deeper aspects of culture being institutionalized in the society as carriers of the cosmology (e.g., religion, food, sex, science, and technology) and internalized in the individuals as assumptions about what is normal and natural. It provides, in other words, the collectively shared subconscious. The double-level nature of the collective megalo-paranoia, in both society and personalities, makes therapy and healing very difficult.

Individual-Level Paradigms and Collectivities

Clearly, individual-level paradigms do not automatically apply to collectivities; there are nevertheless many parallels. To see them, we should apply the aforementioned therapeutic approaches to collectivities, particularly nations, and their relations—in other words, apply them to international relations.

Sociotherapies

These therapies have some obvious, often violent, applications. What was the Nazi extermination of the European Jews about? Not the pettiness of some economic and cultural competition between Jews and other Germans but rather the idea that there was room for only one chosen people on German soil, the "Aryans." Hitler compared Jews to microorganisms[24] and applied the seek-and-destroy strategy that has been used not only to eradicate contagious diseases but also (by the United States) to eliminate communism in Indo-China. Each Jew was seen as a vector for the disease of non-Aryan chosenness and hence had to be eliminated. The process was very similar to the Spanish Inquisition effort to eradicate heresy by eliminating heretics.[25]

Like the inquisition, Hitler also used banishment and institutionalization. Eradication was instrumental to the goal of purifying Germany and occupied Europe; the world came second. Exile was an alternative, with both holocausts making money on that alternative,[26] obviously preferable to potential victims if they could afford it (and as usual, class is a factor). Prison was also used (not only as a prelude to execution) both by one chosen people to eliminate another chosen people but also by the chosen people who wanted to eliminate others.

Not accepted by Hitler were marginalized communities who defined Jewish apartness as normal: the ghetto system that had been used since the sixteenth century. Hitler would not tolerate the assimilation of Jews into society—which had been the liberal approach since the nineteenth century—nor would he allow them into leadership positions.

Recently, that was the approach taken by the United States. One theory, for example, argues that the early United States had emulated the Jewish chosenness as an archetype, as the model for its own existence and social construction (Galtung 1988b). In this view, after an initial period of rejection and anti-Semitism the Jews have since been used as the executive agents of that archetype.[27] A conflict emerges, however, between the intellectual brilliance of the Jews and the high level of U.S. anti-intellectualism, seeing the intellectuals as people who regard themselves as chosen, their deviance being mental (being "eggheads"), and their ghetto being the campus (Jacoby 1987).

Banishment and even institutionalization have been often used in international relations, where the marginalized are made into pariah nations and then isolated through diplomatic and economic sanctions. This has been applied to the socialist countries, South Africa, Nicaragua, Cuba, Iran-Libya-Syria, Iraq, Israel, Serbia—and all of them have or had blossoming CMT complexes.[28]

What about the practice of "kicking the deviant upstairs"? This is precisely what the Western nations are doing with the United States! They insist, "You are our leader," recognizing the United States as themselves in the extremity, as a more powerful expression of their own inner yearnings.[29] Could Nazi Germany have obtained the same recognition had they exercised their violence only outside (Western) Europe and retained parliamentarism?[30]

Somatherapies

The U.S.-led anti-Iraq coalition attempted a lobotomy and electroshock combined.[31] The coalition tried to cut off the functions of Iraqi society, civilian as well as military, exorcising the evil, making it apathetic, punishing it, forcing it out of Kuwait. This was a tall order, requiring a variety of strategies. For example, the ataraxia approach to therapy would correspond to the introduction of television and consumer society as a means of making people passive and even apathetic, inner-directed and concerned with their own material comfort and not with the social change called for by their ideas. This was the therapy that also followed the lobotomy and electroshock of the U.S. invasions of Grenada and Panama.[32]

Psychotherapies

Here, the applicability of individual-level paradigms weakens. Paradigms I and II can only be applied to a heavily "chosenness-myth-trauma"-imbued nation if it is willing to undergo other-directed (Paradigm I) or undertake self-directed (Paradigm II) therapy. The glaring dissimilarity is obvious: it is a matter of power. Society as a whole can handle, literally speaking, a minority of megalo-paranoid deviants, but the international community can only do so as long as the deviant is small and relatively isolated, not when it grows to a full regional or global status, overpowering others.

We should not commit the "realist" fallacy of thinking that effective therapy requires coercive power. The problem is that chosen people recognize only the Almighty who chose them as the authority; only He could order them to undergo "therapy." But there still may be opportunities for therapy in the name of common values in the international system, with the promise of rewards for successful therapy.[33]

Imagine a nation willing to undergo therapy, following Paradigm I. The first condition would be for its people to recognize collectively their tendency to "get into trouble," to get involved in crises that are at least partly their own making. How could they be made to see this in themselves? There may be rumblings in some people's individual subconscious that reject not only overt mainstream ideology but also the nation's covert cosmology; the rumblings might even be consciously shared. Yet this would at most lead to the creation of subversive subcultures within the society, with a countercosmology gradually taking the shape of an ideology with the potential for transformation, such as working-class socialism or female gender feminism. Our concern is not with new power groups or with alternative ideologies and cosmologies but rather with transforming the mainstream cosmology.

The key to how that could occur is as simple in theory as it is difficult in practice. If the leading cosmology is the cosmology of the leading class, then it is from the leading class (and more particularly from the "leader") that the transformation must come, as part of the transformation of the leader or leaders themselves. The usual circulation of elites in and out of leadership is insufficient; that produces only outer not inner change. Leaders, to become leaders, do not always have to confirm the cosmology but rather only never reject it.

For real change, leaders would have to openly reject the cosmology and never covertly confirm it. For signals to reach deep down they have to come from high above. But they can only work if they create a sufficient resonance deep below in the collective subconscious. The formula for successful therapy is the same as the formula for contracting the pathology: transforming leaders and followers alone is insufficient; only together can their transformation produce real change.

What is needed, then, is for the leaders to recognize that they are in a self-rooted crisis (meaning individual and collective self). This is not the same as conceding defeat, such as after an election. In that case, neither cosmology nor ideology is wrong; what went wrong was only that the people failed to become followers. Nor should the admission be confused with a conversion to a new ideology, like some turncoat crossing the floor of a national assembly.

Instead, we are talking about recognizing something fundamentally wrong "in the State of Denmark," as Shakespeare phrased it in *Hamlet.* The best example in modern times is probably the change of heart initiated by Nikita Khruschev at the Twentieth Party Congress of the Communist Party of the Soviet Union in February 1956, followed by Mikhail Gorbachev in a process that continues thirty years after Khruschev. We can see this as a recognition by stages. Khruschev essentially rejected Stalinism, including its "deep structure"; Gorbachev then rejected the deep structure of Leninism. From being mere ideologies, they had both become cosmologies in the Soviet collective subconscious for most people, mixing with the leftovers of the tsarist cosmology, located deep down also in many dissidents.[34]

Why were these cosmologies rejected? Obviously, because the whole system was in crisis, which was arguably rooted in their own program and code. Efforts at blaming others were somewhat effective, such as blaming interventionist wars, counterrevolutionaries, post–World War I hunger and misery, sabotage, the Nazi horrors of World War II (the Great Patriotic War), and poor harvests. But an unexplained residual remains (Galtung, Heiestad, and Rudeng 1978).

Communist formations are better at making crises for themselves; capitalism is better at making crises for others. Neither of these should be confused with Russian imperialism, which is tsarist more than communist. Communism kills upward in an attempt to control middle and upper classes, including those it has itself created. Capitalism kills downward in an attempt to control restless workers, including those created by its own dysfunctions. Capitalism displaces its crises downward, exploiting the inner proletariat of the working class, the outer proletariat of the periphery countries, and nature; communism exploits all three plus itself. After all, Khrushchev spoke mainly of the Stalinist victims in the Communist Party, meaning his own kind.

A "clear and present" crisis, then, is one precondition of national change. The other is an enlightened, honest, courageous leadership taking the moral risk of recognizing and acting on a deep cultural failure. Then comes the problem of healing, of one's capacity for doing so, and of the possible need for the other, even that ultimate Other.

The United States tried to be that other to defeated Germany and Japan after World War II and is today more than willing to play the same role for the former Soviet Union, and now Bosnia, dispensing the triple medicine of pluralist democracy, free-market economics, and Christianity, administered by governmental action, corporate investment, and U.S. missionaries, respectively. But the Germans did not have the requisite inner readiness; that came only through the youth revolt a generation later.[35] Japanese elites probably never underwent any basic inner change. And U.S.-induced change in the former Soviet Union presupposes a submissiveness to the United States, a condition satisfied in the other cases. Soviet self-healing has not yet succeeded, but the process continues.

Let us then try Paradigm II, since it is closer to real politics, and let's assume that the problem of conscientization has already been solved. First, "mobilization" is important because it has a concrete collective interpretation: it is a matter of organizing the people who have been transformed, for the purpose of working on the rest. In the case of a nation that has developed pathological character traits, we are talking about something very concrete: devising a new gender, generation, race, class, nation, or other group to carry a "new message."

Second, there is the process of "confrontation." It is crucial to select the proper test case, the exemplar, that has pedagogical value for contrasting the way things were done in the old days with the way it will be done under the new cosmology. Both old and new are to be tested at the same time. A test case for the former Soviet Union, for example, has been the independence of the republics and the nations within the republics, which has caused change as well as resistance. A second test case has been the attempt to peacefully transfer power through a secret ballot, and a third has been privatization.

All three are efforts, from both inside and outside, to implant Western ideology in Soviet cosmology, thereby changing the cosmology. The leaders were exposed to pressure from both above and below, and they fell; even an effort in August 1991 to restore them, which was probably ritualistic, failed. In the end, Gorbachev, the instigator of the whole process, also fell.

But are these changes basic enough? Do the ex-Soviet people in general and the Russians in particular still see themselves as a chosen people with the same rights and duties that this implies? If they do, a new cause will be found, propagated with the same missionary zeal, and legitimized by myths and traumas—including the recent trauma.

Third, Paradigm II would require "struggle" to become independent of what was before. It may be quick or slow, violent or nonviolent—the slow and nonviolent being the objectives of the peace researcher who wants to explore the conditions for peace by peaceful means.[36] Killing, exiling, imprisoning, or otherwise marginalizing all who might carry the seeds of the old order deep down in their subconscious is megalo-paranoia, not transformation. This was the route taken by Nazi Germany and, on a microscale but with the same structure, by Zionist Israel. Only through deep transformation can the inner coherence of a new cosmology be established, leading to self-reliance and autonomy. It means an independence from any outside healer, equipped instead with a self-healing process, such as when real democracy is firmly rooted.

An example might be Germany, where democracy some fifty years after Nazism seems firmly rooted, as measured by the high participation in and pluralism of the parties, with a real choice among more than two alternatives. But the test will be whether there are still domineering tendencies in the German nation: the way West Germans are treating their own nation in the former German Democratic Republic, with its aggressive and full-scale economic, cultural, and political penetration, should make us wonder.

Can Collective Therapy Succeed?

Evidently something produces change, since many of the empires driven by CMT complexes are no longer around. Probably they became exhausted, victims of their own success, or were simply beaten (Galtung et al. 1978). Whether being beaten leads to the kind of deep self-reflection demanded by both paradigms is another matter. The outcome of the German and Japanese cases is far from clear. And the United States, which was beaten in the Vietnam War, used the Persian Gulf War to "overcome the Vietnam syndrome." In other words, it cleansed itself of any doubts about its right and duty to engage in violent international relations when its leaders deemed it necessary.

A nation may also change more convincingly, either through the hard way of sociotherapy or somatherapy or the soft way of psychotherapy. Spain today, for instance, is rather different from the España—*una, grande, libre*—propagated by the Franco regime, and Spain after the *decadencia* was very different from Spain before.[37]

Something works, otherwise we would have had much less historical change. It would greatly benefit humankind if the gentler rather than the tougher types of therapy could be pursued. Even so, the German, Japanese, and Soviet examples as well as the U.S. nonexample indicate what a painful process this is.[38] How difficult it is to practice the old admonition: to know one's self. For that is the precondition for any therapy, whether of the other-oriented Paradigm I or the self-oriented Paradigm II.

Notes

An earlier version of this essay appears as chapter 5 in Johan Galtung, *Peace by Peaceful Means* (London: Sage, 1996).

1. Like others, Hussein probably tried to do more than one thing at the same time, as Avicenna noted. But in the Arab/Islamic world the rivalry between the old empires rooted in Damascus, Baghdad, Cairo, Tehran, Istanbul, and to a lesser extent, Saudi Arabia was no doubt important. Iraq borders on four of them and is more centrally located than any other Muslim country.
2. This is a basic theme in Galtung (n.d.b), which focuses on power balances, power profiles, and the relationship between the two.
3. But states tend to behave about the same way if they have the same position in the international system, regardless of domestic political formation. Possibly, democratic elites have to be more imaginative when trying to legitimize bellicose intentions.
4. Together with nature, person, society, and the transpersonal, I use space (in the sense of world), time, and knowledge as the seven dimensions to be defined by a civilization.
5. The occidental archetype is Jewish chosenness; the oriental archetype is Japanese chosenness.
6. Leo Beck (1961), the famous German rabbi, came close to defining Jewish specificity in terms of "chosen for suffering." What did this mean for a German Jew abducted by the SS?
7. In my experience in the Middle East, these are the three major Palestinian interpretations. In addition, Palestinians prefer to be their own light.
8. The Sumerians seem to be in this category, convinced about their own excellence but also of their own coming demise.
9. As a consequence, Satan has to be strong, like God, possibly with many apparitions but unified. The only countervailing force that can effectively balance monotheism is monosatanism.
10. Although the defeat in Vietnam played into that kind of thinking for fundamentalist Americans, the Persian Gulf War was the confirmation that they still enjoyed God's favor.
11. This is a basic point in the Dantziger (1989) psychotherapy, according to which many of their patients (1) have the idea that they are better than others in some way, (2) suffer tremendously when evidence to the contrary emerges, and (3) do their best to avoid such situations, which makes social life difficult.
12. The Gulf War was a good war in that regard, giving ample occasion to both Saddam Hussein and George Bush, Iraq and the United States.
13. This was a basic point in the late Norwegian sociologist Vilhelm Aubert's exploration of similarities and differences between the criminal and the patient.

14. But for this to happen the social definition of the deviant is essential, as explored so masterfully by Michel Foucault in his classics, *The Birth of the Clinic* and *Discipline and Punishment.*

15. Bureaucracy is generalizing, not individualizing, as pointed out repeatedly by Weber. The personal is always singular.

16. In other words, the negative faith may be what is called for. A U.S. presidential candidate does not have to say every day that the "United States is a chosen country," but if he says, the "United States is just an ordinary country like any other," not to mention "America is a sick society," he will not last (Jimmy Carter).

17. Thus, if the country is poor and educated the (prospective) leader should have the same profile. I am indebted to the late Swiss sociologist Peter Heintz for this important insight (private communication).

18. These are very high temperature forms of behavior that cannot possibly be sustained over a longer period.

19. This is a basic point made by Kelley (1961), the U.S. army psychologist who examined the Nuremberg war criminals.

20. Norwegian cosmology would have elements of the myths of glory (such as the golden Viking age) and traumas (such as the Black Death and the periods of Danish and Swedish rule), but most Norwegians would take neither statement too seriously at any level of consciousness.

21. If the alternative is incarceration for life or banishment, there may be something to this; but why define it that way?

22. There certainly is interpersonal connection at the level of the mind and the spirit; how it works and its relevance to psychotherapy is another question. In Western cosmology, individualism is a basic assumption, so the interpersonal is usually constructed as traces left on the mind by significant others, such as the parents. In Japanese cosmology, collectivism implies that the interpersonal is open to a more synchronic, less diachronic interpretation. Western psychotherapy would typically try to uncover the traces of the past, while the Japanese might typically try group therapy.

23. "I am the way, the truth, and the life"—very strong words (John 14:6).

24. Hitler actually made comparisons between the "discovery" of the role of Jews in the social organism and Robert Koch's discovery of the role of the TBC bacteria in tuberculosis.

25. In criminology, it is known as individual prevention punishment. Of course, in the Spanish Inquisition there was also an element of general prevention, to scare others.

26. In that traffic, there is also an implicit message about the spiritual quality of "abroad"—impure anyhow, so impure and impure belong together.

27. The archetypal example of this is, of course, Henry Kissinger.

28. Exactly how that works is not so easily explained. What occurred in Eastern Europe in 1989 happened essentially in the relationship between ruler and

ruled inside the countries. But the rulers had been weakened as a result of marginalization; and the ruled had been strengthened through their contacts with outside actors.

29. In these inner yearnings there are fascist elements who enjoy watching the United States doing to a country like Iraq what they might have liked to do themselves but never dared to (for an analysis of the underlying structures, see Galtung 1988a).

30. The answer is certainly; it would probably have been recognized as a normal democracy sacrificing itself to maintain law and order.

31. The expressions "bloodletting" and "surgical cut" bridge the two arenas, making both of them metaphors for the other.

32. The problem is, of course, that the goodies of consumer society are mostly available for the well-to-do; and the well-to-do are not the source of the problem for law and order oriented therapists.

33. This seems to have been the approach of the Group of Seven to the Soviet Union: first, exorcism (of communism), then aid.

34. The basic question now is how that will come out after the exorcism of communism. Will there be a new age of Russian chosenness, recreating myths of the *mir* (the village community), as in Aleksandr Solzhenitsyn?

35. On the other hand, the little-known work by the "German Youth Administration," teaching democracy to Germans in the late 1940s, may have played some role.

36. However, Eastern Europe in 1989 also showed that nonviolence may work very quickly, at least in the last phase. In general, however, the comparison to traditional herbs relative to antibiotics may be a good one: the latter are quicker but may also be more destructive.

37. The question is, of course, whether Spain is now making the same mistake again, gambling so much on tourism rather than the difficult job of sophisticated processing and industry.

38. Thus, when are we to hear a speech from Washington apologizing for the belligerence behind its more than two hundred military interventions around the world?

Works Cited

Beck, Leo. 1961. *The Essence of Judaism.* New York: Schocken Books.

Dantziger, S. R. 1989. *You Are Your Own Best Counselor.* Honolulu, Hawaii: Self-Mastery Systems.

Freire, Paolo. 1981. *Pedagogy of the Oppressed.* New York: Continuum.

Galtung, Johan. 1988a. "The Cold War as Autism." In *Essays in Peace Research.* Vol. 6. Copenhagen: Ejlers.

———. 1988b. *United States Foreign Policy as Manifest Theology.* Berkeley: University of California Press.

———. 1992. "The Emerging Conflict Formations." In *Restructuring for World Peace.* Ed. Majid Tehranian and Katharine Tehranian. Cresskill, N.J.: Hampton Press.

———. 1984. *Hitlerism, Stalinism, Reaganism: Three Variations on a Theme by Orwell* (in Norwegian). Oslow: Gyldendal.

———. n.d.a. *Theories of Peace.* Forthcoming.

———. n.d.b. *World Politics of Peace and War.* Forthcoming.

Galtung, Johan, Tore Heiestad, and Erik Rudeng. 1978. "On the Last 2,500 Years in Western History." In *Cambridge Modern History: Companion Volume.* Ed. Peter Borke. Vol. 13. Pp. 318–61. Cambridge: Cambridge University Press.

Gilligan, Carol. 1986. *In a Different Voice: Psychological Theory and Women's Development.* Cambridge, Mass.: Harvard University Press.

Jacoby, Russell. 1987. *The Last Intellectuals: American Culture in the Age of Academe.* New York: Basic Books.

Kelley, Douglas M. 1961. *Twenty-Two Cells in Nuremberg.* New York: MacFadden.

Parsons, Talcott. 1951. *The Social System.* Glencoe, Ill.: Free Press.

Yablonsky, Lewis. 1990. *The Robopaths.* New York: Bantam.

Conclusion: Untangling the Web of Violence

Lester R. Kurtz and Jennifer Turpin

The argument underlying this volume is that our current perspectives on violence are too narrowly conceived; research approaches, theories of violence, and policy debates must be broadened. We now turn our attention to the implications of these insights for current public policy debates. Recent public attention to problems of violence is heartening, but we are convinced that the debates are narrowly conceived, misguided, and will not solve the problems they are intended to alleviate.

In this conclusion, we argue that the tendency to see violence as the consequence of aberrant behavior committed by deviant individuals at the margins of society obscures the central role violence plays in the very foundations of the social order and the fundamental dilemmas that humans face as they move into the twenty-first century. The problems created by violence will not be solved by acting on the margins but by rethinking the pervasive use of violence in contemporary cultures.

Linking Personal and Global Violence

Current approaches to violence precipitate two conceptual difficulties. First, most people feel forced to choose between a micro- and macrolevel approach to theory, research, and policy. This forced choice leads to two false alternatives, one of which ignores the effect of microlevel processes and individual choices on broad historical trends; the other screens out the impact of broad sociocultural, macrolevel situations on individuals choosing to engage or not engage in violent behavior. Our argument is that violence is caused not simply by individual psychological factors, biological impulses, or social-structural factors alone but by a web of causal connections between personal-level and global-level structures, processes, and behaviors.

Second, current perspectives on violence promote efforts to find a "technical fix" to the problems that violence creates, especially in the pragmatic technical cultures that now dominate much social organization. Technical solutions often provide temporary relief, but they also deflect our attention from the underlying nontechnical problems that are not easily remedied.

A sociology of knowledge-oriented analysis of these approaches suggests that they are unduly shaped by cultural biases and attempts by ruling elites to maintain the status quo. The lack of attention to micro/macro linkages, which has been a primary focus of this volume, is a major difficulty facing the general public, scholars, and policy makers around the world. Although broad generalizations are difficult to make on such matters, our impression is that the collapse of socialist experiments at the end of the twentieth century has narrowed our field of vision even further. Individualistic solutions that ignore larger structural causes of violence now dominate the policy scene, as played out in two related models.

The criminal model of violence distinguishes between legitimate and illegitimate violence and requires the identification of criminals, whether in neighborhoods or geopolitical regions, who transgress national or international law. According to this paradigm, problems of violence are created by outlaws and thugs who deviate from civil norms and make life miserable for decent, law-abiding citizens and nations. According to this theory, we must punish individual criminals: we put them in prison, drive them from power, execute them by the state (or rebel forces), or somehow expunge them from the civil society in which they are wreaking havoc.

A more liberal alternative to the criminal model of deviance is the medical or psychotherapeutic model: miscreants (from petty thieves to dictators) are maladjusted and require treatment. We should rehabilitate or treat (sometimes medicate) gang members and prison inmates for aggressive personality disorders.

A more recent trend is to teach miscreants conflict resolution techniques that can facilitate their dealing with personal struggles in a less violent manner. The conflict resolution movement, which has had dramatic success in a number of spheres, while promising in many respects, is still only a bandaid applied to a deep wound. It usually represents yet another technical fix, so popular in modern cultures that excel in technology. Conflict resolution is similar to the search for the ultimate weapon that will end all war or the frantic effort to build more prisons or improve the treatment that often accompanies individualistic approaches to solving the problems of violence.

These individualistic and technically oriented solutions are rooted in the broader process of cultural framing in which the policy debates are conducted, and it is to that process that we now turn our attention. From our perspective, the analysis of violence, and any proposed solutions to the problems it creates, must encompass a broad frame that includes many voices heretofore excluded from the debate. At the core of our approach is the conclusion that individual propensities to violence are not ordinarily enacted except in what Elias calls a "culture of violent solutions." That is, any psychobiological vulnerabilities to engaging in violent behavior are discouraged and are rarely acted on unless the broader culture allows or encourages such behavior. On the other hand, even in a culture that promotes violent solutions, not all individuals will be violent. Moreover, even the most violent individuals are not so all of the time. Violence, from our perspective, is thus a result of the dialectical interaction of micro- and macrolevel processes. Solutions to the problem of violence must address all levels—as well as the interactions among them. Most of our current struggles with the issue are framed in such a way as to blind us to significant elements of the problem.

In the discussion that follows, we will explore the ways in which people define policy issues and narrow their alternatives. After exploring two mainstream approaches to violence that frame current policy debates, we will outline a third perspective that we believe addresses significant problems with conventional approaches and provides some promising alternatives.

Public Discourse about Violence

Public policy positions on the problem of violence tend to fit within two major frames, although elements of a third, alternative frame occasionally enter the debate. The first frame is a "peace through strength" or "law and order" frame that emphasizes the use of tough measures, usually involving violence against deviant individuals or nations, to solve problems of violence (the traditional so-called conservative position in U.S. culture). A second frame is the traditionally liberal "legal control" frame that emphasizes rational legal procedures that place boundaries around the use of violence (e.g., such measures as arms and gun control). A final, alternative frame that has seldom been part of the mainstream debate is the "common security and nonviolent conflict" approach that combines elements of the first two positions but emphasizes the interdependence of individuals and nations and promotes the use of nonviolent techniques for solving conflicts.

A narrative expresses each frame, linking macrolevel cultural orientations with microlevel motivations and actions, as Smith observes (in this volume). Individuals thus fit events into "moralizing narrative frames" to assess the ethical status and efficacy of particular acts of violence. This process is a political one, although not exclusively within the realm of the state. Collective and individual rituals thus reaffirm the narratives of the frame and express the boundaries of a culture's repertory of acceptable behavior.

People are socialized into a culture; its norms are internalized through a variety of cultural processes, from the mundane storytelling of village folktales or corporal punishment of children by conservative Christian parents (Ellison and Bartkowski, in this volume) to the high drama of political spectacles and denunciation of counterrevolutionaries by Chinese communists (Chu, in this volume). Often the cultural boundaries are so pronounced and the institutions that enforce them so powerful that evidence contradicting the culturally accepted frames becomes almost invisible. Thus, the Chinese official Yuan Mu insists that photographs of violence taken in Tiananmen Square on June 4, 1989, are falsifications (Chu, in this volume). Others contend that the Holocaust is a hoax or that its scope has been vastly embellished.

In the discussion that follows, we will explore the narratives, characteristics, and methods of each approach, as well as its fundamental assumptions and policy implications. We will also evaluate the problems with each perspective and what must happen in order to stop the cycles of violence within that framework.

Peace through Strength and Law and Order

Whether violence is occurring within a community or among nations, the peace through strength position advocates the use of whatever means are required—often violent ones—to stop "illegitimate" violence in its tracks. This approach gives birth to the criminal model of violence discussed above and relies on deterrence through intimidation to mitigate violent behavior, thus strengthening military and police forces and pursuing technological developments such as weapons arsenals, surveillance techniques, and so on that will punish offenders. Advocates call for more prisons, tougher sentences, and the death penalty, or military action against aggressors. For the most part, such actions are carried out by the state—the police or military and the criminal justice system, but at the extreme, if the state is perceived as ineffective, vigilante groups may intervene.

A number of assumptions lie behind this perspective. First, the only way to stop violence is with superior force, usually one that relies on violence.

A second assumption is that the world is inhabited by many evil people who must be deterred from violence through intimidation and punished should deterrence fail. Advocates of the law and order position contend that we cannot appease or coddle aggressors and criminals: the only language such people understand is force, and it will do no good to reason with them. In fact, efforts to deal rationally with "deviants" may allow them to perceive authorities as weak and vulnerable, thus resulting in efforts to exploit the weakness, like Hitler did with the British before World War II.

Finally, peace through strength advocates contend that such measures as arms and gun control do nothing to mitigate violence. On the contrary, they simply hamper legitimate efforts of law enforcement officials and the military, leaving them at a disadvantage. Criminals and aggressors will always obtain the weapons they need, whether legal or not, so that demilitarization will simply disarm legitimate authorities and honest citizens, while criminals and international aggressors will proceed illegally, cheat on treaties, and ignore the law.

Several implications follow from this perspective—most importantly, that military and police systems must have the most advanced weapons available, thus requiring continual force modernization. Second, tough laws must be enacted to enhance deterrence and punish aggressors. The central issue here, as with all frames, is whether the perspective is an accurate depiction of human nature. We contend that the peace through strength approach misreads the dynamics of conflict and inadvertently compels opposing forces to escalate their fights and to proliferate their weapons.

The major problem with the peace through strength frame is that it often perpetuates an upward spiral of violence and thus results in widespread devastation, a police state, war, or—at its extreme—a nuclear holocaust. Moreover, it does not address many of the individual or structural causes of violence, such as fear, greed, and inequality, or foster nonviolent means to engage in conflict or pursue one's desired goals. On the contrary, the peace through strength approaches serve primarily to suppress violent behavior through brute force, regardless of the precipitating factors. Ironically, it is the most effective approach in preventing the weak and powerless from becoming violent, while provoking those with more resources to escalate their aggression. As the military or police become more sophisticated in their ability to destroy, so do their opponents, so that the conflict takes on a life of its own—as it often does—and escalates beyond the control of all involved parties. The most obvious example of this problem is the superpower arms race of the cold war, which escalated to such extremes that the entire planet was placed at risk by a complex system of nuclear weapons and redundant weapons delivery systems. Although the danger appears to have subsided somewhat because of the collapse of the Soviet Union, the weapons system itself is still very much in place, and the perceived increase in security may be as much a consequence of social amnesia as the result of a substantial change in the situation (Turpin 1993).

Although less threatening in its scope, the arms race between police and illegal forces in various urban areas and regions of ethnic conflict in the United States, Russia, the Middle East, and elsewhere mirrors the larger global process, as does the conflict between various parties making overlapping territorial claims from the so-called warlords of Somalia to the street gangs of Los Angeles.

In such situations, ruling civil authorities feel compelled to "up the ante" by "clamping down," "getting tough," escalating the level of armaments, and reducing the civil rights of the populations involved. When the peace is kept by a "balance of terror" within the family, community, or worldwide, everyone feels the pressure to escalate violence and armaments. Terrified citizens who feel vulnerable and unprotected by the state often turn to private systems of security, buying guns for their own homes and—especially among the economic elite—hiring armed bodyguards to protect them.[1]

A major consequence of this situation is the set of high social and economic costs of living in a militarized zone. As C. Wright Mills noted, we all now live in a "war neighborhood" (1958). Although he was referring to what now seems a rather crude set of long-range weapons delivery systems, the proliferation of weapons at the local level—even among schoolchildren—makes his remarks even more salient.

The high cost of the ongoing escalation of violence globally and in many local contexts around the world involves not only the physical consequences of widespread violence, and the psychological toll of the balance of terror, but also what Victor Sidel calls "destruction without detonation" (1981, 36). That is, the militarized context in which we live has its costs even when the weapons are not fired, in terms of the way economic resources are spent, the effect of the threat of violence on children, and the social construction of evil that poisons interpersonal, interethnic, and international relations. A wide range of political costs of this approach includes the growth of the national security state at the national level, police states at the community level, and a vast system of propaganda, deliberate secrecy, and deception that undermines public trust (Herman and Chomsky 1988; Marullo 1993; Kurtz 1988).

The cycles of escalating violence sustained by these dynamics can only be halted by a technological breakthrough that enables the "good guys" to gain control over the criminals and aggressors who threaten the social order. This search for an ultimate technical fix to the problem runs the gamut from the Strategic Defense Initiative (SDI, or Star Wars) and first-strike nuclear weapons of the Reagan era to sophisticated arms and management techniques for police forces. Some thought that the invention of the machine gun would put an end to combat, because it was so ghastly that no one would dare to use it. But, the weapon to end all weapons, like the war to end all wars, appears as a mirage on the distant desert of an increasingly armed planet.

The Legal Control Frame

A second major frame in the violence debate is the traditional liberal position that calls for a rule of law that imposes reason on chaotic forces and aims to stop violence with legal progress and procedures designed to impose rational order. This frame emphasizes arms control negotiations and treaties in the international sphere, effective law enforcement and gun control legislation combined with social programs to treat offenders at the domestic level, and a legal framework to protect human rights. Efficient military and criminal justice systems are necessary but should be combined with such efforts as job training, rehabilitation of offenders, and more recently, programs to teach conflict resolution techniques to "at risk" populations.

Several assumptions lie behind this approach, which follows the Western Enlightenment tradition that places a premium on rational thought and efforts to control both natural and social environments. The core assumption, for our purposes, is that the only way to stop violence is to maintain the rule of law. Disputes among civilized people should be fought in the courtroom, not on the battlefield. Human beings, according to this approach, are basically rational and can be taught to act in a rational fashion when shown the costs and benefits of the alternatives.

Unlike the peace through strength frame, this perspective usually maintains that we already have enough weapons and guns, prisons, and tough laws and that an escalation of arms will not alleviate the problem. Moreover, new opportunities exist in the post–cold war era for the establishment of a reasoned global social order governed by rational discourse, international trade and cultural exchanges, and international law. New techniques of arms verification to enforce treaties at the international level and sophisticated techniques of conflict resolution and behavioral therapy at community and individual levels will enable people to make slow, steady progress toward a less violent world.

The legal control framework has a number of implications for public policy, notably (1) an international legal framework is necessary to sustain a stable global social order, (2) violence would be reduced by improving law enforcement and military techniques, while maintaining civil liberties, protecting human rights, and placing strict limits on military and police authorities, and (3) criminal justice and international peacekeeping efforts need significant reforms and increased resources in order to maintain the peace from local to global levels.

The international legal framework involves the elaboration of an arms control regime that expands the efforts of the last few decades, with interstate negotiations and treaties and mechanisms for monitoring agreements and imposing sanctions on violators. Legal control advocates maintain a wide range of positions regarding the nature of the international order that would best serve the process of legal control. They usually claim that successful international trade agreements and the development of new forms of arms verification provide the foundation on which such an order can be built. Moreover, the structure for negotiating, concluding, and monitoring such agreements has been established through decades of arduous work that could bear fruit in the post–cold war period.

At the community level, the legal control framework would systematically upgrade the criminal justice and law enforcement systems in order to rationalize the entire process of peacekeeping. The effort to make criminal justice a science reflects these kinds of concerns, as does the ongoing professionalization of the police, who in more "enlightened" cities are now armed with conflict resolution techniques and computer databases as well as guns and assault rifles. Hence, journals such as the *Police Chief* attend to such issues as those addressed in Gary Buchanan's (1993) article, "Handcuffing All Arrested Persons: Is the Practice Objectively Reasonable?" (cf. Hudson 1993).

Finally, such reform of the social control system will require a major effort, with the expenditure of substantial resources to upgrade and rationalize police and military forces, establish rehabilitation programs and treatment centers, train police and military officers, and upgrade technological services available to them. From this perspective, crime control is essentially a management problem, in which individuals who fail to cooperate with the larger system are brought back into line.

Similarly, a legal control system at an international level requires the elaboration of international organizations such as the United Nations. Nationally based militaries would give way to a sophisticated arrangement of collective security arrangements. Effective multinational peacekeeping and police forces would be deployed by the international community, and violators of international law—individuals or collectivities, public or private—would be brought before the World Court. Convicted offenders would be subjected to rational sanctions to deter them and others from future violations.

The legal control framework is appealing to many who find the peace through strength approach too aggressive, but its major stumbling blocks are formidable: it is individualistic in its proposed solutions, despite its so-called social programs, and it is ultimately hampered by the "bureaucratic shuffle." That is, the legal control approach must be implemented by large, inefficient bureaucratic systems in which no one takes responsibility. These systems also result in a bureaucratic distancing between officials and the "clients" whom they serve, which ironically results in the hidden bureaucratized violence common in the modern world.

The assumption of this approach—that humans can act rationally—has some serious problems. Although certainly capable of rational calculation, humans often engage in violence precisely because of nonrational motivations, or because of a complex combination of rational and nonrational, individual and social forces, as Lifton suggests occurred among the Nazi doctors. Perhaps the only way to break the cycles of burgeoning bureaucratic administration of violence is the mass mobilization of social movements across national and social boundaries—a mobilization that demands a humanization of large-scale social organizations in much the same way that movements within the civil societies of Eastern Europe challenged their states in the late 1980s and early 1990s. Such movements push us toward the third frame, that of common security and nonviolent conflict.

Common Security and Nonviolent Conflict

All problems could be peacefully resolved if adversaries talked to each other on the basis of love and truth. All through history, the way of truth and love has always won. This was the belief and vision of Mahatma Gandhi and this vision remains good and true today.

Ronald Reagan, speech to the United Nations, September 25, 1984

The final frame has not been central to the mainstream debates in most societies because of its radical departure from accepted assumptions about security. Four recent developments, however, make it a more imaginable alternative: (1) increased doubts, raised by the specter of a nuclear holocaust, about the conventional wisdom regarding security, (2) Mikhail Gorbachev's advocacy of a common security perspective while serving as president of the Soviet Union in the 1980s, (3) the global diffusion of nonviolent struggle from Gandhi's anticolonial movement to the prodemocracy movements of the late twentieth century, and (4) increasing public discontent with the threat of violence that saturates daily life.

The common security approach emphasizes the interdependence of all humans. Although differing in substantial ways from the two previous frames, it also draws upon elements of both of them: it recognizes both the importance of strength and confidence as an element of security and the need for a rational order based on law. In the place of deterrence through intimidation advocated by both peace through strength and legal control perspectives, however, the common security approach emphasizes cooperation when possible and creative nonviolent conflict when necessary.

The common security perspective advocates the construction of institutions that mitigate the causes of violence, rather than emphasizing the organization of social control agents like the military and police. Common security relies on the provision of basic economic security and human rights for all, systematic training of the civil population in the techniques of nonviolent struggle and conflict resolution, and the cultivation of cultural prohibitions against the use of violence to solve even problems of violence. In short, the common security approach would replace a "culture of violent solutions," as Elias calls it, with a culture of nonviolent solutions. New cultural narratives (see Smith) would be woven that delegitimate violence.

The fundamental assumption of the common security approach is that no one is secure until everyone is, because we all live in the same "global village." A second assumption is that strength is necessary in order to maintain the peace, an assumption similar to the peace through strength position. Weakness will be exploited by others, so some form of deterrence must be adopted. Strength is not measured in terms of military might or weapons technology, however, but by means of a variety of other criteria. Thus, the ability to deter is also redefined in this perspective: people are deterred from undesirable behavior by a variety of factors, only one of which is the threat of violence. In everyday life, for example, people are deterred from harming those whom they love, respect, or with whom they wish to maintain civil relations for fear of the consequences that aggressive actions will have for others and themselves. Deterrence results from a complex combination of rewards and sanctions that lie along a continuum between the most violent and the most nonviolent (Kurtz 1994).

That violent solutions may provide temporary relief of a problem, but do not work in the long run, is a third assumption of the common security approach to violence. Behind this notion is the cycle of violence thesis: "Violence begets violence." Those whose aggression is stopped by today's violence may retaliate tomorrow.

This assumption clearly demonstrates the importance of cognitive framing: we readily observe evidence confirming our general frame in order to sustain our preferred argument, while conveniently ignoring any counterevidence that might negate it. Anecdotal evidence can easily be provided to "verify" the cycle of violence thesis, but counterevidence can be provided just as easily by peace through strength advocates who claim that unchecked aggressors are genuine threats. The common security frame addresses this dilemma by offering an alternative to simply ignoring a genuine threat or "wishing it away." Nonviolent struggle with opposing forces, which may seem foreign to some peace through strength advocates, requires standing up to opponents but fighting in such a way as to attack their aggressive or unwanted behavior, rather than the people themselves (Gandhi [1951] 1961; Kurtz 1992a).

A fourth assumption of the common security approach is that structural violence can be as destructive as other kinds of violence. This aspect of the approach is significant, because it shifts the focus of definitions of security and deterrence from attention to strictly military or overt violence forms of violence toward other ways in which people are made insecure or are physically harmed. Emanating from efforts in the field of peace studies to distinguish between positive and negative peace (Brock-Utne, in this volume), this argument implies that solutions to the problem of violence must include more than increased use of force to defend against deviants at the local or global level, exploring such matters as economic security, at least as long as malnutrition and poverty remain major killers.

Fifth, conflict does not have to be a "zero sum game," as it is sometimes perceived (Bell and Kurtz 1991). According to some conventional wisdom, a conflict must end in victory by one party only at the expense of the other; the goal of nonviolent conflict is to conduct a dispute as creatively as possible, so that all parties benefit from its resolution. Whereas violent conflict inherently accentuates differences between partisans, nonviolent struggle seeks to minimize boundaries between people.

Gandhi, for example, argues for separating the "doer from the deed" (Gandhi [1951] 1961, 203); when engaged in struggle, the nonviolent activist seeks to destroy unjust systems but not the people who are involved in them. While this approach may seem idealistic to many, it was both a moral and pragmatic stance for Gandhi, who always treated the British individuals with tremendous respect, and often affection, while standing squarely against the British colonial system.

This principle has become a central element of conflict resolution approaches that emphasize "fair fighting" and respect for opponents as a significant way of changing the nature of any conflict and moving it toward a positive resolution. It also served as a hallmark of the nonviolent political revolutions of recent decades; in the Philippines' "People Power" revolution, for example, efforts to oust dictator Ferdinand Marcos were dramatically assisted by the fact that large sections of the military were persuaded to defect, in part because of the way in which they were treated by the demonstrators, who gave them flowers, food, and cigarettes (Lee, forthcoming; Blanco, forthcoming). It may well be that the massacre at Tiananmen Square in Beijing in 1989 was precipitated in part by a breakdown in the nonviolent discipline of the demonstrators, who had held the square peacefully for seven weeks and, until hours before the military stormed the square, had generally treated the soldiers with respect and dignity.[2]

The differentiation between behavior and people goes to the heart of the link between micro- and macrolevel processes that lead toward or away from violence. Violence may be perpetuated by systems, but it is carried out against individuals. Although we do not have sufficient data to prove it, the highest probability for violence occurs, we would argue, when certain structural conditions and individual motivations converge. When individuals feel threatened or wish to obtain something they do not have (fundamental emotions that are not as different as they might appear superficially) and their sociocultural context proffers only violent solutions to their dilemma, they are more likely to engage in violence to achieve their wishes.

The dynamics of human conflict are such that individuals engaged in it often find themselves swept along by the escalating events in which significant aspects of their personal identities are invested in its outcome. As conflicts escalate, issues become abstracted, opponents are often vilified as part of the rhetoric of the struggle, and the outcome becomes a matter of moral and personal consequence.

Several studies (e.g., Milgram 1975) suggest that violence is more likely to be perpetrated when the distance between the perpetrator and the victim increases. The "social construction of evil," by which opponents are dehumanized and perceived as the personification of evil, enhances the probability that a conflict will become violent.

Violent responses to complex situations have been a fundamental part of human life for thousands of years; twentieth-century technologies have so transformed the consequences of violent response, however, that conventional approaches are now called into question. Moreover, the long range of contemporary weapons means that no personal contact occurs between perpetrators and victims.

A final assumption of the common security approach is that nonviolence is morally and strategically superior to violence. One central dilemma in the issue of violence is the gap between what is often considered moral and that which is defined as effective. In *The Fate of the Earth* (1982), Jonathan Schell remarks that the advent of nuclear weapons forces us to be either a strategic or a moral idiot. On the one hand, that which is usually defined as strategically superior (i.e., the effective use of superior force to deter or sanction one's opponent) becomes morally offensive if it threatens widespread destruction. On the other hand, if one eschews the use of weapons of mass destruction on moral grounds, one opens oneself up to attack and appears strategically naive.

This tension between the moral and the strategic emerged with particular poignancy in the nuclear debates in the United States during the early 1980s. Alarmed by the threat of a nuclear holocaust, the National Conference of Catholic Bishops undertook an extensive study of the ethical implications of nuclear weapons and concluded that nuclear war is morally indefensible because it violates two fundamental principles of the church's traditional "just war" teachings. The principle of proportionality requires that the good caused by a war must outweigh its harmful consequences; the principle of discrimination prohibits the intentional use of violence that kills noncombatants.

Defense Secretary Caspar Weinberger's report to Congress grappled surprisingly, for the first time in history, with the ethical virtues of particular strategic and weapons policies (Weinberger 1983). Ironically, in responding to the bishops' critique of the indiscriminate nature of nuclear weapons, the Pentagon developed an argument that justified the escalation of the superpower nuclear arms race. The new, sophisticated weapons under development—so-called counterforce weapons—were declared moral because they were targeted on military installations, weapons systems, and so on. In contrast, earlier and existing systems were less accurate and were used for targeting cities and other "soft" (i.e., civilian) targets. Thus, a whole set of new weapons delivery systems from the MX missile and the Trident D-5 (submarine-launched) missiles to the stealth bomber were justified by the Pentagon on moral as well as strategic grounds.

The nuclear holocaust debates of the 1980s called into question the strategic relevance of such weapons programs. Ostensibly created for deterrence purposes, nuclear weapons were seen by some as having a limited strategic value, especially in light of the nuclear winter studies that suggested that the explosion of even a relatively small percentage of the world's nuclear weapons could result in the possible annihilation of all human, and most other, life on earth.

In an effort to expand the technical fix approach to the problem of international violence, and to "regain the moral high ground," peace through strength advocates proposed the Strategic Defense Initiative (SDI, or Star Wars) designed to protect against nuclear attack. Questions about its feasibility were raised in many quarters; ultimately, advocates admitted that its purpose was to "enhance deterrence," rather than protect against an actual attack. It merely provides a numerical advantage by destroying some unknown portion of the aggressors' weapons before they reach their targets. Advocates promoting the program, however, questioned the deterrence effectiveness of all advanced weapons systems. The ultimate spokesman for the "peace through strength" approach, President Ronald Reagan, argued that if deterrence were to work, "it *must* work perfectly, because if it doesn't work perfectly, it fails utterly" (quoted by Myer 1984). By promoting a "final solution" that became widely ridiculed, advocates of this frame undermined their position in the public debate. Reagan ended his term by promoting peace through friendship, because of his negotiations and personal relationship with common security advocate Mikhail Gorbachev. One of the great ironies of the 1980s is that Reagan, who was elected on a peace through strength platform and dramatically increased the U.S. military budget in the first years of his presidency, concluded his tenure in office by promoting friendly relations with the nation he had earlier designated the "focus of evil in the modern world."

The moral superiority of nonviolence is seldom questioned; it is the practical side that is problematic, even among many who would prefer nonviolence to violence. Even Gandhi admitted that the effectiveness of nonviolence could not be asserted, only demonstrated. Nonviolent direct action, so foreign to most ways of perceiving solutions to the problem of violence, carries little validity with those who have not experienced its potential power. On the other hand, participants in the Indian Freedom Movement, the U.S. civil rights movement, or recent nonviolent revolutions in Eastern Europe and elsewhere confirm its power. Even in those cultural contexts, however, the efficacy of violence remains strong.

Reframing the Problem of Violence

The common security approach requires a reframing of public policies at all levels, from local to global. This framebreaking implied by the common security perspective requires nothing less than rethinking basic approaches to human relations from the family to the world system.

It is not possible to address the entire range of implications for that reframing process, but we will suggest three significant areas in which the common security approach to violence differs substantially from most conventional frames: (1) it defines deterrence as a broad social process, rather than as a strategy of military and criminal justice systems, (2) it expands the repertory of nonviolent means of struggle (when deterrence fails), and (3) it transforms cultural values and socialization processes, such as the link between masculinity and violence that encourages the socialization of young men in such a way as to require violent behavior on their part in order to prove their "manhood."

Efforts to deter violence would focus not on more effective means of confronting violence with violence but on a broad range of issues that addresses the assumptions just outlined. Deterrence policies would emphasize the cultivation of friendly relations across boundaries that are the site of violent confrontation, from class and race divisions within the community to international, alliance-driven, and ideological boundaries within the world system. Common security approaches contend that aggression is deterred through a variety of means that address the concern that parties will have about protecting their own interests, relationship, or alliance. It does not necessarily rely on altruism, although it does not deny the possibility that people may engage in altruistic behavior, especially when relating with people for whom they care.

At the interpersonal level, people are frequently deterred from engaging in aggressive behavior because they are afraid that they might harm someone who might then retaliate or sever a relationship. Sometimes the motivating factor may even be genuine concern about the well-being and safety of the other. At more abstract levels of social organization, this more humane element may be obscured by the distancing mechanisms of bureaucratic institutions, vilification of certain groups or nationalities, or the politics of international relations. Even at the most abstract levels, individuals act on behalf of structures, which may help to explain why some puzzling events occur, such as the thawing of the cold war. Although many economic and geopolitical factors converged to bring about the development of friendly relations between the United States and the former Soviet Union, even sociologists must take into account the dramatic impact of the personal relationship forged between the two unlikely partners of Gorbachev and Reagan. A relationship of mutual respect and affection seemed to develop between the two when they began meeting face-to-face at the initiative of the charismatic Gorbachev (Turpin 1995). These personal interactions between two leaders who had both a sense of their role in history and reputations for affability apparently broke through the formal structures that defined them as bitter enemies. The valence of the relationship changed from negative to positive, but its intensity did not diminish.

A related element of the reframing of conflict required by the common security approach is the need to expand the repertory of nonviolent solutions to conflict. It is nothing less than a call to transform the "culture of violent solutions," as Elias puts it (in this volume), so that the dominant alternatives to social organization and social conflict are not deeply rooted in violence.

We are quite adept at violence because the peace through strength approach has been so important historically, especially in macrolevel human relations. We have the technical know-how, institutional infrastructure, and a wide range of options in our cultural repertory for carrying out violent conflict in a sophisticated manner on a wide variety of fronts. In fact, the world spends about U.S. $2 billion each day (almost half of that by the United States) on its militaries, and another very large sum on paramilitary and police forces and private arsenals. Compared to that remarkable mobilization of resources, very little is spent on nonviolent means of conflict and on research to address the causes of war and violence.

"If you want to get tough on crime, rock a crack baby," a Catholic bishop remarked recently. Each baby born in poverty and raised in a violent neighborhood without opportunities for meeting his or her basic needs is a candidate for violence. It is not simply a matter of addressing the individual orientation of such a person and providing techniques for dealing with conflict nonviolently—although such a program might help in a number of ways. The fundamental structures that produce a world in which half of the population lives on the verge of starvation, while a small percentage lives in unprecedented wealth, cannot simply be supported indefinitely by force.

Thus, a final implication of the call for reframing in this perspective is the need for a broad transformation of contemporary cultures, so that violence is devalued and nonviolence promoted. Since the vast majority of violence is committed by men (Archer 1994), we must break the link between cultural definitions of masculinity and violence that can be found in most of the world's cultures. It involves the creation of what Eisler (in this volume) calls a partnership, rather than dominator, social organization, making alternative models of leadership part of the cultural repertory. As long as we require that manliness be proven through the adept use of violence and that boys be taught from a very early age that they must demonstrate their strength through violence and the use of weapons, it is difficult to imagine a significant move toward a nonviolent global order (Brock-Utne, in this volume).

The dialectic between micro- and macrolevels again becomes important. On the one hand, the socialization of young men is shaped profoundly by the culture of violence that is imposed from the top. On the other hand, the ongoing process of teaching boys to use violence for solving problems reproduces the culture of violence across generations. It is difficult to tell one's young son not to destroy his enemies on the playground when the country's president uses such methods to solve international problems. By the time our sons become heads of state, they have been taught repeatedly the efficacy of violence in solving problems: by their parents and peers, through popular culture, the media, video games, the political leaders of their respective countries, and sometimes by their religious leaders. These cycles of violence cannot be solved either by transforming individuals on a case-by-case basis or by imposing nonviolent dictums from above but through a complex process of cultural and individual transformation. Although individuals may be taught to "use words" or enlarge their repertory of conflict techniques, such actions will not be sufficiently widespread without a broader cultural shift. Historic cultural changes, however, do not take place without the courageous action of individuals who contradict existing cultural frames. The kind of cultural transformation required by the common security approach is possible only with massive transnational social movements that mobilize public opinion in opposition to existing frames and that cultivate cooperation between civil society and state agencies, from community to global levels.

The common security and peace through strength approaches have some important common threads that may not be immediately apparent. Both share a suspicion toward the state, which is inconsistent in both approaches; each has some ambivalence about the state that results in internal contradictions. Peace through strength advocates tend to oppose excessive state intervention in other spheres but often place a heavy burden on the state to provide the kind of military and police forces necessary to check violence with violence. Common security advocates tend to be oriented toward forging a democratic civil society as a force opposing the state, which is so often hierarchical and violent. Even in the most democratic of political systems, there is no other entity for undertaking the kind of social transformation demanded by social movements, which are usually better at resisting than ruling (witness the difficulties faced by post-Soviet societies in Eastern Europe).

The common security approach also emphasizes the creation of social institutions that promote nonviolence, mitigate violence, and address the sources of potential violence. If the world community could spend $2 billion a day on that process rather than on military training and arms, the world would be much less violent.

Erich Fromm (1961) notes that if people behave the way nations do, we institutionalize them, by putting them in a jail or a mental hospital. Large-scale human social organization is so oriented toward violent conflict, and the amount of resources spent on the conduct of violence is so enormous, that it should not surprise us that we resort so frequently to violence.

One model for this sort of institution building is the concept of nonviolent peacekeeping systems—what Gandhi called *Shanti Sena* (peace brigades)—organized at all levels, from the neighborhood to the world. As Gandhi conceptualized them, local citizen peace brigades would work in a community to address the potential sources of violence. When no overt conflict is raging, the *Shanti Sena* would engage in "constructive work," meeting the needs of the local community: if there is a housing shortage, they should help local residents build homes; if the community needs a water supply, they should help residents dig wells. When an overt conflict breaks out, members of the brigade intervene nonviolently, acting as mediators or placing themselves directly between the conflicting parties, attempting to manage the conflict in a nonviolent fashion (Gandhi [1951] 1961, 86).

Such an approach—advocated only at the margins a few decades ago—has entered into the mainstream, not so much as an idealistic dream but as a concrete form of action, beginning with the Indian Freedom Movement, which culminated in India's independence in 1947, and then elaborated in the U.S. civil rights movement and other nonviolent social movements around the world, such as the Filipino "People Power" movement, and finally, the successful prodemocracy movements of the former Soviet bloc (Kurtz and Asher, forthcoming).

Although we should not expect the peace brigade concept to be adopted by the Pentagon or Kremlin any time in the near future, it has matured over time, and a number of serious efforts to develop a plan for a system of nonviolent "civilian-based defense" have emerged in recent decades, notably in the work of Gene Sharp (1973, 1991). Peace brigade proposals have actually been considered practical policy in a few cases: Costa Rica exists without an army but in relative peace with its violent neighbors; a movement to abolish the army was widely popular in Slovenia before the civil war shattered the peace; the newly independent Lithuania is considering a nonviolent defense system as part of its national security.

Less dramatic, but quite remarkable, measures that emphasize nonviolent conflict and common security include the increasing sophistication and systematic use of conflict resolution techniques in international and ethnic conflicts, such as that between the Palestine Liberation Organization (PLO) and Israel (Dajani, forthcoming).

Finally, many creative ideas about the cultivation of a nonviolent civic culture that promotes free expression, equal opportunity, and mutual support have emerged from resistance movements in various parts of the world (Ackermann and Kruegler 1994). From the essays and plays of Vaclav Havel (Havel 1990; see also, Brinton and Rinzler 1990) to the actions of nonviolent prodemocracy movements in Thailand (Satha-Anand, forthcoming) and Latin America (Pagnucco and McCarthy 1992; Maciel, forthcoming), it may be that the groundwork for a less violent culture is being laid toward the end of humanity's most violent century. At the community level, experiments in nonviolent conflict and its resolution thrive: in Gandhian "constructive workers" in India, Christian-based communities in Latin America, the Quaker "Alternatives to Violence" training in U.S. prisons, and elsewhere around the world.

We are not blind, of course, to the tremendous obstacles to the transition from a violent to a nonviolent culture. We will briefly discuss three major problems with an implementation of the common security approach: (1) cultural resistance and the complexity of such a transformation, (2) our collective ignorance about alternatives to violence and a lack of structures for facilitating nonviolent conflict, and (3) the virtually inevitable resistance by powerful interests who profit from the status quo and will fight to maintain it.

In a global culture saturated with violence, the idea of a nonviolent world sounds like the idealistic ramblings of marginal sociologists and peace activists. Two factors make it possible to imagine. First, the power of nonviolent struggle has been demonstrated for the first time on a large scale in the twentieth century, from the Indian Freedom Movement to various social movements especially in the United States, Philippines, Argentina, Palestine, and the former Soviet bloc. The fact that nonviolent approaches have now been demonstrated changes the nature of the argument in their favor from a primarily moral to a more strategic one.

Second, despite the flaws of a nonviolent approach, conventional approaches look increasingly defective in the nuclear age. As Gwynne Dyer (1985) puts it, violence has been a part of human life for five thousand years; in the twentieth century, it has simply been too costly. Is it really more idealistic to imagine the transformation of human social organization toward nonviolence than to expect humans to survive if we continue down the path of violent solutions? Do increasingly sophisticated weapons of mass destruction, the proliferation of armaments around the world, and the widespread distribution of guns in schools and homes provide more security? Perhaps the shock of the nuclear threat in the 1980s and the violence of daily life for so many (including even the wealthy and powerful) around the world in the 1990s provide the kind of awareness of our addiction to violence that will lead us to seek some therapeutic measures (as Galtung postulates, in this volume).

A second obstacle to the common security approach is our collective ignorance of nonviolent alternatives. For centuries—perhaps millennia—we have cultivated warfare techniques, invented new means of destruction, and rationalized our strategies for violent conflict. In the twentieth century, preparation for the use of violence and its actual practice consume an enormous proportion of human resources. We are very adept at it and getting better all the time.

Nonviolent struggle, on the other hand, while also as old as human life, is less well developed. It is only in the last millisecond of the long day of human history that we have discovered large-scale nonviolent action, systematized plans of action, and laid the groundwork for future development. There is no Strategic Integrated Operation Plan (SIOP) for a nonviolent defense system, and no large-scale system that develops necessary technologies and battle strategies, recruits and trains combatants, and carries out conflicts in a nonviolent manner. We have only the scattered fragments of Gandhi's writings and stories about his work, the teachings of Martin Luther King Jr., Sharp's *Politics of Nonviolent Action,* a few documentary films and scholarly works on nonviolence and conflict resolution, a handful of research institutes studying, and religious organizations promoting, nonviolent change, and the recently developed tradition of nonviolent social movements, with their stories, pamphlets, and collective wisdom. Perhaps we do not need or want a Pentagon for nonviolent struggle, which should be democratically forged and wherever possible homegrown, but we should not be surprised that, when the forces of violence meet those of nonviolence, the latter look shabbily prepared and sloppy compared to the twentieth-century culmination of centuries of discipline and training in violence.

Finally, the interests organized against such a transformation are formidable: the largest block of capital resources available for capital formation exists in the U.S. military budget, and those who control it will not relinquish it lightly. Certainly, it appears to be in the vested interests of those who control the missiles and the guns, as well as those who make them, to resist the sort of dramatic social transformation required by the common security perspective, and perhaps to resist it violently.

Developments since the fall of the Soviet bloc demonstrate the nature of the obstacles to taking the nonviolent path. In the former Soviet Union, just days after Boris Yeltsin led crowds of unarmed demonstrators in the street to challenge the Soviet military troops and tanks with flowers and words, the new Russian president himself was dispersing his new troops around the country and making compromises with his military establishment. Gandhi-reading Lech Walesa requested NATO to admit his new Poland into their military alliance. Self-proclaimed change-oriented presidential candidate Bill Clinton, now in charge of the world's most powerful military machine, called for dramatic reductions in government but asked for only a 4 percent reduction in the U.S. military budget, swollen to nearly twice its pre-Reagan size.

The only way to break this kind of impasse, it would seem, is what we call the "Eisenhower solution": that is, a popular mass movement that mobilizes a social and cultural transformation sufficient to pressure the state into making changes. We call it the Eisenhower solution because Dwight Eisenhower, commander of Allied Forces in Europe during World War II and subsequently president of the United States, claimed that "people of the world want peace so badly that some day governments had better get out of their way and let them have it" (1953, 421).

The Politics of Violence Research

Critics who contend that the problems created by violence are widespread but can only be met with violence are, in the final analysis, correct about the vagueness of the alternatives. We simply do not know enough about how to solve these problems beyond escalating the violence.

Part of our problem is our lack of knowledge, and the current processes for learning about violence and its alternatives are too meager and misguided. We contend that the current myopia in research must be overcome because of four major problems. First, the foundations and government funding now available for research on violence tend to support status quo systems and are locked into disciplinary frameworks. Second, most current research and policy recommendations tend to frame violence in individualistic terms and propose solutions that involve technical fixes at the margins of society, rather than address the fundamental issues. Third, current research is dominated by a peace through strength frame that screens out many of the insights from the legal control frame and most of the common security approach. Finally, even the style of research that is funded narrows our vision by taking a conservative approach to data collection and analysis, a tactic that further reinforces existing paradigms.[3]

Foundations and other institutions interested in advancing our understanding of violence need to "break frame." The most dramatic example of how the current funding process works is the fact that the largest amount of funding for social science research in all fields (not just violence) is controlled by the U.S. Army Research Institute for the Behavioral and Social Sciences, which had an annual research budget of $59.9 million in 1988. Although a small portion of the overall Pentagon budget, that amount exceeds the total *combined* social science research budget of all other sources of federal funding in the United States, including the National Science Foundation, the National Institute of Mental Health, and the Department of Education (Kurtz 1992b).

The individualistic focus of research is underscored by the fact that the Army Research Institute employs 197 psychologists out of its 213 scientists, and only five sociologists (Bynam 1988). Although their research agenda includes a number of topics, a primary objective is how to make members of the armed forces fight more efficiently, manage more effectively, and stay in the military longer. Thus, the military spends vast amounts of money to study itself and to analyze alternative military strategies (Janowitz and Little 1974).

The end of the cold war offers an opportunity to engage in new thinking about violence; indeed, some new government officials seem to be willing to consider alternative approaches. In Eastern Europe, considerable conceptual and practical progress has been made in this area, growing out of the movements resisting communist domination of that region (Havel 1990).

Some new possibilities are also emerging in the West, especially in the field of nonviolent conflict resolution (Kriesberg 1982, 1986), which is rapidly becoming an established field. Similarly, the number of university peace studies programs has escalated dramatically in recent years, especially in Europe and the United States, but elsewhere as well. A handful of peace institutes were founded after World War I and more following World War II, but only in the 1970s and 1980s did the academic study of peace and conflict become widespread. In 1970, there were two peace studies programs at U.S. universities; in 1990, there were about 250 (Elias and Turpin 1994).

Following years of lobbying for an alternative to the military academies, the U.S. Congress established the U.S. Peace Institute in 1984. Although this official agency faced considerable political turmoil from the outset, with its Reagan-appointed governing board sometimes opposing the procedures favored by those influential in the institute's creation. Nonetheless, it has managed to fund a number of important projects, primarily in the area of conflict resolution techniques.

More surprisingly, U.S. Attorney General Janet Reno recently made the following statement, which represents a sharp departure from previous frames emanating from that office:

> One of our greatest challenges in the 1990s is to make the prevention and treatment of violence a top priority.
>
> If we can make peace education and nonviolent conflict resolution a part of everyone's life; if we take it to the housing projects and make it a part of every resident's life; if we can take it to domestic violence programs and prevention programs throughout the United States; if we can say that before anyone gets married they should go through a conflict resolution course, we will make great strides in the 1990s.
>
> If we can bring this program to bear at every level of our society, we will be able to look back 10 years from now and be proud of what we did through education, prevention and showing people how to be peaceful. (1992, 1)

It is no accident that this new cognitive frame at the Justice Department comes from the America's first female attorney general. Similar shifts will occur if we expand our frames of reference in other ways, by including perspectives from various cultures and subcultures around the world other than those that have traditionally dominated research. Papers from "Studying Violence," a seminar held by the Indian Council of Peace Research in 1973, repeatedly identified social, rather than individualistic, causes of and remedies for violence. According to Sugata Dasgupta, for example, "the seedbed of violence" lies "in the disfunctionality of the societal process" (1972, 5).

American scholarship tends to dominate social science approaches around the world and, to the extent to which it shapes U.S. policy, has a global impact. Research on violence in the United States tends, however, to reflect the individualistic culture of the country as well as—even though often unintended—the hegemonic structures of international capital. As long as we remain within the frames provided by conventional scholarship, we will fail to untangle the web of violence we have woven. We hope that this volume will be an initial step toward broadening debate and opening new alternatives.

Notes

1. In residential areas of New Delhi, for example, many homes look like fortresses, complete with high walls and guard towers staffed by well-armed guards.

2. Some have speculated that agents provocateurs planted by the government may have incited the crowds to turn against the soldiers (Sharp and Jenkins 1989, 5).

3. Enlightenment rationality certainly represents a culmination of this sort of thinking, but similar approaches can be found in many other cultures. Confucian thought in Chinese civilization, so influential throughout Asia, for example, emphasizes a hierarchical order and a formal rationality that produces many results similar to the utilitarian rationality of the West, although it did not develop in the same way.

Works Cited

Ackermann, Peter, and Christopher Kruegler. 1994. *Strategic Nonviolent Conflict: The Dynamics of People Power in the Twentieth Century.* New York: Praeger.

Archer, John, ed. 1994. *Male Violence.* London: Routledge.

Bell, Nancy, and Lester R. Kurtz. 1991. "Social Theory and Nonviolent Revolution: Rethinking Definitions of Power." Paper presented at the Peace Studies Association, March, Boulder, Colo.

Blanco, Jose. Forthcoming. "Filipino People Power: An Interpretation in Faith." In *Geography of Nonviolence,* ed. Kurtz and Asher.

Brinton, William M., and Alan Rinzler, eds. 1990. *Without Force or Lies: Voices from the Revolutions of Central Europe in 1989–90.* San Francisco: Mercury House.

Buchanan, Gary W. 1993. "Handcuffing All Arrested Persons: Is the Practice Objectively Reasonable?" *Police Chief* 60:26–34.

Bynam, James. 1988. Telephone interview. 24 September.

Dajani, Souad. Forthcoming. "Nonviolent Civilian Resistance in the Occupied Palestinian Territories: A Critical Reevaluation." In *Geography of Nonviolence,* ed. Kurtz and Asher.

Dasgupta, Sugata. 1972. "Violence, Development, and Tensions." In *Studying Violence.* Pp. 2–11. New Delhi: Indian Council of Peace Research.

Dyer, Gwynne. 1985. *War.* New York: Crown.

Eisenhower, Dwight D. 1953. "Peace in the World: Acts, Not Rhetoric Needed." *Vital Speeches of the Day* 19(May): 418–21.

Elias, Robert, and Jennifer Turpin. 1994. "Thinking about Peace." In *Rethinking Peace.* Ed. Robert Elias and Jennifer Turpin. Pp. 1–12. Boulder, Colo.: Lynne Rienner Publishers.

Fromm, Erich. 1961. *May Man Prevail? An Inquiry into the Facts and Fictions of Foreign Policy.* Garden City, N.Y.: Anchor.

Gandhi, Mohandas K. [1951] 1961. *Non-Violent Resistance.* New York: Schocken.

Havel, Vaclav. 1990. "The Power of the Powerless." Pp. 43–127 in *Without Force or Lies,* ed. Brinton and Rinzler.

Herman, Edward S., and Noam Chomsky. 1988. *Manufacturing Consent: The Political Economy of the Mass Media.* New York: Pantheon.

Hudson, Arthur. 1993. "Special Needs Unit: Probation Program Offers Officer His Toughest Challenge." *Corrections Today* 56(July): 20–23.

Janowitz, Morris, and R. W. Little. 1974. *Sociology and the Military Establishment.* Beverly Hills, Calif.: Sage.

Kriesberg, Louis. 1982. *The Sociology of Social Conflicts.* Englewood Cliffs, N.J.: Prentice-Hall.

———. 1986. "Consequences of Efforts at Deescalating the American-Soviet Conflict." *Journal of Political and Military Sociology* 14(Fall): 215–34.

Kurtz, Lester R. 1988. *The Nuclear Cage: A Sociology of the Arms Race.* Englewood Cliffs, N.J.: Prentice-Hall.

———. 1992a. "Nonviolent War: An Idea Whose Time Has Come?" *Gandhi Marg* 14(October): 450–62.

———. 1992b. "War and Peace on the Sociological Agenda." In *Sociology and Its Publics.* Ed. Terence C. Halliday and Morris Janowitz. Pp. 61–98. Chicago: University of Chicago Press.

———. 1994. "The Geometry of Deterrence." *Peace Review* 6(2): 187–94.

Kurtz, Lester R., and Sarah Beth Asher, eds. Forthcoming. *The Geography of Nonviolence.* Oxford: Blackwell.

Lee, Stephen. Forthcoming. "The Philippines and Nonviolence." In *Experiments in Peace: Student Studies in Nonviolence.* Ed. Margaret Zimmerman and Lester R. Kurtz. New Delhi: Gandhi-in-Action.

Maciel, Crueza. Forthcoming. "Nonviolence in Latin America." In *Geography of Nonviolence,* ed. Kurtz and Asher.

Marullo, Sam. 1993. *Ending the Cold War at Home: From Militarism to a More Peaceful World Order.* Lexington, Mass.: Lexington Books.

Milgram, Stanley. 1975. *Obedience to Authority: An Experimental View.* New York: Harper and Row.

Mills, C. Wright. 1958. *The Causes of World War Three.* New York: Simon and Schuster.

Myer, Alan. 1984. "The Political and Strategic Context of the Strategic Defense Initiative." Address at "Star Wars: The Strategic Defense Initiative," a symposium sponsored by the Southwestern Regional Program in National Security Affairs and the Military Studies Institute, Texas A&M University, 16–17 November, College Station, Tex.

Pagnucco, Ronald, and John D. McCarthy. 1992. "Advocating Nonviolent Direct Action in Latin America: The Antecedents and Emergence of SERPAJ." In *Religion and Politics in Comparative Perspective.* Ed. Bronislaw Misztal and Anson Shupe. Pp. 125–47. Westport, Conn.: Praeger.

Satha-Anand, Chaiwat. Forthcoming. "Nonviolent Practices, Professional Class and Democracy: The Bangkok Case, May 1992." In *Geography of Nonviolence,* ed. Kurtz and Asher.

Schell, Jonathan. 1982. *The Fate of the Earth.* New York: Alfred A. Knopf.

Seminar on Studying Violence. 1972. *Studying Violence.* New Delhi: Indian Council of Peace Research.

Sharp, Gene. 1973. *The Politics of Nonviolent Action.* 3 vols. Boston: Porter Sargent.

———. 1991. *Civilian-Based Defense.* Princeton: Princeton University Press.

Sharp, Gene, and Bruce Jenkins. 1989. "Nonviolent Struggle in China: An Eyewitness Account." *Nonviolent Sanctions* 1(Fall): 1, 3–7.

Sidel, Victor. 1981. "Buying Death with Taxes." In *The Final Epidemic.* Ed. Ruth Adams and Susan Cullen. Pp. 35–47. Chicago: Educational Foundation for Nuclear Science.

Turpin, Jennifer. 1993. "Nuclear Amnesia." Paper presented at the annual meetings of the American Sociological Association, August, Miami, Fla.

———. 1995. "Gorbachev, the Peace Movement, and the Death of Lenin." In *Why the Cold War Ended: A Range of Interpretations.* Ed. Ralph Summy and Michael Salla. Pp. 69–80. Westport, Conn.: Greenwood Press.

Weinberger, Caspar W. 1983. *Department of Defense Annual Report to the Congress, Fiscal Year 1984.* Washington, D.C.: Government Printing Office.

Contributors

JOHN P. BARTKOWSKI is a doctoral candidate in the Department of Sociology at the University of Texas at Austin. His areas of interest include the sociology of religion, gender, and the family, and sociological theory. His previous research has appeared in *Sociology of Religion*, *Review of Religious Research*, and several edited volumes.

BIRGIT BROCK-UTNE, professor at the Institute of Educational Research, University of Oslo, is a Norwegian social scientist with a doctorate in peace studies. She has written several books on peace studies, women and education, and women and peace, including *Feminist Perspectives on Peace and Peace Education* (Pergamon, 1989) and *Educating for Peace: A Feminist Perspective* (Pergamon, 1985).

RIANE EISLER is the author of *The Chalice and the Blade: Our History, Our Future* (HarperCollins, 1987) and *Sacred Pleasure: Sex, Myth, and the Politics of the Body* (Harper San Francisco, 1995). She is cofounder of the Center for Partnership Studies (P.O. Box 51936, Pacific Grove, CA 93950), has taught at UCLA and Immaculate Heart College, and is a founding member of the General Evolution Research Group.

ROBERT ELIAS is professor of politics and chair of the peace and justice studies and legal studies programs at the University of San Francisco. He is the editor of *Peace Review*, an associate editor of *New Political Science*, and the author of *Victims of the System* (Transaction Books, 1983), *The Politics of Victimization* (Oxford University Press, 1986), and *Victims Still* (Sage, 1993).

CHRISTOPHER G. ELLISON is associate professor of sociology at the University of Texas, where he is also affiliated with the religious studies and Afro-American studies programs and the Population Research Center. Much of his current research focuses on religious variations in childrearing and family life, with particular attention to the distinctiveness of conservative Protestant family ideology and practice. His recent work has appeared in the *American Sociological Review, Social Forces, Journal of Health and Social Behvior, Journal for the Scientific Study of Religion, Review of Religious Research,* and numerous other journals.

JOHAN GALTUNG is a mathematician, sociologist, and professor of peace studies at universities at Witten/Herdecke, Hawaii, Tromso, Alicante, and at the European Peace University, Austria. He established the first peace research institute, PRIO, in Oslo, and served as its director for ten years. He has authored many books and articles, including *Human Rights in Another Key* (Polity Press, 1994).

LESTER R. KURTZ is professor of sociology and Asian studies at the University of Texas at Austin. His research focuses on social conflict and the sociology of religion. He is the author of *Gods in the Global Village: The World's Religion in Sociological Perspective* (Pine Forge/Sage, 1995), *The Nuclear Cage: A Sociology of the Arms Race* (Prentice-Hall, 1988), and editor-in-chief of the *Encyclopedia of Violence, Peace, and Conflict* (Academic Press, forthcoming).

ROBERT JAY LIFTON is Distinguished Professor of psychiatry and psychology, City University of New York, and the director of the Center on Violence and Human Survival at John Jay College of Criminal Justice. He is the author of dozens of books, including *Hiroshima in America: Fifty Years of Denial* (with Greg Mitchell, Putnam Publishers, 1995), *The Protean Self: Human Resilience in an Age of Fragmentation* (Basic Books, 1993), and *The Genocidal Mentality: Nazi Holocaust and Nuclear Threat* (with Erik Markusen, Basic Books, 1990). Lifton is a founding member of the International Physicians for the Prevention of Nuclear War, which was awarded the Nobel Peace Prize in 1986.

PHILIP SMITH teaches in the anthropology and sociology department at the University of Queensland, Australia. His articles have appeared in *Contemporary Sociology,* the *Journal of Narrative and Life History, Historical Social Research,* and *Theory and Society.* He is the coauthor of *Sociology: Themes and Perspectives* (Collings, forthcoming). His current interests focus on a cross-national analysis of discourse, comparing the Suez Crisis of 1956 and the Persian Gulf War of 1991.

JENNIFER TURPIN is associate professor of sociology at the University of San Francisco, where she is also affiliated with the peace and justice studies program and is chair of the women's studies program. Her teaching and research interests include the sociology of conflict, gender and violence, peace and war, and Russian society. She is the author of *Reinventing the Soviet Self* (Praeger, 1995), coeditor of *Rethinking Peace* (Lynne Rienner Publications, 1994) and *The Gendered New World Order* (Routledge, 1996). She is the senior editor of *Peace Review* and associate editor of the *Encyclopedia of Violence, Peace, and Conflict* (Academic Press, forthcoming).

YUAN-HORNG CHU is associate professor of sociology at Tunghai University in Taiwan. He has authored many articles on issues of rhetoric, narrative forms of national memory, risk communication, aesthetic speech, and postmodernism. He is currently directing a three-year research project on lifestyles in Taichung City, including ethnographic studies with aboriginal and foreign laborers, prostitutes, and slum families.

Index